CONTENTS

Everything you wanted to know about the EU

But were afraid to ask

Robert Oulds

www.BretwaldaBooks.com
@Bretwaldabooks
bretwaldabooks.blogspot.co.uk/
Bretwalda Books on Facebook

Please note that this book draws extensively on documents and sources
not generally available to the public. For a list of these sources and where to
access them please refer to the publisher's website page for this book:
http://bretwaldabooks.com/book.php?p=173

First Published 2013
Text Copyright © Robert Oulds 2013
Robert Oulds asserts his moral rights to be regarded as the author of this book.
All rights reserved. No reproduction of any part of this publication is permitted
without the prior written permission of the publisher:
Bretwalda Books
Unit 8, Fir Tree Close, Epsom,
Surrey KT17 3LD
info@BretwaldaBooks.com
www.BretwaldaBooks.com
ISBN 978-1-909698-05-5

Printed and bound in Great Britain by
Marston Book Services Limited, Oxfordshire

Introduction

"Sometimes I like to compare the EU as a creation to the organisation of empire. We have the dimension of empire."
José Manuel Barroso, President of the European Commission, EUobserver, 10th July 2007

In Britain the long held principle of free speech still stands with two traditional exceptions; firstly it is seen as irresponsible to shout fire, or its modern equivalent – Allah Akbar – in a crowded cinema and secondly it was uncouth at best and dangerously crazy at worst to advocate in polite society the case that Britain should leave the European Union. The latter point has now drastically changed. We have the responsibility to question our EU membership and - as it is almost inevitable that the UK will have a referendum on EU membership at some point - it is irresponsible not to consider the options for life outside the European Union.

The EU is not some abstract and irrelevant international organisation; it affects every man, women and child in Britain, Ireland and on the continent. And has a poignant influence on developing nations which are affected by its policies.

The EU has been seen as a complicated subject. It is true that some looks at this topic leave the reader feeling like they have had their brains scrambled by some dastardly secret euro-weapon, but it does not have to be so. This book aims to make the EU accessible and will tell you what you need to know to navigate your way through the debate that has seized the nation's airwaves. A debate that will only become louder and more complex as the referendum approaches.

The story of the EU begins with the drawing to a close of a world war, the greatest conflict that mankind had known. Yet, contrary to what many believe the war that led to many concluding that Europe should unite was the First World War, not the Second. At the heart of the drive to award powers from national institutions to those based in Brussels where much of the EU is based is the belief that,

'National sovereignty is the root cause of the most crying evils of our times... The only final remedy for this supreme and catastrophic evil of our time is a federal union of the peoples... '

In fact they are the words of a British civil servant called Philip Kerr and are emblazoned on a wall in the visitors centre of the European Parliament.

There are other ideological underpinnings, in fact all those involved in the "European Project" have their own reasons to support the principle of an ever closer union being developed under auspices of the European Union. Each supporter or opponent seems to project their own hopes and fears on to the EU and analyses it according to their own prejudices. This is especially the case in Britain where the UK's approach towards the EU is schizophrenic but this was not always so. Previously people in Britain knew how to approach the issue of European unity.

British, originally English, foreign policy since the time of Elizabeth I sought to prevent the continent of Europe being dominated by one major power. First the power of the Spanish whose Imperial power was projected across large parts of the continent was resisted. Later, one Churchill, the 1st Duke of Marlborough, fought against the French hegemony of Louis XIV. Later Britain opposed the domination of Bonaparte. The ambitions of the Kaiser Wilhelm II were also thwarted by Britain as were the near identical aims of Hitler just a generation later who was opposed by another Churchill. This approach endured beyond the Second World War when the UK lead in the formation of a rival to the EU known as the European Free Trade Association.

In this modern era the UK does not collectively know whether or not to embrace European union or reject it. Some British politicians such as the Prime Ministers Harold Macmillan and Edward Heath supported the ideals of a union between the once belligerent nations of Europe. Macmillian who presided over the end of Empire saw this as an opportunity for a new role for Britain, naturally he thought the UK would become the leader of the soon to be united Europe. However, the days of the mythical British newspaper headline, and once regular common phrase during weather reports, which read 'Fog in the Channel, Europe cut-off' are long gone.

Attitudes towards Europe were not just a matter of foreign policy but were also a matter of jurisdiction and sovereignty. The 1532 Act in Restraint of Appeals, passed during the time Henry VIII, banned legal appeals outside of the Kingdom of England. This made the Monarch in Parliament the highest authority in the land.

Now there is a legal industry seeking to take courses to apparently higher judicial authorities on the continent. It is not just politicians who have sought to constrain British sovereignty into web of international legislation. The judiciary has even played its part. The legal system even established the innovation of 'Constitutional' Acts of Parliament in order to reconcile a conflict that emerged over which set of laws have supremacy; those coming from the EU or legislation made by the British Parliament.

Clearly the EU is having a major effect on life in the UK; but Britain is a part of the EU and has a say, perhaps even influence, over developments in Brussels. What we see as European legislation may have been inspired by the UK, developed in the UK and merely projected back onto the UK via the prism of the EU institutions. That would certainly be the case if the UK has substantial influence in the European Union; but does it?

And so before asking if Britain should stay in the European Union or leave it, we should first ask "What exactly is the European Union?"

Chapter 1

A Snapshot of the EU

'If the distribution of power among the several parts of the state is the most efficient restraint of monarchy, the distribution of power among several states is the best check on democracy.'
Lord Acton, The History of Freedom in Antiquity, 1877. He is also known for his famous quote "Power tends to corrupt, and absolute power corrupts absolutely."

The European Union, also known as the EU, is a collection of supranational institutions that are created by treaties between its member states. These have voluntarily been signed by the 28 democratically elected governments of the nations that make up the EU. As has each new treaty which passes yet more power to the EU.

The EU is therefore the creature of the member states and one in which they pool or share their sovereignty. Prior to entering the EU each state was an independent sovereign entity. A bachelor is like a sovereign power; whereas a married man enjoys the benefits of shared sovereignty.

The institutions

There are numerous Presidents within the European Union; President of the Commission, President of the European Council, President of the Parliament and the six-monthly rotating Presidency of the Council of Ministers. The various bodies known as courts have their own Presidents, as does the EU's central bank. In Britain one President would be considered more than enough.

There are seven main institutions of the European Union. The EU has a Court of Auditors which reviews the EU's accounts and it has its own central bank ingeniously known as the European Central Bank.

The European Union has its own system of courts officially called the Court of Justice of the European Union. Its most important part is the European Court of Justice or ECJ for short. There is also a general Court originally known as the Court of First Instance. The roles of the court are to give rulings on the validity or interpretation as to the extent or meaning of European Union law. It can also apply fines against a member state for failing to apply EU law. It can also strike down national legislation that is incompatible with EU law.

The EU's executive, or government, is known as the European Commission. This has the sole right to propose EU legislation which it drafts, however the European Parliament can request that the Commission submits a proposal. The Commission also manages and implements both the budget and the EU's many policies. It sees itself as the guardian of the treaties and along with the Court of Justice it enforces European Union law. The Commission represents the EU around the world. It is unelected.

There is a European Council whose membership is drawn from the heads of government or heads of state of the countries which are part of the EU. The President of the European Commission and the President of the European Council attend European Council meetings. Its purpose is to identify important issues that need to be addressed and it can invite the Commission to produce proposals on a given topic.

There is also a separate Council of the European Union which is often referred to as the Council of Ministers. Confusingly the Council of Ministers is actually several different bodies depending on what is being discussed. The Agriculture Minister of each state attends meetings about agriculture, the Transport Minister of each state attends meetings about transport and so forth. Debates are held behind closed doors and are not recorded. This is in effect one of the legislatures of the European Union, which along with the European Parliament votes on legislative proposals from the European Commission. The European Parliament has limited powers to monitor the work of the Commission but has a role in approving the Commissioners and can call on the entire Commission to resign; a rarely used 'nuclear option'.

There are other important institutions such as the European Investment Bank which supports EU projects and aids development by borrowing money on the international financial markets and loaning it to munipalities, businesses and even the BBC. The member states are liable for any losses.

To advise on legislation there are the European Economic and Social Committee (EESC) and the Committee of the Regions (CoR). The EESC is actively involved with lobby groups and seeks to help align future EU legislation with its social and economic goals.

The Committee of the Regions frequently bypasses the central institutions of the member states and seeks to have a dialogue between the EU and regional government. Its aim is to represent in Brussels the interests of regional government. Its role hollows out the nation state from within. Such a system of regional government below the nation-state but above the local council is common in many European states. In contrast, it has been anathema in the UK since 1657 when the rule of Cromwell's Major-Generals ceased. This rule was a system that for nearly two years divided up Britain, including Ireland, into twelve regions which were governed by the military under the leadership of Oliver Cromwell, the Lord Protector. Ironically, the twelve major generals are reflected in the same number of regions that were recreated in Britain in the 1990's following the constituencies of the European Parliament.

Interestingly under regulation 2052/88 EU economic spending has to be spent on a regional basis via the European Regional Development Fund (ERDF). The nine regional development agencies that existed in England were, however, abolished in the UK in 2012 being replaced by Local Enterprise Partnerships.

Both the European Commission and the European Parliament are mandated to consult with the CoR. The CoR not only has the right to offer its opinions but can also take cases to the Court of Justice if its advice in the process of law making has been ignored.

The EU also has numerous agencies that both enforce and develop specifics of EU law. In addition to these there are hundreds of committees which aid the development of the European Union's body of law.

How EU laws are made

Before the Commission produces the final draft of its legislation and long before it goes to the European Parliament and Council for decision it is developed through a host of committees in which the proposals are discussed. This is known in EU jargon as Comitology.

There are Advisory Committees which are chaired by an official from the Commission. The membership includes national civil servants who travel to Brussels on all expenses paid regular busman's holidays. They have no power to prevent the Commission from taking action or to mandate it to do so. However, they do have influence.

There are working groups known as Legislative Committees. These are similar to the Advisory Committees but there will be voting on specific proposals by qualified majority vote. They can delay and even reject a proposal from the Commission but can be overruled by the Council.

There are also management Committees which develop policies that are already in existence. National civil servants are also involved here and voting takes place according to qualified majority.

Lobbyists and businesses are also regularly consulted during the Comitology process. There are also separate committees of MEP's which assess and amend proposals from the Commission.

When the proposals are being considered in the Council stage the draft law is discussed by the Committee of Permanent Representatives known as COREPER. Each national government has civil servants which serve on this body. The proposals which the civil servants on COREPER consider to be non-contentious are considered as being ready for adoption and go to the next Council meeting. Assuming a measure is approved there (and the vast amjority are) it goes through the European Parliament are usually approved without further discussion. Those measures on which the representatives on COREPER cannot reach agreement also go to the Council, but they are flagged up to be discussed and voted on. Even so, they are usually eventually adopted albeit after amendment.

Under what is known as the 'ordinary legislative procedure' equal weight is applied to the votes of the European Parliament and the Council. A Commission proposal first goes to the European Parliament where it can be amended or adopted. It then goes to the Council. The ministers may then decide to accept the Parliament's changes and pass the legislation, or it may make its own amendments and send it back to the Parliament for what is known as a second reading. Parliament then reviews the Council's amendments and either accepts them, with the proposal becoming law, or it proposes amendments and returns the new draft to the Council for its second reading in that chamber. The Council will then either accept the amendments or reject them. If it does not approve the views of the Parliament the matter is passed to a conciliation committee.

The conciliation committee has an equal number of Council Representatives and MEPs. They attempt to reach an agreement. If they cannot the legislation fails. If there is an agreement on a final text it goes back to both the Council and Parliament. Here they can either accept or reject, but not further amend, the final text.

Throughout these debates what goes on in the European Parliament is open to the public. What is said in Council remains secret.

Most EU laws are passed through this process of ordinary legislative procedure. However, there is also a special legislative system called the 'consultation' procedure. In this the Council is not legally obliged to take the amendments of the Parliament into account. The Council must not act before having received the views of the European Parliament, but may then ignore those views if it wishes. This procedure is used in exceptions from the internal market and competition law.

There is also what is known as the 'consent' procedure. Legislation that deals with discrimination can be passed with the European Parliament only having the right to reject or approve the proposal. This process is used to approve international agreements, including the withdrawal agreement should an EU member state wish to leave the EU.

In short the EU's system of law making is complex, secretive and largely hidden not only from the general public but also from their elected representatives.

There is little input from national Parliaments. Traditionally the representatives of Her Majesty's Government have not been open about how much legislation is originating from the EU and denied that Brussels is imposing legislation; but they are complicit in this process. First they say it isn't happening, then Ministers admit it is happening but that it isn't important, then they say it is important but it doesn't apply to us and then they admit it does apply to Britain but there is nothing we can do about it.

This system of law making sharply contrasts with how legislation is conducted in the UK where there are more checks and balances. In all democratic systems draft legislation is proposed by elected politicians. It will then be subject to a great deal of scrutiny both from the media, publically interested organisations and especially Members of Parliament. Before becoming law it must pass through several stages, often in two separate chambers, where it will often be amended if not rejected by those who have been directly elected by the people who will be affected by the laws.

Whilst the Executive branch of the state in the UK, the British government, has too much power vis-à-vis Parliament since 2010 it has suffered a number of defeats. Most notably over the proposal to take military action in Syria and particularly on votes in the House of Commons on EU matters. The British Parliament has proved that it can still act as check on the authority of the government and at times be a real impediment to the government.

The same cannot be said for the European Parliament which on most occasions rubber stamps proposals from the Commission and supports the transfer of power from national democracies to the EU binding the member states under its writ.

EU law
EU law comes in three forms: Regulations, Directives and Decisions.

Regulations are directly applicable in the UK. They do not need to be approved by national parliaments before coming into force. Once made and published in the Official Journal of the European Union they automatically become law. Regulations, are very specific and are the Commission's preferred method of producing legislation.

Directives are still binding on all EU countries but are more general leaving the national institutions to develop the precise wording to suit national conditions. They must go through the Parliament of each member state before becoming law. However, directives must be enacted according to a strict timetable and any delays or misinterpretation of its aims leaves a state open to a legal challenge. What is more, the courts can give a Directive 'direct effect' if a Member State fails to transpose it into law.

Decisions do not require the approval of national parliaments. They refer to specific cases and require the relevant party, a national authority and even an individual, to do something or cease doing something. Alternatively decisions can grant rights. This form of legislation can come from the Council, on occasions in conjunction with the European Parliament, or from the Commission.

There also exist 'Recommendations' and 'Opinions.' They do not have legislative force as they lack the ability to compel a member state to take action they have influence over national governments. They are often used to steer a member state's policies in a certain direction before legislation is actually introduced. What is more, they are intended to supplement existing EU law and are to be taken into consideration. They have what is known as 'indirect effect.'

The extent of EU law

Most areas of national life are now affected by EU law. In most years, across the EU the majority of laws and statutory instruments put through national Parliaments now come from Brussels. There are over 100,000 EU rules, international agreements and legal acts binding on or affecting citizens across the EU. In 2013 there are in force:-

- 8,937 EU Regulations;
- 1,953 EU Directives;
- 15,561 Decisions;
- 2,948 Other Legal Acts;
- 4,733 international agreements;
- 4,843 non-binding legal acts, which may however bind if agreed;
- 52,000 agreed EU international standards from CEN, Cenelec, Etsi etc. and
- 11,961 verdicts from the EU Court of Justice.

The rules of the European Union codified in the EU treaties prevent national democratic procedures - be they votes in parliament or referenda - from amending let alone abolishing a single one of these previously mentioned legal measures.

This complete body of EU law is known as the acquis communitaire, or just acquis for short, and translates from French into English literally as acquired but in effect means 'that which has been agreed upon.' The entire acquis runs to more than 170,000 pages of active legislation which is in force.

The importance of legislation from the European Union cannot be understated. In Judge Bruce Morgan's comments in the Sunderland metrication case are telling. Here traders were being prosecuted for selling groceries in Imperial measures against an EU directive, he noted in his judgement on 9th April 2001 that,

"This country quite voluntarily surrendered the once seemingly immortal concept of the sovereignty of parliament and legislative freedom by membership of the European Union ... as a once sovereign power, we have said we want to be bound by Community law."

EU law is enforced in the UK as a result of the European Communities Act 1972 and its later amendments which bring into force the numerous treaties that have been agreed between Britain and the other EU states.

This has been clearly recognised by the Courts in other legal cases. As Lord Denning observed in the case of Macarthys Ltd v. Smith 1979,

"Community law is part of our law by our own statute, the European Communities Act 1972. Community law is now part of our law: and whenever there is any inconsistency, Community law has priority. It is not supplanting English law. It is part of our law which overrides any other part which is inconsistent with it."

This body of law is added to at the rate of around 3,000 new pieces of legislation put into force each year. Yet, how many of Britain's new laws originate or are influenced by the EU? A study by the House of Commons found that more than 50% of the UK's new laws come from Brussels or are influenced by the requirements to adopt EU rules.

British politicians have in effect outsourced their role to the institutions of the European Union. What is more, the British Parliament has to produce criminal sanctions if an EU law has been contravened. The British authorities will then enforce this law. EU legislation is therefore the law of the land and is not an abstract set of arrangements to facilitate trade.

The EU does not just have a legislative effect on its member states; it also has some regional influence.

The EU in the wider world
The influence of the EU is not just upon its member states it has both a foreign and economic policy agenda that ripples around the world. The largest impact is felt by the states which neighbour the European Union. If states which border the EU are not making preparations to

join, which include adopting the acquis communitaire, they are increasingly subject to agreements which bind them for good or ill into the EU's economic orbit. Iceland, Liechtenstein and Norway have a requirement to reach common standards with the EU. Switzerland is asked to adopt similar legislation to that which is in operation in its neighbours. The European Union has also opened up economic relations to its South and East.

As part of its European Neighbourhood policy, the European Union has instituted the Euro-Mediterranean Partnership, which includes the countries stretching from Morocco to Turkey. and the Eastern Partnership (EaP) which runs with the exclusion of Russia from Belarus to Azerbaijan. These partnerships with the European Union include the development of free trade areas, the elimination of customs duties on cross border trade, yet the agreements also carry duties. There are obligations to apply EU standards. These policies are consistent with the beliefs of Karl Ernst Haushofer, the German General whose political philosophy of Geopolitik advocated the creation of regional power blocs under European hegemony.

The EU is not without its supporters in Europe and beyond in other continents. The United States originally saw the EU as a bulwark against Soviet Communism. Since the collapse of the USSR, which cannot be attributed to the EU, Russia's former satellite states have either become part of the European Union or Brussels' Eastern Partnership.

Henry Kissinger, the former US Secretary of State, is reported as saying "Who do I call if I want to call Europe?" In fact he has denied that he actually said this. Yet the EU is indeed slowly developing one voice and regional influence.

This has the support of the American government. The US President, Barack Hussein Obama, certainly supports the UK's continued membership of the European Union. In fact he sees it as a guarantee of American interests. On 13th May 2013 the US President said in answer to a question from the BBC's James Landale during a discussion on Britain's continued EU membership that "we believe that our capacity to partner with a United Kingdom that is active, robust, outward-looking and engaged with the world is hugely important to our own interests as well as the world."

This expanded on a statement by the US Assistant Secretary of State for European and Eurasian Affairs, Dr Philip H Gordon, who on 9th January 2013 said that Britain's "voice within the European Union is essential and critical for the United States… "

The United States of America also supports the Single Market. This is perhaps not surprising as American firms export more to the EU than the UK does. Its total EU exports in goods alone amounted to more than $265 billion, with a further $9.9 billion coming in terms of the sale of agricultural products. In terms of services the figure is $194 billion. Clearly the US sees the EU to be in its commercial as well as its geopolitical interests. It is noteworthy that both the EU and the European Central Bank have followed and enforced US sanctions against Iran.

Whilst the European Union may well be in the interests of the USA, and has the overt support of successive American governments, it is questionable whether the process of 'ever closer union' in Europe is to the benefit of the people governed by Brussels. And the EU is not the only international body that is relevant to the continent of Europe. There exist other bodies such as the United Nations Economic Commission for Europe (UNECE). Its members include not only all European states, but also several Asian countries that were once part of the Soviet Union and even Canada, the USA and Israel. And there are many other institutions which have the name Europe in their title but are not directly related the EU apart from often being mistaken for another of its many arms.

What the EU is not
The word 'Europe' is the widely used noun for the European Union. The EU, however, is in reality a system of governance and nearly 20 European states do not belong to the EU. What is more the EU is not the only international organisation that exists on the continent of Europe. It needs to be stated what the EU is not.

The institutions of the EU are often confused with a number of other European institutions and organisations. The Council of Europe is separate to the EU and predates it. And where the EU has 28 member states the Council of Europe has 47. The European Court of Human Rights (ECHR) is also not a part of the EU. The ECHR was created by the European Convention on Human Rights and operates within the context of the Council of Europe.

The European Union does, however, work closely with these international organisations which overlap. What is more, the EU does mandate its member states to be part of the ECHR and therefore follow its rulings.

The European Free Trade Association is also separate to the EU. This was founded in 1960 to provide tariff free trade without the loss of sovereignty that came with membership of the European Economic Community, the forerunner of the EU. Clearly there is much more to 'Europe' than the European Union.

EFTA, as it is known, does however work closely with the European Union. Three of its four members – Iceland, Liechtenstein and Norway – form with 27 EU members, Croatia being the exception, what is known as the European Economic Area (EEA). The EEA is the EU's internal market with many standardised regulations free movement of goods, services capital and people. It is known in Britain as the Single Market. Switzerland an EFTA state has its own separate relationship agreements with the EU which grants them rights to access the EEA's internal market.

The EU is also not a simple trading relationship. It is a system of law making whose rulings bind its member states and influence the laws of some other countries beyond the EU's borders.

Whilst power is being handed to the European Union whose laws have supremacy over national law it is technically incorrect to describe the EU as a United States of Europe. Its Executive branch is not a directly elected institution. What is more, whilst it does resemble a federal system and a state with its own flag, incidentally borrowed from the Council of Europe, and an anthem, sovereignty in the EU ultimately rests with the nation states. The opportunities for the member states to use their sovereign rights is however extremely limited and mainly exists in the right to leave. Until such time the EU institutions bind its member states under it rules and regulations. This transfer of power encompasses many areas ranging from trade to an increasing amount of criminal justice legislation.

The EU is not just a source of law it also has a policies and programmes which are not conceptual ideas but must in fact be paid for.

How the EU is funded

In 2013 the EU had an annual budget of €150.9 billion (£126 billiion). 1% goes towards supporting its policies relating to citizenship, freedom, security and justice. 6% is spent on meeting the EU's administrative costs and a further 6% goes towards its foreign policy and international commitments. 42% is related to the Common Agricultural Policy with approximately a quarter of that going on rural development and the remainder funding direct aids and market related expenditure. And the final 45% is intended to fund projects to create economic cohesion and to create growth and employment.

There are a number of funding streams from where the EU obtains money from the member states.

One funding stream is known as 'Traditional own resources.' This is mainly the customs duties on imports from outside the EU and the taxes on importing for example sugar. Member states are allowed to keep 25% of this to cover the costs of collecting this money on the EU's behalf.

Indirect taxation, that is the EU's version of a sales tax known as Value Added Tax, is under the control of EU law. National governments only have the right to raise the level of the tax in certain areas beyond a standard minimum level. The EU takes a small proportion of this 'own resource from value added tax (VAT).' This source of funding gives the EU approximately €14 billion.

The largest source of revenue is known as the 'own resource based on gross national income (GNI). This was originally intended to be simply a financial balancing system, but is now the largest source of revenue for the EU. In 2010 it took from the member states €92.7 billion.

These own resources are 1.23% of the gross income of the EU and it accounts for 99% of the total EU budget. Other revenue comes from contributions from non-EU countries to certain EU programmes which they can take part in, fines on companies for breaching European Union law, and taxes on EU staff salaries. The EU's bureaucrats in Brussels pay a mere 12% tax. They are not the only ones who are benefitting from the EU. Members of the European Parliament can earn more than massively higher salaries than their compatriots in their home state where people are often less well-off in particular Bulgaria and Romania.

The budget of the European Union is over a seven year cycle known as a Multiannual Financial Framework; the next running from 2014 – 2020. In the member states the financial proposals come from the elected governments. In the EU the system is quite different.

EU budget proposals come from the unelected European Commission. The draft budget is then discussed by the European Council, which consists of EU member-state leaders and if a majority under the Qualified Majority Voting procedure request that the Commission's proposal be modified then the matter goes before the European Parliament who can chose to stick with the Commission's request or make their own amendments to the wishes of the Council. The matter then has to be put before what is known as a conciliation committee. This consists of the members of the Council and an equal number of MEPs which will then thrash out a common proposal. And the final say on the common proposal rests with the deeply federalist European Parliament, and not with national leaders. There is not an effective national veto over the budget. If no agreement can be reached then the previous year's budget stays in force. However, 2% is added onto its total and it therefore automatically increases.

Despite there being an agreed level of funding it does not stop the European Commission from regularly claiming the need to take yet more money. This adds more costs onto the taxpayer.

Chapter 2

The Trouble with the EU

"People crushed by law, have no hopes but from power. If laws are their enemies, they will be enemies to laws; and those who have much to hope and nothing to lose, will always be dangerous."
Edmund Burke, British Parliamentarian and political theorist, 8th October 1777

There are a number of ways in which EU membership directly impacts upon people in the UK. Supporters and opponents of Britain's membership routinely exaggerate or play down these factors to support their point of view. They are able to do this largely because the true facts are so difficult to get hold of and because the ways the EU works are so frustratingly opaque.

One of the most often referred to costs of the EU is that it places a direct charge on the British taxpayer; they have been net contributors to the EU in all but one of UK's 40 years of membership. The only year when Britain was a net beneficiary was 1975. In real terms the total contributions since joining amount to £401 billion gross, with the British taxpayer only received back £134 billion in the form of EU spending in the UK and the budget rebate.

In 2012 gross payments to the EU amount to more than £15.02 billion, however, the UK is entitled to a rebate of just over £3.17 billion. This makes a net payment of nearly £11.85 billion per year. However, the EU spent inside the UK more than £4.95 billion. This still leaves a sizeable deficit of nearly £6.9 billion in 2012. What is more, gross payments are set to increase and in the 2014–15 financial year will reach more than £18.7 billion with a net contribution, less the rebate and EU spending in Britain, totalling nearly £9.37 billion per year.

The EU's spending in member states goes towards aid for the farming sector, EU projects involved with education and regional aid. However, this spending has to be match funded by the British government. It is worth noting that the EU's own Court of Auditors has never signed off the EU's accounts citing numerous instances of fraud and mismanagement.

It is not a matter of contention how much the UK has to pay the EU, the issue here is what exactly is the UK getting in return for the large membership bill. There are other costs and benefits associated with EU membership.

A core principle of the European Union is the free movement of peoples between member states of both the EU and the European Economic Area. This is, apart from the higher taxes that have to be paid and noticeable in deductions from monthly pay packets, one of the main areas where people will see the effects of EU membership.

EU Directive 2004/38/EC gives free movement without the need for a visa to all members of both the European Union and the European Economic Area. It came into force on 29th April 2004 just prior to the enlargement of the EU when it expanded to the east taking in 8 Eastern European states as well as the Mediterranean countries of Malta and Cyprus.

This rule covers all citizens regardless of their background and even if a criminal offence has been committed. Contrary to a popular misconception the reason why criminals from other EU states cannot be deported is not because of the Human Rights Act and the European Court of Human Rights. It is because Directive 2004/58/EC allows even those with criminal records to enjoy the benefits of free movement between EU members. Deportation can only happen when 'The personal conduct of the individual concerned must represent a genuine, present and sufficiently serious threat affecting one of the fundamental interests of society.' It also states that, 'Previous criminal convictions shall not in themselves constitute grounds for taking such measures.'

One of the few Europeans to be denied entry was the Dutch politician Geert Willders MP. He was due to attend a meeting at the House of Lords where issues of Islamic extremism were due to be discussed. The exclusion order led to objections from the Dutch Ambassador to the UK.

Other areas on controversy concern the economic impact of migration. One a half million non-British citizens of other EU member states work in the UK, This constitutes around 5% of employment in Britain.

According to the a report from November 2013 by the Centre for Research and Analysis Migration between 2001 and 2011 immigrants to the UK from the EU, plus Iceland, Liechtenstein and Norway, contributed 34% more in taxes than the British state spent on supporting them.

Whilst that report shows a fiscal benefit to the British exchequer in tax receipts there is evidence that suggests wider economic harm.

According to the respected think tank specialising in issues relating to immigration, Migration Watch UK, an immigrant will have to earn approximately £27,000 to make a positive financial contribution to the British economy. This figure is based upon the average earnings in Britain with an additional amount added on to make up for the cost of the additional infrastructure to support the new entrants into the UK - such as schools for their children. Housing is also affected since an increase in demand without a corresponding increase in supply will drive up both rents and house prices. Immigration also has an effect on depressing the average wage of existing British residents.

The less well off existing residents lose the most from immigration. For each 1% increase in the number of working age immigrants there was a 0.6% decline in the pay packets of those in the bottom 5% of the pay scale. The lowest paid ten per cent suffered from a 0.4% decline in their wages. What is more, the least skilled existing British workers had a reduction of 0.5% in their salaries.

Another cost of immigration is the transfer of money that migrants have earned in the UK back to their country of origin. According to the World Bank each year $1.2 billion is sent from Britain to Poland alone.

This is money that is leaving the UK and benefitting another state. This transfer of funds out of the UK to family in home state their home state, or to fund investments in their country of origin, is of enormous economic importance to many who reside in Eastern Europe.

Much of these costs, however, rely on the immigrants being economically active. According a report by the European Commission the number of non-working immigrants from the EU had risen from

2006 to 2012 by 42% to more than 611,779. According to the same report between 2008 and 2011 there was a 73% increase in the number of people from the EU coming to Britain without a job. Dry economic numbers are not the only considerations when assessing the impact of immigration from the EU to the UK. There are also social considerations in particular matters of community cohesion. The former Labour Home Secretary, Rt Hon. David Blunkett MP, warned on 11th November 2013 that the influx of Roma from eastern Europe may cause riots on the streets.

The European Union is much more than the establishment of a set of principles that establish the free movement of goods, services, capital and movement. It is also a system of governance that that sits above the nation states but its rules apply to all. One of the most well-known and costly is the EU's system of agricultural support, payments and protection against competition from producers outside the EU, in particular developing nations. This is called the Common Agricultural Policy (CAP).

This policy makes up more than 40% of EU spending. In 2013 the EU spent €57.5 billion on subsidies to farmers and rural development. More than ten billion euros The CAP as it is also known is a prime example of a policy that is not in the economic interests of British consumers. Whereas the UK only receives 7.6% of the European Agricultural Guarantee Fund, France receives 20%, the largest amount of any EU member state.

According to written evidence provided by the charity Oxfam to the House of Commons Environmental Audit Committee it is not just the British taxpayer that is losing out. Across the EU the CAP places €36.2 billion on to consumer's food bills. According to Oxfam, this costs a typical European family of four almost €1,000 a year in higher food prices. That is €20 per week on the average family's food bill. This approximate figure is supported by the Paris based Organisation for Economic Co-operation and Development (OECD) this international organisation exists to promote trade and economic advancement. The OECD have estimated that the higher taxes and food prices caused through agricultural protectionism costs the family of four $1,000 per year. With food prices being as much as 30% higher than food which is traded internationally.

To whose benefit are these resources being spent? It is believed that the CAP's agricultural support payments are intended for small farmers, however Oxfam make the case that 80% of the support goes to the wealthiest land owners and the largest agricultural businesses. The OECD also argue that in the European Union under the CAP system the richest 25% get 70% of the payments. And that 'Tens of thousands of small farm households benefit little from current farm policies.' And that 'Of every $1 in price support, only $0.25 ends up in the farmer's pocket as extra income. The rest is absorbed by higher land prices, fertiliser and feed costs and other factors.'

It is not just consumers that are losing out, with British families paying a disproportionally high price for food imported from outside of the European Union which must face EU customs taxes. Many of these producers are in developing nations and the Commonwealth; this prejudices trade with the famers in those countries which also face quota restrictions. The CAP therefore has the notoriety for hurting both first world consumers and third world producers, whilst giving little benefit to small farmers.

This is not the only costly common policy that works against Britain's economic interests.

The Common Fisheries Policy is also considered to be a drain on the British economy. A condition of entry into the EEC, as it was then, the British government was required to surrender control over its fishing waters on 1st January 1973. Under United Nations rules a country has the right, even the responsibility, to control the sea around its coast stretching out for a total of 200 miles or until the median line between two adjacent nations.

The European Commission also opened up UK waters to all other member states' fishing fleets, apportioning fishing rights as they saw fit. The Common Fisheries Policy costs Britain more than £3.7 billion per year caused through the EU depriving the UK of its fishing grounds.

In 2012 UK fishing vessels landed 627,000 tonnes of sea fish (including shellfish) this yearly catch has a value of £770 million. This is 13% of the value for the total EU catch. In 2012 British vessels account for approximately 12%-13% of the total size of the EU catch. This figure remains relatively constant. In 2010 the total EU catch amounted to 4,923,000 tonnes, the share of this going to UK fishermen is 608,000 tonnes. The British catch in 2010 was again approximately 12%-13% of the total for the EU.

This means that the EU fishing industry is worth £6.4 billion. Approximately 70% of this catch is taken in what were once British fishing grounds, now governed by the EU and open to vessels from other EU member states. This means that if these waters were fully reserved for UK fishermen, which would be legal under international law, then British fishing vessels would be able to land nearly £4.5 billion worth of fish. Yet the vast majority is being lost to our partners in the EU, with British fisherman only being able to land £770,000 worth of fish.

Other estimates suggest that 80% of the total EU catch comes from what are, by United Nations standards, British waters. This would put the figure of the total resource taken from UK control by the EU at more than £5 billion.

The problems of the CFP are not just economic. The EU's quota restrictions have had a disastrous environmental impact. If a vessel lands more than its allotted amounted then they must discard the fish that exceed the EU's legal limit. The result is that as much as two thirds are returned to sea dead and subsequently fish stocks have significantly declined; further reducing the bounty of the sea. This policy has turned the once abundant North Sea into an ecological crisis area.

The devastating industry can be measured in a human impact. In 1970 there were 21,443 fishermen in the UK; by 2012 that figure had been cut back to just 12,445. The loss of jobs and the once active fishing fleet will also have had a detrimental effect on secondary industries that supported the fishing fleet and benefitted from the proceeds from this once sizeable business.

The effect of EU control via the Common Fisheries Policy has been to seriously damage a once strong industry. Landings into the UK have fallen from 1,039,100 tonnes in 1970 to just 489,100 in 2012. This steady decline has led to a growing dependency upon imports. In 2010, a total of 687,054 tonnes of seafood worth £2.23 billion was imported into Britain. This subsidising of foreign fleets by British consumers could be reduced if UK fishermen had their exclusive rights restored to them.

Fish is not the only area where since joining the EU where there is a significant trade deficit. Throughout the UK's membership of the EU, apart from years 1980–1984, Britain has had an ever growing trade deficit with the other EU member states. In short, businesses in the EU sell more to the UK than businesses in Britain sell to the other 27 EU members. In 2012 the trade deficit reached an astonishing £46 billion. This is money that is leaving the UK, subsidising employment on the continent. Conversely, the UK has a trade surplus with the rest of world of £17 billion.

The Customs Union and Free Trade
In terms of international trade the EU is what is known as a 'customs union'. This removes tariffs on trade between members but creates an external tariff against imports from outside, unless a free trade agreement is in place with the exporting country. These are not decided by individual member states but are arranged by the European Commission and are subject to agreement by both the Council and the European Parliament. The UK has to accept what is negotiated on the UK's behalf.

Here a stark difference develops between supporters and critics of the EU. The divergence between those who perceive that the EU's control over trade and investment policy has benefits and those that believe it has significant costs is one of fundamental outlook. Those who see that the EU is beneficial are pessimistic about what would have been achieved had it not been for EU membership.

Those who are sceptical about the EU are optimistic about what Britain can achieve outside of the EU. Britain, they think, could be doing much better. Despite the UK being a smaller market than the entirety of the EU, an independent Britain may be able to reach trade agreements with states in the rest of the world more in tune with what Britain needs, than the deals reached by the European Commission which take account of the needs of France, Germany and others.

Negotiations conducted by Britain alone will be more straightforward than those undertaken by the Brussels bureaucracy. The UK, representing its own national interest, will not be encumbered by the diverse and at times contradictory interests that exist within the EU and its different member states; considerations that have at times held up the EU reaching trade deals with developing nations.

The greatest net profit from international trade is with states that are outside of the European Union. The UK has a £22 billion surplus on trade with the United States of America, £9.7 billion with Australia and £8.5 billion with the non-EU state of Switzerland.

Despite the disparity between exports and imports, with the benefits predominantly going to the other EU members, it is often reported that half our exports to the EU. The reality is somewhat different. The amount of British exports to the other EU states in 2012 including trade in goods and services, with income transfers taken into account, was 41% not 50%. What is more, 41% includes exports to customers outside of the EU that go via ports on the continent.

The Office for National Statistics counts goods shipped to Rotterdam and Antwerp as an export to the EU, even if they are promptly reshipped out to Brazil, China or elsewhere. When this so-called 'Rotterdam-Antwerp effect' is taken into account the true figure of exports to the EU is just 38%.

The gathering of trade statistics between EU member states is governed by EU Regulations (EC) 638/2004 and 1982/2004. It is these rules which mandate that the recipient of the exports is recorded as the first port the goods arrive at, regardless of whether they are re-shipped to a third destination.

This is still significant but trade with businesses on the continent is declining and trade to the rest of the world is increasing. With the emergence of fast growing markets on the continent, and the continuing economic crisis in the eurozone, this trend will only continue. Yet as members of the EU Britain is banned from negotiating trade deals with other countries.

Despite all this, there is research which makes the case that membership of the EU has been beneficial for all concerned. This largely rests upon the presumption that trade would not have opened up between the members of the EU without this being demanded by Brussels. This ignores the fact that a free trade area had been established and originally contained more members than the predecessor of the EU, the European Economic Community. There were originally seven members of the British inspired European Free Trade Association (EFTA) and just six within the EEC. EFTA may well have grown as an organisation if it were not for the defection of one of its leading members, notably the UK in 1973, in search of improved trade with the EEC. Yet, just four years later the remaining EFTA members were to agree tariff free trade in industrial goods with the EEC with further agreements that followed. The EU also has free trade agreements with a host of other states around the globe.

It is reasonable, therefore, to presume that preferential trading terms would exist between the EU and the UK even if Britain had not become a member.

What is more, it also fails to take account of the fact that there is an on-going global trend where restrictive trade practices are being eliminated across the world. Globally there has been a steady lowering of taxes on imports and quotas banning imports beyond a predefined level are being replaced with a system whereby additional tariffs are placed on imports that exceed the given quota.

Even the EU's external tariff, which adds duties onto some imports from outside of the customs union, has an average tax of just 1% on the sale price, for some products this is considerably higher. The EU's customs union may have become an almost pointless burden which costs more to administer than what it takes in customs duties.

Political unions are not needed for trade in fact far from enhancing trade politics and politicians actually create barriers to trade. Businesses have to operate in the environment that has been set for them which can be problematic if barriers to trade are created.

Whereas the EU seeks to facilitate trade between its member states it does place obstacles in the way of businesses exporting to the European Union from outside. Whereas it is correct that the European Union, and therefore, its member states, have free and preferential trade arrangements with at present 45 nations outside the European Economic Area these are often complex with many conditions attached.

From the European Commission perspective, free trade agreements are not just to encourage the export of goods but also exist to export its regulations. A condition of tariff free trade access and the faster transit through customs is for the non-EU state to apply common technical and health and safety standards. Compliance with EU environmental rules is also a requirement. There is also the requirement to commit to ensuring that competition is not being distorted by state intervention, as well as the protection of intellectual property rights and that public procurement will be open to all.

There is a price to be paid for accessing the EU's internal market from outside the EU. Still the level of compliance with EU rules will be less than those enforced on the member states of the European Union. However, free trade with the EU does not necessarily mean easy trade. It refers to the elimination of customs duties not of red tape.

One tangible benefit of EU membership for businesses that export to the other EU states is that they have collectively been freed from the requirement to complete hundreds of millions of forms when selling goods and services across the EU. Businesses outside of the European Union must, under EU rules, influenced by the Brussels based World Customs Organisation , undergo a number of significant administrative burdens. The WCO is the intergovernmental organisation which establishes the system of international trade. 179 countries around the globe operate under its aegis covering 98% of international trade.

Even countries that have free trade, either via the European Economic Area or through bilateral trade treaties which eliminate tariffs still have to comply with the EU's bureaucratic procedures.

While trade is easier if a trade agreement is in place, and certainly less expensive, those states must still complete paperwork in particular a EUR.1 movement certificate which must be processed by customs agents. Similar requirements for documentation providing evidence on the origin of goods must be submitted for the states of the Euro-Mediterranean Partnership.

EU membership frees exporters from having to prove the origin of the goods they are selling. If a business is sending produce to the EU from a country that has a free trade agreement it must prove that they were mostly manufactured or re-worked in a country that had a free trade agreement with the EU. If the business cannot confirm the origin of the goods then the tariffs will apply. This can be sidestepped by making some modifications to the products in the exporting state, yet this may be subject to investigation.

The requirement to clear customs and complete documentation, known as an ATA Carnet, to validate the origin of goods and confirm that they are free from tariffs even applies to Turkey. This country is a member of the EU's customs union and therefore has tariff free access for industrial products but it is not bureaucracy free access.

Even where tariffs are eliminated when importing from outside of the EU there is still the requirement to pay Value Added Tax. If the exporter is registered for VAT then this can be claimed back but only if they registered and there is a requirement for an input VAT certificate.

Businesses in EU member states that trade across the EU are also free from having to pay anti-dumping duty. If an exporter to the EU sells its products at a cheaper rate than in its domestic market then this is considered dumping and will face a charge to force an increase in its price. Even the threat of applying these charges can force an exporter to raise its prices thus losing market share in the EU.

At the end of September 2013 the EU was undertaking 33 investigations and undertaking 84 separate cases of anti-dumping measures against products from more than twenty countries, including; China, Malaysia, Thailand, India, Ukraine, Russia and Belarus. A particular issue at present is the EU's anti-dumping action against solar panels being imported from China.

Membership of the EU and the EEA also opens up public procurement to businesses in all EU states. This gives business the opportunity to access a market in public procurement that is worth €2,150 billion per year - around 16% of the EU's entire GDP.

One of the main benefits of membership comes through the principle of mutual recognition. This allows businesses to export to the entire European Economic Area, the internal market, without having to seek approval for the goods to be sold in each member state. As the Single Market is still not complete some member states still have differing standards. The principle of mutual recognition is that if a product has been approved as safe and saleable in one member state then it can be sold in all. This bypasses costly and time consuming safety and regulatory checks in each country where the good is sold. This applies to those that are members of the European Union and the European Free Trade Association states that are in the EEA.

Inside the EU exporting to Berlin is effectively not any different from sending goods to Birmingham, just that the transportation will, due to the distance involved set a slightly greater logistical challenge. There is no requirement for burdensome bureaucracy when moving goods between member states. This will have helped smaller firms to export as there is no administration involved in sending goods across national borders. In fact national borders in terms of trade can be said to no longer exist within the European Union. This eliminates an administrative and therefore a financial cost on trade which non-EU states have to pay regardless of whether trade is 'free' or not.

Membership of the European Union and the European Economic Area also allows businesses to sell their services across the EU and in

Iceland, Lichtenstein and Norway. This should be of particular benefit to the UK with its strong services industry, however, barriers to trade in services, as well as some relating to goods still exist. The government believes that if these can be eliminated, creating one internal market with all rules indistinguishable between member states then economic output could be as much as 7% higher.

After the EU's Single Market had been in operation for 10 years the European Commission estimated that it had added 1.8% to the EU's GDP. A less than 2% increase in economic output is, however, hardly stellar. The European Commission apportions these benefits to the Internal Market opening up national economies to competition, which incidentally should have had downward pressure on prices.

Burdens are further reduced through the establishment of a one-stop-shop for patents. These are a legal title given to the owner of the patent, usually those who developed the technical product, from preventing others from marketing the same technology which others had spent resources on investing in it. This protects their investment and therefore encourages innovation; that is if patent law is not manipulated to drive out legitimate competition. According to the European Commission this gives businesses 'uniform protection' and provides 'huge cost advantages and reducing administrative burdens.'

It is clear that EU membership does ease trade between its member states. However, this works both ways and helps competitors on the continent brings imports into the UK. Importing is not in itself undesirable since many jobs will depend upon bringing resources into the UK – some of which cannot be produced in the UK's domestic markets. However, such a large imbalance as £46 billion remains a drain on the economy. Importing on such a large scale is ultimately exporting wealth and jobs to other territories.

However, if the British economy was more competitive then there would be less need to bring in imports, exports will also be maximised. Does the EU harm Britain's competitiveness? And does the European Union prevent the UK from having a competitive advantage over other EU member states and redress the imbalance in trade?

Regulation

One area of considerable contention is the issue of regulation; this is seen as placing burdens and costs onto businesses. The EU produces legislation which with a few exceptions, known as derogations, apply across the entirety of the EU in such circumstances Britain has limited room for manoeuvre when seeking to reduce the regulatory burden.

The Single Market is not just to enable the easy trafficking of goods, service, capital and labour. It is also a single regulatory area, some of which may be considered beneficial. Consumer protection is an area which EU law safeguards. Such rules, however, could be implemented by the nation states without the need for the higher authority of the EU to demand compliance. Conversely, whilst some will benefit from an individual regulation, excessive rulemaking imposes costs on businesses which will ultimately be paid by consumers and employees.

The European Union is not the only source of such regulation. Nation states also add to the abundance of laws affecting businesses as do agencies of the United Nations. Overregulation is stated as a substantial cost to the economy but a case can be made that the standardisation of technical specifications and standards is of economic benefit and increases trade.

A case can be made that common standards actually boost trade and make it easier for both service providers and manufacturers. Value is added to goods through an increasingly complex chain of production over many jurisdictions, with different parts and programmes originating in a number of countries. Global production, it is argued, requires global regulation. The Brussels bureaucracy is not the only organisation that promotes this position. It is shared by some in the United States of America and is espoused by the influential US group the Council on Foreign Relations.

What is more, the setting of different standards in one country can be used as a protectionist measure that makes it more difficult for one country to produce products for the recipients market. This is especially the case if the exporter has to pass costly and time consuming safety checks.

The standardisation of regulation will therefore remove these technical barriers to trade. Certainly it is the case that supply lines are always improved if there is interoperability. The difference between domestic and export markets will also be reduced making it easier for businesses to operate in one environment. The effects are not just one of ease and convenience for businesses.

The joint European and US mission to send a satellite to Mars failed when it was approaching the red planet's atmosphere due to a simple technical issue. The European systems were programmed in the continental metric system, invented after the French Revolution, and the American software used the traditional Imperial system. The two systems ultimately proved to be incompatible. The Mars Climate Orbiter was lost on 23rd September 1999.

The long serving Premiere of Communist China, Zhou Enlai, was famously asked by US President Richard Nixon during his 1972 visit to Red China what he thought the impact of the French Revolution was; the answer from Zhou was "It is too early to say." The Mars metric mix-up was another consequence of the 1789–1799 upheavals in France.

The arguable increase in trade does not take into account the probability that some businesses can reach agreement themselves making the regulation unwarranted. The desire for regulation also fails to consider the costs of compliance. The level of interference does reach a point where it becomes excessive and arguably this stage has been reached. Standardisation is also monotonous and impinges on creativity harming innovation.

Contrary to the trade argument there is substantial evidence which suggests that overregulation is holding back economic growth. These conclusions which place the costs higher than has been estimated by some Eurosceptics have reached the highest levels of successive governments. A report on the burdensome cost to business was commissioned by the pro-EU Prime Minster, Tony Blair, during his time in office. The 2005 report by the Better Regulation Task Force for the then premier estimated that regulation cost the British economy 10-12% of GDP. That amounts to approximately £150 billion per annum. This cost is divided between, administration which entails 'familiarisation, record keeping and reporting, including inspection and enforcement.' This accounts for around a third of the burden with the remainder coming from the 'costs directly attributable to the policy goal.' At least half of this regulation, and therefore at least half the costs, originate from the EU; with this amount steadily growing. Half the cost equates to £75 billion pounds per year.

Other arms of the state have, however, come to different conclusions with civil service impact assessments reaching a different figure. These have been analysed by the British Chamber of Commerce in their

Burdens Barometer 2010 report. According to this he annual cost of EU regulation is £7.5 billion per year, still not an inconsiderable sum.

Who is correct?

The figure derived from the British civil service may well underestimate the costs of regulation. Their impact assessments have been criticised by the Business Regulation Task Force. This report argued that the evaluations by Whitehall are inadequate. They lack a full cost benefit analysis of how the regulation is to be implemented and enforced. What is more, the impact assessments do not include other, less costly, alternatives to regulation.

The EU also produces its own impact assessments on the advantages and disadvantages of its own regulations. Just as the EU habitually regards that the appropriate level for law making is at the European level, so it also regards its rules to be always beneficial with affordable costs. The fundamental flaw at the heart of EU impact assessments is the fact that the Commission, the body which produces the legislation, also conducts the cost/benefit analysis of the proposals. The bureaucracy, which incidentally leaves implementation to the EU's arm's length agencies and the member states, are unlikely to consider their own ideas as defective.

What is more, the monitoring of the legislation once in force also rests with the European Commission, the same body that has the monopoly on introducing the directives and regulations.

The Roman poet, Juvenal, in his satires famously asked Quis custodiet ipsos custodes? This translates as "Who will guard the guards themselves?" When it comes to law making in the EU the answer is that the EU is its own guardian. The future of enterprise in Europe rests with the benevolence, or perhaps, malevolence of the European bureaucracy.

Even supporters of the EU and some senior figures in the European Commission have admitted that the overregulation of business is harming the economy.

Peter Mandelson, the Secretary of State for Trade, told Confederation of British Industry conference on 8th November 2004 that the cost of EU regulation amounts to holding back GDP in the EU by as much as 4%. He was soon to become the EU Commissioner for Trade, taking up that post just two weeks later. This regulatory burden did not decrease during his time at the centre of the EU.

Those in the UK who believe that EU regulation is seriously to the detriment of enterprise are not alone. The Netherlands has also come to the conclusion that the EU is bad for business. As long ago as 2002 the Dutch government estimated that the administrative burden of regulation alone, which they define as 'the costs imposed on businesses when complying with information obligations stemming from government regulation' cost them 3.6% of GDP.

Other Dutch reports have come to similar conclusions. In 2004 a report commissioned at the request of Gerrit Zalm, the then Dutch Deputy Prime Minister who also served at that time as the Netherland's Finance Minister, estimated that the administrative burden on business in his country cost 3.7% of economic output. These conclusions were supported by the Organisation for Economic Co-operation and Development (OECD). In 1997 they predicted that regulatory reform in the Netherlands could boost Dutch GDP by 3.5%.

Like the UK, not all Dutch regulation, comes through the imposition of European Union directives and regulations. In the Netherlands, it is estimated that the EU element amounts to 40%. The proportion for the UK is higher, now as much as 60%.

On 10th October 2006 Günter Verhuegen, the European Commissioner for Enterprise and Industry and a Vice-President of Commission stated that,

"Many people still have this concept of Europe that the more rules you produce the more Europe you have. The idea is that the role of the commission is to keep the machinery running and the machinery is producing laws. And that's exactly what I want to change."

Verhuegen's bid for reform was, however, blocked according to the Commissioner by the EU's administrative culture. Even the Vice-President could not stop the legislative avalanche.

Günter Verhuegen also estimated that the annual cost of EU regulation across the EU amounted to €600 billion per annum (around 5.5% of GDP), while the benefits of the Single Market amount to only €160 billion: therefore the costs exceeded the benefits by a staggering €440 billion. Later, in a letter from Commissioner Verhuegen to Bill Newton-Dunn MEP, on 18th June 2007, the Commissioner gives the overall figure of just the administrative burden of EU level legislation as costing 3.5% of GDP for all member states and this sum would be similar for the UK. What is more, the figure of three and a half per cent actually excludes the costs that directly relate to the policy goal making the final figure on EU regulation much higher.

It appears that even these, now former, Commissioners have a better recognition of the harm that EU rules have on competitiveness than British civil servants whose analysis of the costs of regulation in their recent impact assessments clearly underestimate the burdens that are being placed on businesses. Neither, however, could stop the ever-growing amount of EU rules. If the EU has not changed this damaging practice after more than a decade of governments recognising there is a problem what hope is their of change now?

All measures of the cost of EU regulation show that there is indeed a significant price that business and therefore consumers have to pay as a result of EU rules; it is merely the final figure that is a matter of much debate. The costs of EU red-tape are excessive, and Eurosceptics are not alone in highlighting this cost as even the EU's proponents admit to concern about it. Across the EU enterprise, production and entrepreneurship have been replaced with regulation, inspection and compliance. Even the Confederation of British Industry mentioned in a report on the European Union that, 'The EU has moved too far from 'adding value' to 'adding functions', resulting in 'mission creep' in several areas.'

Yet why at this difficult economic time is it still in place and continually being added to? Or, more specifically, cui bono; who benefits from the EU?

The reasons for regulation
Sir John Robert Seeley, the historian and writer on religious affairs, in his 1883 book the Expansion of England wrote of the British Empire that 'we seem, as it were, to have conquered half the world in a fit of absence of mind.' The Empire of the European Union, a realm of regulation, has conversely been deliberately established. It is not a free trade area that has been on an accidental legislative binge. The higher authority of the EU uses law to achieve its goal; that is the building of a monolithic system of political control that is aimed, rightly or wrongly, at reining in the excesses of the nation states. By implication the nationalist passions of the citizens of its member states are also kept in check. Or so the thinking goes. Building Europe requires the establishment of a body of law known as the acquis communautaire.

A new political power cannot be said to exist unless it is an active law maker. The European Commission recognises that its political governance cannot be established in an absence of law.

Whilst the EU is largely immune to influence from national democratic institutions it is very much open to lobbying for new legislation from both environmental groups and multi-national businesses alike. Small and medium sized enterprises, who suffer most from red-tape, do not have the finances nor the time to defend their interests. This is not surprising; since 2010 there have been 3580 new EU rules on business that would take 92 days to read. Naturally the bigger the business the greater the resources it can spend on both being consulted by Brussels on future legislation and on lobbying for laws that are in their interests. This can include regulations that add costs on to competitors. Despite the apparent quest for harmony between the people of Europe, EU law making can also be manipulated to raise the costs of a rival country.

According to the German economist, Professor Roland Vaubel,

"Under qualified majority voting, the majority of highly regulated countries (say, France) have an incentive and the power to impose their high level of regulation on the minority of more market-oriented countries (say, the UK) in order to weaken the latter's competitiveness. In the political economy literature, this is called "the strategy of raising rivals' costs". The common level of regulation that is imposed on the minority is even higher than the level originally prevailing among the majority because the majority is no longer constrained by the competitive pressure from the minority."

The City of London and the UK's financial services industry has borne the brunt of this legislative assault. Recent regulations concerning; Credit Rating Agencies, and the establishment of the European Systemic Risk Board, the European Banking Authority, the European Securities and Markets Authority the European Insurance and Occupational Pensions Authority are prime examples. As is the Alternative Investment Fund Managers directive.

The French economist, Professor Jean-Jacques Rosa, shares this opinion. The centralisation of power over 500 million EU citizens resting with the institutions of the EU also maximises the potential effects of lobbying. It does not, however, produce good law.

'A lasting effect is detrimental to consumers. When there is an increase in spending for lobbying, and new lobbies are formed, individual firms get used to work more intensively and more efficiently together, to get "better" regulations passed by the authority. And so the incentives for forming cartels, the collusion between firms, are much increased. As we know, cartels are good for business and bad for consumers: they result in higher prices and lower quantities.'

Professor Rosa further argues that the handing of power to the EU not only dilutes democracy but also produces bad law because it stops competition between different regulatory agencies with control resting with one organisation that is unable to react to changing circumstances.

The elimination of competition and the imposition of vertical lines of control from the European Commission down is anathema in the modern information age with its horizontal lines of communication. In the EU it is becoming difficult to observe and learned from other countries best practice.

Professor Rosa further states that the effect of regulation and its elimination of competition is harmful for consumers. It is, he argues,

'not good for the creation of new firms and for the general dynamism of the economy. Indeed, it is the source of what I call the sclerotic organisation in the EU. It enforces and enhances the rents of large, older business firms and bureaucracies and freezes the hierarchical structure of both industry and political production at a moment when innovation, new small firms, and lighter government are required. It is a recipe for accelerated decline.'

At times corporations in the EU may, conversely, push for light touch regulation. The European Union, after lobbying from the food industry, introduced in 2002 a new food safety regulatory system. This new regime did not include the member states having control. Food safety, as well as labelling, came under the power of the European Union and its European Food Safety Authority, this EU quango sits above the national food safety agencies which receive instructions from the central body. EU Council regulation 178/2002 did not, however, lead to more regulation but less. It gives the primary responsibility for food safety and quality in all EU member states to the food producers and retailers themselves. This removed it from the control of member states and created a system of self-regulation where the retailers policed themselves.

There is an international dimension at work and remains behind the initiation of many EU rules. There is a plethora of UN sponsored standard setting agencies which produce proposals for legislative standardisation across continents and beyond. An increasing amount of what we know as EU legislation is originating above the EU. The EU as part of the case law underpinning the workings of the European Union recognises that international law is to be incorporated into EU law which therefore, via Brussels, becomes the law of each and every member state. The legal decisions of the European Court of Justice which confiorm this are: Case 104/81, Kupferberg, Case C-192/89 Sevince and Case C-277/94 Taflan-Met.

Yet the EU is not just a passive receives of diktats from the international organisations that sit above the EU and are even more opaque than the workings of Brussels. The EU also seeks to export its regulations beyond its own borders.

The European is reticent about letting goods into its jurisdiction unless its safety standards have been met. This is largely a protectionist measure that is designed to protect its highly regulated market from more competitive produced products from more liberally managed economies.

According to Professor Ragnar Löfstedt the Director of King's Centre for Risk Management whenever a new endeavour or product is proposed the European Commission believes that any uncertainty requires shifting the burden and standard of proof. It holds that uncertain risk requires forbidding the potentially risky activity until the proponent of the activity demonstrates that it poses no (or an acceptable) risk. This attitude is at the heart of EU regulation and largely responsible for the growing complexity and rigidity of European Union law.

Members of the EU's customs union, such as Turkey which is outside of the EU, must as part of the agreement which gives them tariff free market access apply some common EU standards on industrial products destined for European markets. The requirement for this to be in place also stretches to the most important potential trade deal in EU history. Instead of allowing European businesses to innovate more freely the Commission is even attempting to make the USA apply what is known as the 'precautionary principle.'

The stubborn requirement for this and not allowing free access to goods which do not comply with the precautionary principle may have the effect of scuppering the Transatlantic Trade and Investment Partnership between the EU and the USA. The United States of America has a different approach to risk-management which is more open to innovation. Incidentally the European Commission estimates that the free trade agreement with the USA has the potential to boost EU GDP by 0.5% which will annually add €120 billion to the economy.

The precautionary principle stymies innovation and harms economic growth. It is this concept - well-intended in theory, but pernicious in practice - that is responsible for the march of health and safety legislation.

The origins of the precautionary principle come from the World Charter for Nature, adopted by the UN General Assembly in 1982. Since then it has been fully embraced by the EU with damaging effects.

According to William Mason, a leader of the 2005 Better Regulation Taskforce advising the former Prime Minister Tony Blair during his Premiership, the EU aggressively uses the precautionary principle and,

'increasingly seeks to manage the risks that affect citizens as they pass through life. This is bad for society. Risk has a value, not just commercially, but also at an individual level. We have sleepwalked into an over-regulated society where communities are increasingly dysfunctional — the state, via regulation, is destroying a culture which valued self-help, personal responsibility and community action.'

Conveniently the precautionary principle gives the EU wide ranging powers to produce yet more law. Its use has been upheld by the European Court of Justice in legal cases including Pfizer Animal Health SA v. Council 1999 E.C.R. II-1961. This allows the Commission to have an extremely low burden of proof for it to apply the precautionary principle and ban products from the market at will.

Other factors that have led to the growth of regulation include the expansion of the EU. The accession of the once Soviet dominated states did not lead to a new European paradigm where excessive regulation would be resisted. Far from leading to a liberalisation of the EU, as many hoped, the eastward expansion became another excuse for yet more law making. In the opinion of the Commission the former communist states of Eastern Europe had insufficiently developed law for a capitalist free market. Apparently their economies were in need of stewardship by the EU. The standardisation that followed led to even greater EU interference.

The former President of the Czech Republic, Václav Klaus, said, during his time in office that, "every time I try to repeal some Soviet-era directive, I'm told that whatever I am trying to scrap is a requirement of the European Commission."

The European Commission is not the only EU institution that is adding to the legislative morass. A member of the Commission Legal Service blames another branch of the EU, the European Parliament. 'The European Parliament, under the co-decision [ordinary] procedure, is allowed to propose uniformed, irrational, impractical amendments, safe in the knowledge that they have no responsibility for implementation.' Other EU institutions are also part of the problem as any ambiguity is clarified by the European Court of Justice who inevitability add evermore complexity to EU law; which once in place is extremely difficult to repeal. EU rules resemble the complicated financial devices bankers use like their debt swaps and derivatives. Few in the banking sector understood how they operated in practice let alone the risks involved. Complex EU law is equally economically damaging.

At the heart of EU law making is a desire to eliminate national differences. The European Union quite clearly establishes a system of law that demands conformity above the interests of diversity. Those who speak out against harmonisation are criticised as being uncommunitaire and working against solidarity in the EU. There is no better example of this than the policy of Economic and Monetary Union.

The monolithic Euro

When the Euro currency was established in 1999 its aim was made clear what the intentions were. Dominique Strauss-Kahn, who was then the French Finance Minister, described the euro as "a conquest of sovereignty." He was not alone in holding such an opinion. Yves-Thibault de Silguy, the EU's Economic and Financial Affairs Commissioner, described the introduction of one currency for the eurozone as "the first time Europe will have its own currency and the first time we have achieved such a result without arms." It is the EU's most well-known folie de grandeur.

Establishing a single currency, known as the Euro, for many of the states in the EU has removed from national democracies the ability to manage their own economies.

It conceals an inconvenient truth that the countries on the continent of Europe have incompatible economic needs. Having one currency takes away the ability of the eurozone states to react independently as their needs demand and meet the different challenges that each nation will face.

The Euro, which is primarily governed by the European Central Bank (ECB) based in Frankfurt, has followed a path that has been prejudicial to the interests of some states while benefiting others. When Germany needed a looser monetary policy to stimulate growth the countries of the Mediterranean-Rim conversely needed their inflationary boom to be reined in. Frankfurt's policy, however, favoured Teutonic interests.

Now the German economy is benefitting from the euro being undervalued by approximately 20-30%. This helps German exports both outside of the EU but also to other member states in the eurozone. Conversely, the Euro is at too high a value for the countries of Southern Europe. It thus makes their economies less competitive, less able to export and importantly their markets become susceptible to imports from Germany whose goods are made especially competitive. It is not surprising that the needs of the eurozone's largest economy will be placed before that of the struggling nations primarily in Southern Europe.

There has been, however, another factor at work that in European terms is more important than economics. That consideration is politics. The stable Deutschmark had been the cornerstone of their successful post-war strategy of pursuing inflation free and therefore competitive economic growth. Germany gave this up on the understanding that its replacement under Economic and Monetary Union would not cause inflation at home.

As Germany became more competitive with a continuing search for high productivity and a squeeze delivering lower Unit Labour Costs it could export more cheaply to the other states in the eurozone which were becoming increasingly uncompetitive by the inflation at home. The growth that did exist was debt fuelled and sucked in imports from the north. This lack of real sustainable growth meant that the states of

Southern Europe were essentially borrowing to fund Germany's trade surplus. The difference in competitiveness between the increasingly divergent economies of the eurozone has been exacerbated by the Euro which was at too high a value for domestic producers in countries such as Portugal, Italy, Greece and Spain. This further added to the divergence between north and south increasing the competitiveness gap. Each factor behind it became mutually reinforcing.

The result was that by 2012 German exports reached a record high. A leading German industrialist, Frank Asbeck, commented on the Eurozone crisis arguing that,

"From a German standpoint we don't see any crisis ... Germany is the industrial heart of Europe and as long as the Euro is weak, I think for Germany, it is a good situation."

Klaus Schweinsberg, a leading German economist, also sees that Euro has been of advantage to the eurozones biggest economy. He stated that,

"The big winner of the Eurozone is German industry ... the view of the German industrialists is that ... it makes us relatively more competitive within the Eurozone."

He has further argued that the German economy "has boomed to such an extent that Germany can afford to pay off the debts of Greece, Ireland and Portugal and should do so to preserve its export markets in those countries."

It is the strength of Germany that is unbalancing the euro. It raises the value of the Single Currency so much that the exchange rate is too high for the less well enough nations of the Mediterranean-Rim. Their producers are then hit with a double-whammy. They are unable to compete by lowering the value of their currency thus making exports to nations such as Germany less profitable than they would otherwise be. And imports from Germany into their domestic markets are thus made less expensive.

The growing crisis in larger countries such as Spain and Italy, with even France becoming less competitive vis-à-vis Germany, has the potential to create a further crisis that not even the German taxpayer can bailout on their own. Keeping the embattled states of Southern Europe in the straightjacket of the euro will also not deal with the issue of competitiveness. It is that divergence between the rich and the poor nations of Europe that is at the heart of the problem, the debt is merely the symptom of a system that is in breakdown. The euro may ironically result in such economic ruination of Southern Europe that nations such as Italy and Spain will eventually cease to have the purchasing power to continue buying Germany's exports. Ultimately all may lose from the euro and the one-size-fits-none policy designed to underpin it. The north will have to pay to the south money that few can afford and the Mediterranean-Rim states will be permanently locked into a vicious cycle of uncompetitive exchange rates and vicious austerity.

The bailouts are another example of EU measures compounding, rather than curing, existing problems.

The members of the eurozone share a common currency, which by definition is of the same value, across its constituent members; this fact rules out the option of using the currency devaluation to restore a nation's competitiveness. It also prevents these states from using inflationary measurers to alleviate the growing debt burden.

The option that remains has been to force the struggling and indebted nations of Southern Europe and Ireland to implement policies designed at creating what is known as an 'internal devaluation.' Instead of making domestically made products cheaper in relation to imports by devaluing the currency and affectively making labour more competitive an internal devaluation seeks to increase competitiveness by cutting wages at home. This allows for the workers of a state to take the strain rather than the currency.

Belief in this approach has been the common condition of the bailouts, known as austerity. They have suppressed internal demand by tax rises coupled with real reductions in public expenditure. Incidentally the 'cuts' in the UK have only been in the rate of growth of public expenditure and not in the actual amount spent. Following the great recession which began in 2008 the UK has benefitted from being outside of the Euro and had a 40% devaluation helping to preserve the export base. The UK was also able to use its central bank, the Bank of England, to produce money to purchase government debt thus lowering the burden on the nation's finances and reducing interest rates for the government, businesses and mortgage holders alike. This was not an option open to the governments and enfeebled central banks of the eurozone states whose monetary policy is at the whim of the ECB in Frankfurt.

Both the European Commission and the European Central Bank cite their belief in the policy of internal devaluation. Austerity seemingly worked for Germany. Under the aegis of the government, employers and unions had agreed a compact to keep people in employment, the so-called 'Bündnis fur Arbeit'. In exchange for jobs being preserved the German workers have been party to an agreement whereby they will accept wage restraint and more flexible conditions. This approach has been built-on during the crisis that followed in 2008 with unemployment being contained through workers accepting 'mini-jobs' and short time working known in German as Kurzarbeit. This victory over the threat of unemployment was described Chancellor Angela Merkel as a 'minor miracle'. These policies succeeding in further reducing labour costs and thus increased productivity and profits.

However, not all can win in this race to the bottom. The German success was achieved against the backdrop of the average German having greater purchasing power than their counterparts in the Mediterranean-Rim nations and a currency that supports Germany's genuine export led economy. The German austerity measures, and the exchange rate favouring their exports, helped it to thrive at the expense of the less competitive nations.

Germany is not the only country that has performed well under the conditions of an internal devaluation. The Baltic state of Latvia is another example. Despite not being in the Euro it is a member of the Exchange Rate Mechanism and has its currency, the Lats, pegged to the Single Currency and must not diverge in value from the Euro by more than 1%.

Until the 2008 credit crunch Latvia's economy had been growing rapidly, yet this was an unsustainable debt fuelled boom. Following the crisis the Latvian economy shrank by a ¼ in just two years. This was exacerbated by the Lats being unable to float and find its own level at a lower and more competitive value. Rather than leaving the straightjacket of the EU's Exchange Rate Mechanism, as Britain had successfully done on 16th September 1992, the Latvian government rejected the option of abandoning the EU's precursor to the Euro that would have allowed for a devaluation of the currency. Instead they choose to impose significant spending cuts in areas from schools to hospitals. Wages were cut and unemployment grew rapidly and by 2009 it had passed 17%. The building boom stopped abruptly as the money had run out. With half-finished properties littering the capital,

Riga. Latvian's who could find no work then left the country seeking opportunities in Western Europe and a budget crisis develop forcing the state to seek a €7.5 billion bailout.

Economic growth soon returned and was as much as 5.5% in 2011. This signalled to some that the policy of cuts had been successful. However, unemployment remains high at 14% and economic output is still below the pre-crisis level. However, the country's creditors are being re-paid so the financial system remains intact as does the EU's policy of pegging together currencies. The EU is therefore happy with Latvia's progress.

Despite the limited progress Latvia is used as an example of how internal devaluation can work, though not eliminate joblessness. The European Central Bank and the European Commission have sought to replicate this model by imposing it upon the struggling states in Southern Europe. However, Latvia is very different to countries such as Greece and Spain. Worker's rights and active trade unionism had been supressed in Latvia under communism and there was little organised labour to resist the harsh austerity measures.

Another difference is that Latvia, despite the Lats being pegged to the Euro, remains outside of the Single Currency and is at a more competitive value than the Euro. Latvians also enjoy higher purchasing power parity (PPP) than countries in the eurozone. Portugal, Italy, Greece and Spain have the overvalued euro as their sole legal tender. Latvia is therefore not a fitting example yet it forms the basis for a set of policies that have impoverished millions.

Unemployment reached alarming proportions. Greece had 27.8% unemployment, the rate of joblessness is 26.3% in Spain, 17.3% in Cyprus, and Portugal has 16.5% unemployment. The young are suffering particularly badly with Greek youth unemployment at 62.9%. The best and the brightest are now leaving these nations further damaging economic growth for a generation. The free movement of Labour, also an exodus of talent, can work against a country.

This is far from what the EU predicted. The "Troika", the three economic institutions that so often work together - the EU, the ECB and the International Monetary Fund - predicted that Greece would only have a short recession in 2010 with a decline of economic output of just 2.6% and would then quickly recover. The economy actually contracted by nearly a quarter. The recession is still deepening. What is more, the debts of Greece, Italy, Ireland and Spain actually became more severe despite the austerity measures, or perhaps because of them.

The cuts and tax rises actually led to a decline the economy and higher unemployment which reduced tax revenues whilst at the same time the costs of welfare payments to those without work increased. Italy's debts increased to more than 130% of GDP. What is more Italy a sizeable nation of nearly 60 million people is considered too big to bail out. The debt is becoming too great. At the heart of the growing problems in Italy is the fact that the value of the euro is too high for Italy, making it 40% uncompetitive against their competitors in Germany. This disparity cannot be addressed by labour market reforms which will only marginally add to Italian productivity.

The problem is ultimately political. The EU has prescribed one solution, which may have worked for two nations, or at least only caused limited harm, have been applied to all. The failure to consider the different circumstances that exist in other diverse economic areas are a fundamental flaw at the heart of the European project to centralise power in the EU.

The example of the bank bust in Cyprus whose banking sector suffered from losing investments in Greece had a proportion of savers' deposits seized to fund the EU's 'rescue' package. The Cypriot economy is now going from bad to worse. The EU has just one approach to the crisis which it has started through the failed experiment to share a common currency.

Nations outside of the EU and its Single Currency can follow the reverse strategy. Iceland provides an example of a small island economy which recovered after a banking collapse. Instead of pursuing the policy of internal devaluation the Icelandics allowed their currency, the Króna, to take the strain and devalue thus making the economy more competitive. To the chagrin of the EU the Icelandic population voted to default on their debts in a referendum. Social spending was also protected keeping money in the local economy.

The policies of unity are having an ironic affect; far from creating conformity of economic growth across the continent it is actually creating disunity. The disparity between the wealthy states of Europe and the struggling Mediterranean-Rim nations is growing ever wider. One size does not fit all. Whatever the solution it is not disputed that the German economy is the winner of the euro era.

With the continuing economic crisis, and growing divergence between the rich and the increasingly poor nations the EU is left with just two alternatives. Romano Prodi, the former President of the European Commission, described the emerging economic catastrophe,

"When the euro was born everyone knew that sooner or later a crisis would occur... We are therefore at a crossroads. The only alternative to greater co-ordination of economic policies is dissolution of the euro."

As coordination allows for the debt to be managed it does not resolve the competitiveness issue. This leaves but one option, the break-up of the euro. This logical conclusion to a flawed monetary union is however vigorously being resisted by the EU. The economic crisis will therefore continue and where these conditions exist a political crisis will soon follow.

Conformity and conflict
The process of building Europe from the roof down is not having the effect that the founding fathers of the EU intended. Opposition to the project to centralise decision making in the EU is growing. Seizing the commanding heights of decision making is not creating a European demos, one people. It is instead only adding to the belief that decisions should be made at the national democratic level.

According to a Eurobarometer poll, conducted on behalf of the European Commission trust in the EU has fallen dramatically and not just in Britain. In Spain, once amongst the most pro-EU of countries, trust in the EU has collapsed from May 2007 when 65% trusted the EU to as little as 1 in 5 in November 2012. Those who mistrust the EU ballooned from just 23% in May 2007 to 72% five and half years later. Spain is not the only country that seen such a dramatic turnaround.

Germany has also seen change. Over the same period the percentage of those who tended to trust the EU and now mistrust it had seen full polar reversal. In 2007 56% of Germans trusted but now 59% mistrust the EU; the suspicion rising from 36% half a decade before. Now even a total of 56% of the French mistrust the EU and increase of 15% in five years. The situation in Italy has seen a near doubling of mistrust 28% to 53%. Poland where once mistrust was the smallest out of these six nations which make up the bulk of the EU's population, has increased from a low of 18% in 2007 to 42 per cent in November 2012.

In the UK over the same time period mistrust has risen from 49% to 69%. And these are the EU's own figures.

If Britain were to leave the EU, the people of Europe may well be on our side. Or at least appreciate our reasons for what has become known as "Brexit" - British Exit. According to an opinion poll conducted by French market research agency, BVA, 52% of French people support the UK leaving the EU. However, this may not be for reasons of international solidarity.

The political divergence between the nation states and the EU is important. The currency union can only work when there is a transfer of funds from those nations which benefit from the Single Currency to those areas which are suffering from the wrong exchange rate. This will need to be an on-going arrangement to offset the harm caused by the euro. However, there will come a time when the nations of northern Europe will become unwilling to guarantee the debts let alone subsidise the impoverished nations of the south. To offset the lack of competitiveness caused by the Single Currency the fiscal transfer from Germany to Southern Europe will exceed the amount paid by the German Weimar Republic after the First World War.

Other European Commission opinion polls also show that across the continent people do not feel a sense of belonging to the EU. According to Eurobarometer, few people see themselves as European. As little as 46% of respondents from across the European Union felt attached to the EU whilst 52% felt unattached. The strength of attachment to their locality was significantly greater. 88% felt attached to their town or city. Attachment to their country was greater still with 91% saying that they felt attached to their nation.

The same research shows that 87% of those who responded to the survey identified themselves according to their nationality. Only 9% said they saw themselves as primarily as European.

As power is being increasingly centralised by the institutions of the EU and the nations states are becoming emasculated by Brussels the populations of many member states may ask for self-government to be restored.

Conversely some states do have a strong attachment to the EU. 72% of Luxembourgers according to this poll feel attached to the EU. The micro-state of Luxembourg is however unique. It disproportionally benefits from many EU institutions being based in the Grand Duchy such as the European Court of Justice, the Court of Auditors and the European Investment Bank. The European Parliament also has a third, but unused seat, in Luxembourg. The small state also has a significant banking sector.

Despite this strong attachment to the Europe Union, 89% are still attached to their nation-state and 74% of the largely multilingual population still see their identity as being Luxembourgers. A much smaller minority of just 24% identify themselves as being European first and foremost. This shows that even the most pro-EU states lack any real and significant European identity, let alone the more Eurosceptic nations.

Respondents from Britain recorded the lowest level of attachment to Europe. In the UK only 27% said they felt attached and as many as 93% identified themselves as being British above European and 60% saw themselves solely as British. According to the European Commission's own survey only 5% of people in the UK regard themselves as European above being British.

There is clearly not a single European population or demos. There is not even a single significant continental wide media that can help make the same issues to be understood in more than one country.

English, the international language of business air transport and now diplomacy, is the lingua franca of the EU. Even so it is far from being a universal second language. According to the European Commission's Special Eurobarometer 386 which reported on Europeans and their languages found that just 54% of respondents can hold a conversation in a language other than their own. Of these bilingual and multilingual respondents; 38% have English as their second language, 12% French, 11% German, 7% Spanish and 5% Russian.

Belgium, whose capital is incidentally Brussels, is a prime example of the divide between linguistic groups creating disunity in the country. French is predominantly spoken in the South of Belgium and Flemish in the North. The divide and the difference in political outlook between the two groups led to a paralysed political system where they went 589 days with no elected government.

Other examples, such as the former Yugoslavia, have produced far worse results than the stagnation in Belgium. To expect the different peoples of Europe to live under one form of governance, which fails to recognise their diverse interests, will ultimately be doomed to fail.

Language and national identity are not the only international dividing lines. The policies of the EU are likely to provoke opposition from the people of Europe who do not share a collective endeavour. People in different countries want contradictory policies which EU control cannot deliver.

Comparing political and economic culture

Just as the project to centralise power in the EU alienates those who favour national democracy the European Union will also ultimately fail to please both the political left and the right. The EU's austerity measures have run counter to the economic thinking of John Maynard Keynes which saw a role for increased government expenditure during a downturn in the business cycle to restore economic growth. The EU's policies have worked to reinforce the bust. The ECB's restrictive monetary policy followed by its former President's Jean-Claude Trichet and Wim Duisenberg and the inability for eurozone states to devalue alienated those that see the need for competitive devaluation and monetary easing.

Likewise the Treaty of Rome's outlawing of state support for industry and the opening up of national markets to competition in the aim of building a fully-fledged EU internal market can alienate those who favour interventionist economic policies. The other side of the EU's Single Market, excessive regulation resulting from governance by Brussels, adds burdens onto businesses. This estranges those who favour laissez-faire economic policies. If the EU had abolished all regulation it may have won the support of classical liberal economists and libertarians. However, such an approach is anathema to the Brussels bureaucracy. European governance cannot be established through a scarcity of laws. The EU's breaking down of national barriers and freeing up national markets is more about kratos than competition.

European centralisation will therefore only succeed in alienating both those who support the approach of John-Baptiste Colbert and Adam Smith. Colbert was the French Minister of Finances under King Louis XIV; he advocated what are known as dirigiste policies with intervention from the state to support industry and the picking of national champions. Adam Smith was the Scottish economist advocated the antithesis of this. He supported free markets and its so-called 'invisible hand.'

Economics is not the only source of division in Europe. Centralisation is not just a matter of the occasional treaty handing power to the institutions of the European Union. It is the exercising of that power, often referred to as competences, which counts. Building the system of control by the higher EU authorities is a continually developing process that happens each time a new regulation is passed and each time that the meaning of EU law is clarified by the European Court of Justice.

Such an approach to governance is alien to the Anglo-Saxon tradition of limited government; but also to the traditions of a number of other European nations.

The significant states of the European Free Trade Association; Iceland, Norway and Switzerland have a strong democratic tradition. The former members of the alternative trade alliance known as EFTA which includes the countries of; Denmark, Sweden and Finland also set a robust by European standards example of democracy. Only the nations of Austria and Portugal, which were members of EFTA before joining the EU, as well as the micro-Monarchy of Lichtenstein, have a less than stellar history of producing democratic politicians. The UK was also a member of EFTA and shares, if not pioneered, the principle of liberal-democracy which is prevalent throughout Northern and North-Western Europe.

Bar the honourable exception of the Netherlands many of the continental countries that formed the original European Economic Community had a political culture that is quite different. Belgium, France, Germany, Italy and Luxembourg had within living memory a tendency to support a system of government that was very much in line with how the European Union operates. This system operates with an unelected ruling elite paying attention to organised interest groups (such as aristocrats, business leaders and trade unionists) while ignoring the mass of the population. Yet ultimately no one is winning in the EU apart from a series of vested interests that have excessive influence in Brussels.

Wolfgang Schäuble, German Finance Minister, told the New York

Times on 18th November 2011 that 'We can only achieve political union if we have a crisis.' Currently the EU is lurching from crisis to crisis and the drive for centralisation is continuing to increase.

Whilst one size does not fit all, especially as the people are distinct with many diverse interests and needs. Yet why is the EU still being tolerated in other countries?

Why EU control endures
The way law is made in the European Union benefits politicians who begin to enjoy the benefits of being independent of their electorate. If agreement can be reached in Brussels then their whims will be written into law. These rules cannot be tampered with by a troublesome national parliament or electorate; both of which may want legislation be changed. Should the EU leaders be removed by their own populations they can rest assured that the legislation they helped put in place via the EU cannot easily be undone. It is incorrect to believe that the EU has a democratic deficit, it's system of law-making has a deliberately inbuilt democratic bypass.

There are other reasons why the EU is supported by the political class. Otto von Bismarck, the 'Iron' Chancellor of Germany who united what become known as the Second Reich, said, "I have always found the word "Europe" in the mouths of those politicians who wanted from other powers something they did not dare to demand in their own name." Incidentally Bismarck established a public health care system sixty-five years before the National Health Service was created in Britain under the Attlee administration in 1948.

Indeed a more contemporary German Chancellor, Helmut Kohl, said in October 1996, "The future will belong to the Germans... when we build the House of Europe. In the next two years, we will make the process of European integration irreversible. This is a really big battle but it is worth the fight."

The top down approach of the EU is traditional in many European countries and in theory their citizens should have less of an objection to how the EU operates. Nevertheless, this does not rule out the possibility that some will resent other countries, acting via the EU, overruling their own national interest.

It is important to understand why so many across the continent support EU membership. European integration has come about largely through a failure to object to centralisation. One reason is that the arcane workings of the EU receive insufficient scrutiny from national media. Instead of focusing on the complex policies and policy-making processes generated in Brussels the media often report EU affairs through the prism of national politics and its personalities.

The European Union is not shy in propagating the alleged benefits of integration and actively uses education and academia to sell the concept of EU centralisation. For them, the main issue will always be economic.

Effectively, populations across the continent of Europe have entered into a Faustian pact with the EU. National democracy has been replaced by EU governance on the promise of economic prosperity. The same belief has for years been held in UK government circles. However, the costs of the EU are now beginning to turn public opinion.

To paraphrase the political theorist and 6th President of Pennsylvania, Benjamin Franklin, they that can give up essential liberty to purchase a little temporary prosperity, deserve neither and will lose both. This situation is certainly coming to pass.

So far the economic harm has not yet resulted in the total repudiation of the EU, memories of Brussels largesse with other people money and the hope of yet more subsidies keep the dream of the EU alive.

There are also political factors at work. Many Europeans wish to insulate their country from their own politicians. The history of some EU countries in the 20th Century is not one of harmonious democracy. Countries that have only relatively recently emerged from dictatorship have profound suspicions of their own politicians and see the EU as a tool to protect themselves from their own, often corrupt, governments.

This ignores the fact that liberal democracy is the best guarantor of both peace and prosperity and the protection of civil liberties. Yet, when a country has a history whereby national politicians have a tendency to be more demagogue that democrat then it is not surprising that many do not trust their own national political institutions.

Yet in time memories of a brutal past will fade and the unemployment crisis will focus attention on the failures of supra-national governance.

At Nurembourg Hermann Göring, the former President of the Reichstag and head of the Luftwaffe, said (quoting Roosevelt) in defence of the Leadership Principle practiced under the Nazi regime,

"Certain peoples in Europe have forsaken democracy, not because they did not wish for democracy as such, but because democracy had brought forth men who were too weak to give their people work and bread, and to satisfy them. For this reason the peoples have abandoned this system and the men belonging to it."

Thankfully for Britain and Europe the British democracy finally brought to the forefront someone who possessed more resolve than the politicians in the Weimar Republic before Göring's kind came to power. The present problem is that the EU and its emasculation of national politicians has created a system that is intended to be politically inflexible. This has important economic consequences. The EU is designed to eliminate competition between nation states, yet this means that some nation democracies no longer have the powers that are essential to adjust their economic policies as individual needs dictate.

As legislation is increasingly made beyond the remit of national parliamentarians national elections will therefore not be able to deliver meaningful change. The danger is such circumstances is that the public will have little choice but to give their support to extremists, not only as a protest but also to get their voices heard. Nationalist movements show that alienation can be a substantial threat to the status quo.

Some states in Europe have a particular restriction on their thinking towards the EU. These are the countries that were less than a generation ago subject to Soviet rule. The lack of democracy is tolerated because having been cut off from the West for generations all things Western are viewed as being benign if not beneficial. What is more Eastern Europeans may prefer the writ of Brussels to rule by Russia.

The EU's ability to negate the threat from both internal and external threats to civil liberties is one significant issue. Another is that some believe that European integration is a means of multiplying their national influence. For others the hope of financial support remains an ever present feature in their countries dealings with the EU. Agricultural subsidies and the European structural funds are understandably thought to improve the lives of citizens in countries across Europe. Or it can be the combination of these considerations. The financial factor has been a clear calculation and will lead both politicians and the public alike in net recipients of EU spending to believe that the EU is in their national interest. The evidence, however, increasingly suggests otherwise.

The different national approaches and the more bottom-up system of governance in the UK make the UK the most likely to renounce the EU. Eventually the shift of power from elected national politicians and the economic harm caused by the EU will be considered as a cost too far and EU membership will be seriously called into question. Can the moment when demands for national sovereignty be restored be predicted?

The future of the European Union
The European Union is most definitely in relative, if not actual, economic decline. According to a report by the European Commission titled Global Europe 2050 in the year 2000 the EU accounted for 25% of world economic output. However, by 2050 its share of global GDP will be 'as low as 15%.' The EU's own report goes onto say that, 'By 2050, Europe's share of global economic product may be lower than it was before the onset of industrialization, hardly a trend leading toward global economic dominance.'

The loss of jobs across the continent will lead to a loss of both prestige and popular support. Under these circumstances can the EU survive, or will some of the member states seek to align themselves with the rest of the world that is prospering?

Will the break-up of the EU really come to pass?

The issue of whether or not a country is a net contributor to the budget of the European Union will be a factor but so will the level of unemployment. A severe lack of economic opportunity is a sign of an economic crisis and such problems endure then a political crisis will eventually follow especially as citizens will seek alternative economic policies to those enforced by the EU. Interestingly the word crisis originates from the Greek term krisis and entered the English language as meaning the "turning point in a disease." It refers to the time when a patient will either be cured and return to health or they will expire.

Unless there is homogeneity the answer is clear. If the time line is extended long enough then all transnational empires fail. Yet there is another factor that can add to the may be a catalyst for change in the EU. This is the almost perpetual square peg in the round hole, the role of the UK. In the European equation the choice that the UK makes can be decisive for what happens next. Certainly, this has happened in the past.

William Pitt the Younger, British Prime Minister, commented on 9th November 1805 about the fight against Napoleon's earlier attempt to unite Europe. He said,

"England has saved herself by her exertions, and will, as I trust, save Europe by her example."

Chapter 3

A Question of Influence

"Isolationists think of sovereignty as being rather like virginity; something that comes under severe strain in a close relationship and something that once gone is lost forever..."
Rt Hon. Jack Straw MP, as Foreign Secretary, 11th December 2001

"Ministers often end up nobly accepting responsibility for laws which they actually opposed in Brussels... they prefer to claim paternity rather than admit impotence, the fate of the cuckold across the ages, which is to take responsibility for what others begot."
Rt Hon. Peter Lilley MP, Speech to the Bruges Group on false claims of British influence, 24th February 2009

Central to the debate about Britain and the European Union is the issue of whether or not the UK has power inside the EU to effect change. The EU has clearly evolved, or more accurately followed a path of predestination, so that it sharply contrasts with what an increasing number of British citizens are comfortable with. Is the surrendering, or pooling, of sovereignty a price worth paying to gain more influence in the European Union or is it a symptom of a distinct lack on authority in the EU?

There are a number of formal ways that a member state can have some degree of sway over developments within the EU. Does engaging in the EU institutions give the UK enough influence to block ever-closer union and defend British interests from encroachment by the EU; let alone drive forward its own agenda?

The effect of MEPs

Less than 10% of the MEPs in the European Parliament represent the UK, just 73 out of 766. These alone, even if they did act in unison, cannot block any EU legislation. A simple majority of MEPs voting in the chamber is required to pass legislation or to suggest amendments to proposals from the European Commission during the first reading of the proposed laws. However, an absolute majority of MEPs is needed, that is 384 votes in favour, to approve amended legislation or to recommend further amendments during the second reading of a proposal from the Commission before it becomes law. Votes on international treaties with states outside of the EU and the budget also demand that an absolute majority of MEPs vote in their favour before they are approved.

Despite the higher bar to pass legislation in these circumstances the ability of MEPs representing Britain to block damaging rules is still highly limited and massive support from MEPs representing other states will be required to block legislation. It is also the case that the Members of the European Parliament do not initiate legislation, this being the preserve of the unelected Commission.

Whilst it is true that the UK is just one country out of 28 and has little formal power to reject proposals that it does not agree with this is not the full story. Some influence, for good or ill, is exercised by Britain's MEPs. Individual European parliamentarians may on occasions reach positions of influence. This is through the power of persuasion. It does not come though the ineffectual and limited debates in the chamber during a plenary session but through a member holding the Chairmanship, or even just belonging to, a committee of the EP. Here the parliamentarian can have the very real opportunity to show leadership and amend proposals from the European Commission and to make their own which may indirectly result in future legislation binding on all member states. Most MEP's, however, favour further European integration and are not directly mandated by the British government, let alone the British House of Commons. Therefore, if the nation-state is the main – if not the only – effective democratic political entity then the system in the European Parliament will always be lacking. Its democratic influence and ability to hold the executive arm of the European Union to account is highly limited.

The cost to the British taxpayer of each Member of the European

Parliament is £1.79m a year; this is triple the cost of a British MP in the House of Commons. A value for money audit is dependent very much upon the individual and will include; their activity, their ability to persuade, their views on European integration and of course their attendance. All of which can be highly variable. What is more, voting in European elections does not produce a government for Europe; this remains the unelected European Commission.

Britain's Commissioner

Although they are proposed by each of the member states' head of government, in Britain's case the Prime Minister, the UK's Commissioner is not a delegate of the British Government; in fact far from it. There always exists the probability that the delegates will put the European Union first above that of the national interest. This tendency was first noticed by Margaret Thatcher who observed that one of her appointments to the Commission had begun 'to go native' and was excessively 'communitaire'.

These powerful people, who lead the EU's legislative agenda, have to swear an oath to the European Court of Justice which determines where their interests lie. They have to state;

"I solemnly undertake:

• *to respect the Treaties and the Charter of Fundamental Rights of the European Union in the fulfilment of all my duties;*

• *to be completely independent in carrying out my responsibilities, in the general interest of the Union;*

• *in the performance of my tasks, neither to seek nor to take instructions from any Government or from any other institution, body, office or entity;*

• *to refrain from any action incompatible with my duties or the performance of my tasks.*

"I formally note the undertaking of each Member State to respect this principle and not to seek to influence Members of the Commission in the performance of their tasks.

"I further undertake to respect, both during and after my term of office, the obligation arising therefrom, and in particular the duty to behave with integrity and discretion as regards the acceptance, after I have ceased to hold office, of certain appointments or benefits."

Furthermore, according to Article 245 of the Treaty on the

Functioning of the European Union 'Member States shall respect their independence and shall not seek to influence them in the performance of their tasks.'

The importance of having a commissioner is trying to persuade the other EU leaders, and the European Parliament, to agree to the appointment of a right minded individual to become a member of the European Commission. In December 2009 the British government, after failing to secure the Presidency of the European Council for former PM Tony Blair, accepted the sop of having the high-profile but legislatively impotent position of High Representative of the Union for Foreign Affairs and Security Policy (the EU's Foreign Minister). This was awarded to Baroness Catherine Ashton of the UK. Given the importance of issues relating to financial services and the City of London to the UK and the EU's annexing of the power to regulate this area it would have proved better for the UK if a British citizen had been appointed as the Internal Market and Services Commissioner. The person who ended up with responsibility for financial services was Michel Barnier of France. It can be argued that the French do not appreciate the importance of financial services to the EU but they recognise its importance to Britain... this is the concern. It is feared that EU rules will drive firms out of the City of London and stop the UK leading the global market in the trade of euros.

The President of the Commission, who is proposed by the European Council and ratified by the European Parliament, determines which role is assigned to an individual commissioner. The President therefore has the ability to appoint a candidate that conforms to his policy positions. Therefore the other EU states cannot only select a President whose opinions run counter to the interests of Britain but also the President can then appoint an individual to a post who may be thoroughly unresponsive to the needs of the UK government. It is this appointee that will be driving forward the EU's legislative the agenda, not the government of the member state.

The British staffers that work as bureaucrats, shaping legislation, within the European Commission do have an influence. Whilst many are seconded from the British Civil Service they too are not delegates of Britain's democratic system. It is a matter of debate if they are when employed at home, let alone when working in Brussels for the 'European' interest whatever that may be. However, the fact that UK citizens are placed in the European Commission means that their ideas, British ideas, are being placed at the heart of the European Union; but in whose interests? Cui bono?

Judgement in Luxembourg

As the European Court of Justice (ECJ) is an activist court that favours European integration and makes sure that EU law applies equally across all EU member states it therefore expands the power of the European Commission further into the lives of the member states.

The European Court does not have a good track record of defending the British national interest. That is apart from the notable exception in the year 2000 when the European Commission took the French government to the ECJ for refusing to lift its ban on British beef, following the BSE (mad cows disease) food scare. This resulted in a judgement in 2001 ordering France to lift the ban. However, the French government did not allow British beef imports until 2002. The fine that was imposed on France for its illegal ban was never paid. Apart from that diplomatic 'success' for Britain the victories have been few and far between. At times its rulings relating to business taxation have cost the British Treasury billions of pounds. The ECJ has allowed companies making profits in the UK to offset these against losses and costs incurred in other EU states thus reducing the corporation tax bill. The European Court's recent decision of 14th November 2012, which ruled against Britain and its rules on the taxation of dividends in the Franked Investment Income Group Litigation case, is yet another example. This ruling cost the treasury hundreds of millions of pounds.

Quite clearly its judges are not national delegates, and what is more it is thoroughly against the British tradition of judicial independence to expect the ECJ's British judge to be otherwise. Judges should not respond to the whims of the government. However, the nature of the court and its pan-European remit creates a situation where it seeks to standardise law across the EU; idiosyncrasies in the nation states will therefore rarely be tolerated. Judicial activism, the process of driving a certain agenda forward, rather than merely interpreting the law is also common in the ECJ's rulings. At times it invents the law. This politicking is not always the result of its hubris. The character of the EU treaties and European Union legislation, particularly vaguely worded directives which set broad-brush policy goals, which arise out of political compromise, often do not set a clear set of rules for the judges to interpret. This not only leaves much room for interpretation as to what the law means but forces the ECJ to be legally creative in its rulings and add to the development of EU law rather than just clarifying it. Arguably the Court of Justice of the European Union has even made decisions that are quasi-political in nature. It allowed France and Germany to breach the rules that underpinned the euro and has tolerated the proliferation of power, particularly in the area of the bailouts, which have little basis in European law.

What is more, even if the British judge did wish to expand the authority of the UK there is no guarantee that this judge will be presiding over a case that is of particular importance to Britain. The judges usually sit in panels of 5, 7 or 13 judges; the UK representative may therefore be absent from the proceedings.

Technocrats in the Agencies

The increasingly important European Union agencies employ citizens of all EU member states including Britain. Some of the 30 plus agencies are even based in the UK; such as the European Medicines Agency, the European Police College and the European Banking Authority. The European Bank for Reconstruction and Development is also based in Britain. Just because an agency is based in a member state and will therefore predominantly employ staff from that state it does not mean that the population of that country has the ability to exert influence on the implementation of EU law through a democratically elected government. In fact far from it, the EU's system of agencies exists outside of democratic accountability.

Whilst the existence of some British staff in these organisations gives a few British citizens influence over the enforcement of EU policy and the development of the technical and scientific aspects of the European Union's rules. This does not mean that Britain itself has influence over the EU; in fact far from it.

Whilst they take their broad objectives from Brussels the purpose of many of the EU's agencies is to implement EU policy away from the influences of the member-states' national governments. These organisations exist under European law but are even decentralised away from the institutions of the EU and any democratic input, however small that may be, that can be derived from them. They are most certainly independent of the national authorities. What is more, it is actually the case that they diminish the influence of the nation states vis-à-vis the European Commission. The agencies make sure that the activities of national civil servants are coordinated and brought into line with common European standards.

The European Union's Executive Agencies, such as for instance the Trans-European Transport Network Executive Agency (TEN-T EA) and the Education, Audiovisual and Culture Executive Agency (EACEA), manage on behalf of the EU half a dozen important programmes. These do little to enhance the role of the nation state and its government. These give the European Commission directorate responsible for each of the various agencies policy areas more ability to develop the projects which deliver their policy goals across the EU. Some national governments may find that these give a certain utility to their citizens such as the Erasmus programme which helps enable students to study abroad and is under the remit of the EACEA. However, the delivery of policy objectives by another organisation which may, or may not, be desirable does not increase the influence of nation state. What is more, participation in the these programmes is also open to non-EU members such as Norway and Switzerland.

Financial influence
The history of Britain's involvement in the EU has been one of diminishing control over one of the key areas that defines both a nation state and a democratic society; that is the right to democratically control the raising of revenue from its citizens. Through treaty change Britain has not only lost some control over the funds it has to pay to the EU; but also over some financial matters in the UK itself.

Whilst the British veto officially remains in areas such as foreign affairs and taxation; is this enough to defend the UK's national interest in those vital areas? The claim that taxation has been a red line that has been successfully defended from EU control, such as during the UK's negotiations on the EU Constitution and the Lisbon Treaty, does not tell the full story. This wilfully ignores the fact that large areas of business taxation legislation has fallen under the remit of the EU. What is more, the customs duties that are imposed on many, but not all, imports into the EU also constitute a tax. Another highly important area which is a major whole in Britain's tax sovereignty is indirect taxation policy. In the EU all businesses in the member states must apply what is known Value Added Tax (VAT) – the EU's version of a sales tax – on most products according to directives agreed in Brussels. In the 2012-13 financial year VAT receipts totalled 21% of the UK's tax revenue which amounts to around £100 billion. It is interesting to note that the states in the USA have more autonomy over their sales tax policies than the member states of the EU.

Britain's influence over taxation policy has been further partially undermined even in the Council of Ministers. If a proposal has taxation as a secondary measure, such as using it to achieve a green goal in a piece of environmental legislation or any other item, then the vote will be taken under the Qualified Majority Vote procedure. Furthermore the EU's code of conduct on taxation is beginning to lead to the standardisation of tax systems. Under the guise of eliminating 'harmful tax competition', i.e. low taxes, the EU has established a process where tax systems across the EU are being standardised by stealth. The Code of Conduct group assesses member-states tax systems approximately six times a year and produces reports advising on the elimination of 'harmful tax competition'. These are then are submitted to the European Council of Finance Ministers (ECOFIN). Furthermore, as long ago as 27th March 2007 ECOFIN approved a strategy document titled "Coordinating Member States' direct tax systems in the Internal Market". This requests member states to begin the process of coordinating their tax codes so that they are compliant with EU law. The European Court of Justice also actively seeks to force member states to comply with European rules on taxation. Therefore, the emerging reality is that in the field of taxation Britain's ability to defend its interests from inside the EU is being lessened.

Influence in the Council of Ministers

Taxation is not the only EU relevant matter. As a result of the Lisbon Treaty it is now the case that many areas are unequivocally under the control of the EU institutions. 90% of votes in the Council of Ministers are now taken by Qualified Majority Voting (QMV). This system does not allot the UK an opportunity to veto legislation that is not in Britain's interests. It allows the EU to drive through regulations and directives in many important areas and Britain cannot block these rules.

To pass a proposal from the commission in the Council of Ministers any group of member states voting for the measure must control at least 260 of the 352 votes. They must also represent 62% of the population of the European Union. The minimum blocking minority that is required is, therefore 92 votes. Legislation can also be blocked by a group of states so long as they comprise over 38% of the European Union's population. Does this mean that Britain can block the EU's plans and preserve the British national interest? As Britain has just 29 votes, this represents an influence level of just 8.24%. The UK does have 12.48% of the European Union population; but this is some way short of the 38% that is needed to block legislation.

From 1st November 2014 the Qualified Majority Voting system will change. To pass legislation a qualified majority will be defined as 15 states that represent 65% of the population of the EU. Thus a blocking majority will need to represent more than 35% of the population so long as there is a minimum of four states making up the 35%. The UK's share of the vote will also rise to 12.48%. Until April 2017 a transitional period applies where member states can demand that the previous voting system applies. Yet after April 2017 the new rules will be fixed in place and Britain's share of the vote rise will also be locked in.

Whatever the system that is used, it is clear that the UK will need many allies to block a proposal and often the bar is simply too high. What is more, as the British vision of how the EU should work and develop is at odds with other EU member states then the allies will be increasingly difficult to come by.

Possession of around 10% of the votes in the Council of Ministers is not a significant amount; in fact it is much closer to zero than any number that may be considered substantial. Therefore, it needs to be asked; what formal real influence does Britain have? Yet, voting is not the only area that matters and therefore not the only area where the UK can protect its interests and affect change.

Influence in Comitology
The British government does exert a great deal of influence in the EU's working groups that propose and are employed on the adjusting and developing of EU law in a whole range of fields. These committees, consisting of representatives from the member states, are chaired by a

representative of the European Commission. The UK as a major economy and perhaps more importantly a major contributor to the EU budget has a significant voice in these discussions. The British civil servants that attend are listened to, in comparison the representatives of the smaller EU members will not speak; instead they will formulate their positions in private usually aligning themselves to a larger nation. In the EU some states are more equal than others.

Is it possible to quantify this influence that the UK has behind the scenes? And if so does it show that the UK's interests on the continent are being well served by working inside the European Union?

The answer can be found in the voting records of the EU member states in the Council of Ministers. These Brussels based meetings often strive to reach a consensus, with dissent being frowned upon. This culture inside the EU coupled with the fact that the byzantine process of EU decision making can be manipulated by the European Commission, which has the monopoly on proposing the legislation, helps drive the process of law making forward in the face of any national reservations. The Commission can make the necessary concessions to whittle away at any blocking minority. This can be done through a number of methods. Firstly, the Commission can reform the regulation. Or secondly it can give some victory in one part of the law to one, or even all member-states, so that they can claim some measure of success. This leaves the mess to be clarified and resolved by the European Court of Justice. Alternatively, the third method is to make a promise of future measures that will conform to one country's agenda over another. Through such tactics, with the process of negotiation overseen by the Sir Humphreys as opposed to the Jim Hackers, the unelected permanent professional bureaucrats have a greater influence than the elected here today gone tomorrow hapless minister voting in the Council.

The process of passing legislation is further helped by the political culture prevalent in the corridors of power. Instead of rejecting a proposal that is not in the national interest a member-state's negotiating team will seek to mitigate the harm as far as possible without going so far that they risk their reputation of being constructive and committed good Europeans. Obstruction is seen as not being communautaire and against the principle of solidarity. This approach is not just driven by political sycophancy to the aims and ideal of European construction; it also has a practical purpose. Goodwill is a highly valued currency in Brussels.

Through the work in the committees the positions have already been established so it is often the case that the result of a vote on particular piece of legislation is a foregone conclusion. This is known well in advance. In such circumstances continued opposition becomes futile. What is more, losing a vote and therefore being forced to adopt a legislative instrument which was opposed in Council is to admit impotence. Both for the EU and domestic audience it is seen as better perhaps to acquiesce and fain influence by claiming that some aspect was in the best interest of the country. The alternative will display that a country is actually losing in Europe. In fact 65% of votes pass without any opposition. In such circumstances a member state will either abstain or go to the extraordinary length of voting for the proposal but then issuing what is known as a 'formal statement' criticising the new EU law even though they voted for it in Council. On occasions the differences still erupt into the open.

From July 2009 to June 2012 Britain voted against the majority more often than any other state. The UK finds itself in a minority in nearly 10% of votes. France, however, has always voted with the majority. What is more, Britain's position has been in the majority on the fewest occasions. This shows where influence truly lies. And it signals that the UK is often without influence in Europe, whereas other nations, namely France, are getting policies they favour passed through the Council of Ministers. In the votes that were not unanimous Britain was in the minority on nearly 30% of the votes. Of the votes where reservations were recorded; 10% came from the UK. And when formal statements of concern were issued, again the highest amount came from the UK.

It is clear therefore that the battle over influence has been lost before the vote actually takes place. Therefore it appears that the UK actually has little influence and only a limited amount of authority in the EU. It is not a system that is working in the British national interest.

Britain's isolation within the EU is further supported by research into the voting groups that emerge in the Council of Ministers. According to Dr Wim Van Aken there are four distinct groups in the Council of Ministers. The first alliance, which displays a related voting pattern consists of; the Netherlands, Denmark, Sweden, Finland, the

Czech Republic and Malta. These states are described as the 'vocal minority.' A second group consists of Germany and Austria who vote quite differently to the former but form a pivot between the minority and the larger coalition in the Council. The next grouping is largely made up of the other member states, bar the UK. These other states are termed by him as the 'silent majority.' Britain, however, does not fit into any of those groups. In fact Dr Aken considers that the UK is already isolated in a group of its own.

This process of isolation inside the EU has accelerated since 2004. Despite the delusional hope that the enlargement of the EU would lead to its decentralisation and to new British allies joining the union this scenario did not come to pass. After the enlargement of the EU in 2004, when 10 new predominantly Eastern European states joined along with Malta and Cyprus, the UK found that the dynamics of the EU had changed but not in its favour. Remarkably it was since then that Britain found that there was no longer a group of countries that were voting as a de facto group alongside the UK. Clearly the enlargement of the EU did not bring into the orbit of Brussels nations who share the British values as to how the EU should develop.

What is more, Britain's voice in the European Union is not the only international arena that matters.

Global Influence

It is argued that membership of the EU gives Britain a greater influence in world affairs. The theory proclaims that twenty-eight nations speaking as one can have more authority than acting alone. According to this belief 'pooling sovereignty' creates a global voice that is greater than the sum of its parts. It is certainly the case that more decisions are being taken at the supra-national level even above the institutions of the European Union. However, does EU membership enhance or diminish Britain's role in the world?

Currently the UK is a member of NATO, the World Bank and the International Monetary Fund and has a Permanent Seat on the United Nations Security Council and as such a veto over UN resolutions. The UK is already a leader within the Commonwealth. Britain is therefore far from being alone in the world.

The EU seeks to enhance its global standing through the Common Foreign and Security Policy (CFSP) but how does that effect Britain?

Arguable the European Union's CFSP far from advancing the UK's voice in the world actually subsumes Britain's international strategy into the arcane workings of the EU. Most areas of EU foreign policy decision making requires unanimity; this does partly protect Britain's interests. However, some areas are decided by qualified majority voting. What is more, whilst the policy is overseen by a British citizen in the person of Baroness Catherine Ashton (Vice-President of the European Commission) she is not a delegate of the UK. Furthermore, her original appointment to the Commission came through being proposed by the then Prime Minister Gordon Brown. Prior to that she was made a Life Peeress and a Minister by Tony Blair; as such her views are very different to the current elected British government. What is more under Article 17 7. of the Treaty on European Union the UK does not have a veto over the appointment of the High Representative.

A common defence policy is also being formulated. Under Article 43 2. the High Representative of the Union for Foreign Affairs and Security Policy will also have the authority to propose EU military missions. Article 42 3. gives the EU the power to begin the process of standardising the military forces of the member states via the European Defence Agency (the EDA) making the UK comply with EU defence programs.

The EU's foreign policy also restricts the UK's voice in the wider world. Currently the UK benefits from its permanent seat on the UN's Security Council. However, according to Article 27 2. 'The High Representative shall represent the Union for matters relating to the common foreign and security policy. He shall conduct political dialogue with third parties on the Union's behalf and shall express the Union's position in international organisations and at international conferences.' Furthermore, Article 34 2. reads,

'Member States which are members of the Security Council will, in the execution of their functions, defend the positions and the interests of the Union... When the Union has defined a position on a subject which is on the United Nations Security Council agenda, those Member States which sit on the Security Council shall request that the High Representative be invited to present the Union's position.'

The EU also has its own diplomatic service and embassies around the globe. The European External Action Service (EEAS) as it is known is now a world-wide network with 140 embassies and ambassadors with more than 1,400 staff in Brussels and a further 1,900 in other countries around the world. The EEAS now has a budget of more than half a billion euros per year. Article 35 of the Treaty on European Union dictates that national embassies and diplomatic staff will have to cooperate with the EEAS and ensure that 'decisions defining Union positions and actions adopted pursuant to this Chapter are complied with and implemented.'

As a result of the common foreign policy the UK diplomatic service will be receiving direction from the EU's High Representative. With the EU's ever burgeoning foreign and defence policy the question is no longer whether or not Britain will be able to have influence if the UK leaves the EU. Instead we need to ask if the British government can hope to have its own opinion if the UK stays in the EU.

Britain has had for centuries a great deal of global influence and this continues within organisations such as NATO and the United Nations. Perhaps other smaller European countries that do not have the benefit of the UK's traditional global links are in need of the EU and its European External Action Service.

There are two European states that are not in the EU that make interesting case studies on the question of global influence. These are Switzerland and Norway. Arguably the Nordic state has a greater influence in world affairs because it is not in the European Union. A Norwegian ambassador explained how rejecting EU membership actually enhanced Norway's global role. The ambassador explained that,

"Our worst time was just before the 1994 referendum [on EU membership]. Since everyone assumed that we were going to join, I was always being asked to meetings with my 15 European counterparts. Often, I wouldn't even get to speak. Once we voted 'no', people had to start dealing with me separately again."

Furthermore, its influence exists in the first place because Norway can advocate its own position. Inside the EU it risks having its foreign policy determined away from its citizens in a distant meeting room in Brussels with an apparatchik from a different state representing Norway.

Outside of the European Union its diplomatic service makes a virtue of its independence. They are rightly seen as independent intermediaries in international disputes. As such Norway's diplomats have played a key role in seeking to find solutions to many of the world's conflicts from the Middle-East to South East-Asia, from Sudan to Sri Lanka.

The Swiss position is also very interesting. Whilst retaining their sovereignty and direct democracy by keeping out of the European Union, they also host not only one of the world's major financial centres but also many international organisations. Ranging from sporting institutions such as the Fédération Internationale de Football Association (FIFA) based in Zurich and the International Olympic Committee (IOC) based in Lausanne. The Swiss also host humanitarian organisations such as the International Red Cross and Red Crescent Movement and Médecins Sans Frontières (Doctors Without Borders) both of which have their headquarters in Geneva.

Switzerland is also home to the Bank for International Settlements which has its base in Basel. The European Free Trade Association (EFTA) has its headquarters in Switzerland.

Even more significantly Switzerland hosts a number of United Nations organisations and specialised agencies of the UN which produce regulatory instruments which govern the rules in their respective areas. The treaties which have created these organisations have delegated national jurisdiction to these supranational committees. The rules they make are then considered binding upon the states which are members of the organisation. Most states around the globe are members of such bodies.

These organisations discuss, develop and direct the production of technical rules in areas ranging from maximum working hours to regulations governing the specifications for boiler flues. They include bodies such as;

The International Labour Organisation, from where many of our employment laws originate include the controversial 48-hour average working week which on behalf of the ILO the EU is attempting to force onto Britain.

The International Organization for Standardization, the Universal Postal Union regulating postal services, the International Telecommunication Union, International Electrotechnical Commission and Intergovernmental Organisation for International Carriage by Rail are all based in Switzerland outside of the EU. The

World Intellectual Property Organisation and the World Meteorological Organisation are also in Switzerland. These supranational organisations, specialised agencies of the UN, are increasingly standardising global rules in their respective areas. In Europe one of the most important is the Swiss based United Nations Economic Commission for Europe (UNECE or ECE). This has several subdivisions including the World Forum for Harmonization of Vehicle Regulations. Together, this myriad of supranational organisations are not only determining the rules governing the conduct of how nations interact with each other but also seeking to determine their domestic laws.

The International Bureau of Education, the International Organisation for Migration, the World Health Organisation, the Global Alliance for Improved Nutrition and the International Union for Conservation of Nature; are again based in Switzerland. What is more, these organisations are also globally relevant.

Not all of these UN sponsored agencies are based in Switzerland. The International Maritime Organisation is not based there - for a very good reason – instead it has its headquarters in London. However, the UK still has to comply with common EU positions in the creation and development of maritime law. There are a further host of specialised organisations.

The process of international law making for European Union members has become one where a common EU position is aimed at. This limits the UK's ability to present its own viewpoint. Without this a nation cannot have any real influence. EU member states then conform to that position when negotiating international standards in the numerous transnational organisations. Once these bodies propose the rules the EU then adopts these regulations and imposes them on the UK. Through this system Britain is hit by a double-whammy of influence impediments and loses out twice. Firstly in discussions with member states where the British point of view may not necessarily prevail and the agreed common EU negotiating position may not represent the UK's national interest. Then secondly the new international standards are adopted by the EU and proposed as an EU regulation which then becomes law. And regardless of whether or not these rules suit the UK as the new standards are now European Union regulations they have to be obeyed and will be enforced by the courts.

What is more, they cannot be undone by the UK's democratic process.

For non-EU countries the situation is quite different. Whilst these transnational, also known as supranational, organisations acting in a quasi-legislative capacity create legal proposals which are intended to be binding and should be ratified by the participating member states. There are however few mechanisms by which the UN agencies can coerce sovereign states to comply with their strictures let alone enforce them. However, when their rules are adopted by the European Union they then become a part of EU law and as such become binding on its member states. The European Court of Justice and the UK's own domestic courts, backed up by the full force of the state, will enforce these regulations. Therefore, as the EU is increasingly becoming a clearing house for the establishment of an international legal code of regulations it enables even more power to be handed to organisations few have heard of let alone have influence over.

In some instances the UK does not even have a seat at the table where international matters are decided. Often the debate surrounding the European Union centres on the issue of trade. However, as a member of the European Union the UK is not even part of the discussions on matters surrounding the exporting and importing of goods and services. In world trade talks Britain, along with other EU states, is represented at the World Trade Organisation (WTO) by a member of the European Commission; not by a representative of the UK.

Contrast this with Norway's and Switzerland's position. They have 100% of their own vote on global bodies passing global trade rules. Within the EU the UK has just around 8% say in the formulation of the European Union's position. Interestingly both the WTO and the Advisory Centre on WTO Law are also based in Geneva.

Having the EU speak for the UK is only effectual if Britain's interests align with those of the other EU members. Although the UK and nations on the continent are geographically close many European states have differing needs and a different world outlook. The predominantly French desire to protect its politically important agricultural sector is a prime example. This has led to not only the bulk of EU legislation and Brussels' focus being overly concentrated on agriculture but also a significant proportion of spending going towards this inefficient industry. This not only distorts the economy but has also led to a trade policy that is not open to developing nations. Therefore, it does not necessarily make sense to act as one bloc, especially if some nations have very dissimilar views especially in areas such as international commerce.

The evidence from Norway and Switzerland is that even small countries have a significant presence on the world stage without having to surrender, or pool, sovereignty with the EU. There is reason to believe that being inside the EU diminishes the UK's voice in the world.

Despite Britain's lack of influence in international law making the fact remains that the EU is not adrift in a sea of its own decrees randomly reacting to events and stumbling upon a plethora of powers. The European project has an overt agenda to create ever closer union in Europe. So far Brussels has been politically, though not economically, successful in this role; but what is influencing this and driving that plan forward. If any degree of substantial authority does not rest with Britain, where does influence in the EU come from?

Where does influence lie?

The reason why British governments have been ineffectual at shaping developments in the EU is that the reality is that membership affords little opportunity to shape the direction of the EU let alone block damaging regulations from Brussels and from the myriad of mystifying supranational institutions sitting beyond the reach of democratic governance. Any desire to resist centralisation, which has been the raison d'être of the EU and its previous guises and incarnations since 1957, will run into the strong belief held by the leadership of other European countries. This shows where influence truly lies and it is not with Britain.

Whilst the popularity of the EU is at an all-time low in countries such as Britain and Spain the dream of Brussels remains alive in the minds of its bureaucrats who operate as the vanguard of a European class. The mind-set of the Brussels bureaucracy is a key, but hidden, driver behind European integration. Their motivations and ideals are a major influence on the EU. These apparatchiks do not simply exist to do the bidding of the member states governments as one would expect, or perhaps hope.

The commitment of the staff at the commission to the cause is not just driven by their generous terms and conditions on which they pay just 12% income tax.

It is natural that those who work for the Commission will support the organisation. The fact that people choose to work there suggests that they may have an interest in and at least tacit support for the European project before their employment or secondment begins. Although many may perhaps be primarily motivated by the economic reason – which is thoroughly legitimate – especially if they come from an Eastern European state as they will have a significant step-up in living standards the support will soon emerge. In fact Jean Monnet the ideological founder of the post-war European Economic Community saw the Commission as a 'laboratory' where the new 'European Man' will be conceived.

The very nature of the Commission being a supranational body, the higher authority existing above the nation state, puts them more outside of the nation states than would be expected in an intergovernmental organisation. In fact its purpose is to control the nation states of Europe. The European Commission staff have a strong esprit de corps and its fonctionnaires have a degree of dominance over the EU that exceeds merely being the agents of the nation states. In fact they monitor national governments. They are the professionals and the Commission is known as the 'motor of integration'. According to Dr Cris Shore, the staff in the Commission have traditionally seen themselves as 'Far from being mere public servants, officials tended to view themselves as an elite corps of 'policy-makers', 'intellectuals' and 'diplomats' rather than mere 'public servants'.

And it is supported not just by the European Court of Justice but also by the European Parliament. During the wrangling over the 2014-20 Multiannual Financial Framework, the EU budget, MEPs initially sided with the view of the Commission that the budget should not be cut. The Commission originally proposed a 5.9% increase. European leaders, however, eventually sought a minor reduction in spending.

The basic process of how Brussels works shows that much influence rests with the political, but unelected, bureaucrats. The Council of Ministers, the representative arm of, and from, the member states including Britain, receives proposals from the appointed Commission, asking them to take powers away from their governments thus depriving their own citizens of power. From then on, the Commission having been given the power, it keeps it, to exercise as it sees fit.

Does the Council maintain an oversight over how those powers are exercised?

No.

Has the Council any power to call the Commission to account over the way it uses its powers?

No.

Can the Council remove or modify those powers, if it is unsatisfied with the way the Commission is performing?

No.

Does the Council even have the power to ask the Commission for information on its performance?

No.

That is not a system where the democratically elected governments of the nation states can hold the Commission to account. The other 'democratic' arm of the EU is also lacking. The European Parliament is certainly junior to the Commission. The European Parliament elections do not produce a government, so the Parliament has no power or authority to execute a mandate. It cannot, for instance, decide to repeal any EU laws – it cannot even directly initiate any laws. No matter what the European Parliament thinks about an existing piece of EU law it cannot force a change. The unelected Commission can completely ignore the European Parliament.

Ultimately the power play between the member states is not the only dynamic in play. The unelected European Commission also has a strong hand at the table and an undoubted great deal of influence in its own right.

The audience that Brussels seeks to address and engage with is another factor that deprives influence from all member states in the EU. The EU is becoming less influenced by the national states operating through the paradigm of the committees, commission, parliament and council but more from what it calls civil society. Input from the nation states has long been, in the eyes of the Commission, tainted by issues being looked at through the lens of national issues. This is especially the case amongst the citizens of the EU whose only participation in the project is at the time of the European elections and then their involvement is usually through the prism of national politics.

Despite being conscious of the rejections of European integration at numerous referenda in Denmark, Ireland and then France and the Netherlands the EU attempted to square the circle of having European integration whilst addressing the ever widening democratic deficit. The EU did not, however, accept the limits of centralisation and acquiesce to the return of powers to the nation states, or allow for an à la carte Europe. Nor did it seek a significant enhancement of the power of its representative institutions or suggest the introduction of direct democracy. Instead the EU is seeking to bypass national democratic institutions and engage directly with organisations that represent groups of citizens across Europe. The numerous bodies range from interest groups that campaign on specific issues, to non-governmental organisations, pro-EU think tanks, trade unions, corporations and even the specialised agencies of the United Nations. The list goes on; but does not include EU-critical groups. The representatives of the civil society organisations who may well be unelected are still considered to speak for many of their members on issues of importance. They represent the tip of a pyramid which feeds into discussions on EU legislation amongst the EU expert groups and even has access to the Commissioners. In the committees of the EU they are placed on a par with the representatives of the nation states. Their input bypasses the member states and dilutes their influence in the formulation of legislation further limiting the authority of the UK.

Such insider groups do not just have a right to be consulted on but also to be recognised experts in their fields. As such they have access to the European Commission and the opportunity to lobby in Brussels. In return for their input and assistance with policy making, these groups receive funds from Brussels. In effect, Brussels is paying lobbyists to lobby itself to do what it wanted to do in the first place. As ever, this is to produce policies whose outcome produce ever closer union in Europe. Less EU governance in never the answer.

The largesse shown towards these organisations is telling. The funding towards the EU's Civil Society Contact Group in 2011 amount to more than €3 million and made up the bulk of each organisations funding. The European Public Health Alliance received €681,536 which constituted 61 per cent of its funding. CONCORD (The European NGO confederation for relief and development) was granted €691,345, 51% of its funding. Social Platform (Platform of European Social NGOs) was granted €654,289 86% of its total income, the

European Civil Society Platform on Lifelong €200,000 which equals 74% cent and Culture Action Europe was granted €110,500 and made up 45% of its proceeds.

Environmental organisations especially benefit from Brussels. As in the previous list the recipient organisation is listed followed by the size of taxpayer funding from Brussels and the percentage of their income that comes from the EU.

Birdlife Europe €332,163 (35%); CEE Bankwatch Network €836,238 (45%);

Climate Action Network Europe €295,022 (33%); European Environmental Bureau €894,000 (41%);

European Federation for Transport and Environment €275,516 (16%); Health and Environment Alliance €362,992 (59%);

Friends of the Earth Europe €1,195,259 (46%); Naturefriends €365,735 (41%);

WWF European Policy Office €599,954 (13%).

There are nearly a further three dozen organisations engaged with the EU's social platform. These range from; the European Association of Service Providers for Persons with Disabilities to the European Council for Non-Profit Organisations (CEDAG) to the European Region of the International Lesbian, Gay, Bisexual, Trans and Intersex Association (ILGA Europe). And more than a dozen pro-EU campaign groups such as; Centre for European Policy Studies, Pour la Solidarité and Friends of Europe each receiving the bulk of their funding from the European taxpayer. The list goes on and the financial cost increases.

In return for involvement at the heart of the EU's policy making process the participating organisations are encouraged to promote the European ideal to its network of citizens in the member states and across Europe. The crux of the issue is the effect of the benefits of pro-EU integration propaganda reaching potentially millions of citizens and sidestepping existing national structures. It is ironic that as the bulk of EU money comes from the nation states the citizens of those countries are effectively paying these organisations to make recommendations that lead to power being taken away from their country. What is more, for the EU member states influence has a cost associated with it, the member ship fee; yet for civil society groups influence actually pays.

It establishes a formal, even institutionalised, system of lobbying. This gives this myriad of organisations and businesses access, and therefore influence, direct to where power really lies. That is straight to the heart of the European Commission. This entrée to Brussels' key decision leaders, without having to go through the filter of a national government's political process nor even its civil servants, allows for the easy lobbying of the EU. This no doubt goes some way to explaining why many multinational businesses and civil society groups overtly support Britain's membership of the EU. When they speak of the importance of having influence they are referring to their opportunity to engineer legislative outcomes in the internal market, not the democratic institutions of the UK.

In other national democracies lobbying is seen as somewhat of a dark art. Indeed the £2 billion industry of lobbyists operating in Westminster was described by the British Prime Minister, David Cameron, whilst he was Leader of the Opposition as "the next big scandal waiting to happen". And he pledged to reform the "far-too-cosy relationship between politics, government, business and money." Yet, in the EU there is a very different attitude towards access to senior figures in Brussels which can formally seek to influence Brussels as part of its civil society engagement activities. It is considered as a positive substitute for democracy. Only in the world of European politics can lobbying be considered a virtue.

Whilst the important minutiae of legislation and policy formulation is being left to the assorted civil society organisation the big strategic picture of treaty changes is still left to the European leaders.

Traditionally the most significant driver behind the absorption of the nation state into the EU's system of governance has been the Franco-German Axis. The relationship between France and Germany has, since 1870, been one of the key factors in European politics but there have been others. The orientation of Paris looking towards Berlin was not always so. Prior to the Suez debacle France was closely aligned to the UK. In 1956, going even beyond the closeness of the 1904 Entente cordiale the French Prime Minister, Guy Mollet came to Britain to see his UK counterpart Anthony Eden on 10th September 1956 to suggest a Franco-British Union. When this was rejected the French head of government suggested having joint citizenship between the two nations and that France should join the Commonwealth. History could have been very different. The final nail came after the UK announced a ceasefire in Egypt without consulting Paris the French ended their flirtation with Angleterre and looked towards a new alliance. The Franco-German axis was born. It became the motor for European integration.

Is the alliance between the two major Gallic and Teutonic nations in Europe still at the forefront of European integration? Can the UK muscle in on this and drive forward its own alternative vision for Europe? There are hopes that a new axis between Britain and Berlin can emerge.

Chapter 4

The Choices for Britain

"There are only two coherent British attitudes to Europe. One is to participate fully, and to endeavour to exercise as much influence and gain as much benefit as possible from the inside. The other is to recognise that Britain's history, national psychology and political culture may be such that we can never be anything but a foot-dragging and constantly complaining member, and that it would be better, and would certainly produce less friction, to accept this and to move towards an orderly, and if possible, reasonably amicable separation."

Lord (Roy) Jenkins of Hillhead, former Home Secretary, Chancellor of the Exchequer and President of the European Commission, Speech in London, 1999

Britain has been and remains fully engaged with the Byzantine institutions of the EU. Yet throughout few can actually believe that Britain's heart is really in the European project. Both the main British political parties, the Conservatives and Labour, are, with differing levels of sincerity, committed to reform the EU to varying degrees of change. What are the different routes available to Britain to restructure the UK membership and can they deliver?

Allies and alienation

At one point in time it was hoped that the small but numerous in quantity eight Eastern Europe states which eventually joined on 1st May 2004 would organically change the EU. These were the once so-called 'New Europe.' Britain was not alone in labouring under this misapprehension. Michel Barnier, as the Commissioner responsible for institutional reforms, when speaking to the European Parliament's Foreign and Security Committee in 2003 described some of the soon to be joining states as lacking a "European reflex". Eventual access to phased in agricultural payments and the benefits of structural funds have outweighed any reservations about democratic accountability. The voting records in the Council of Ministers show that the EU has not inadvertently let in the Anglocentric Trojan horses.

It was hoped that reform would take place organically through the unworkable geometry of an enlarged EU; the so-called 'wider and shallower' hypotheses. The reality has been very different. Taking on new members has been used as a political pretext for more centralisation most notably the treaties of Nice and the Constitution finally introduced as the Lisbon Treaty. The enlarged EU is not a reformed EU; integration is now simply both wider and deeper. On 20th April 2004 when the then British Prime Minister presented the centralising EU Constitution to the House of Commons he stated that, "The new constitutional treaty is designed... to answer the challenge of enlargement."

Enlargement has brought political difficulties for the UK. Britain is not footing the bill for the bulk of the bailouts. It is also not seen to be paying its fair share towards the East, claiming a rebate, and has supported restrictions on the new member states right to claim common agricultural policy payments. As such why should less well-off nations in Eastern Europe listen to Britain above the voice of their near neighbour Germany?

This leaves the UK looking around for friends that will support reform. Yet British influence is low so a new strategy is unfolding.

It is now hoped that Germany, the dominant half of Europe's chief partnership, will support British calls if not for wholesale reform of the rigid EU at least for a repatriation of powers to nation states which want less centralisation. The creation of a Franco-German axis is the raison d'être for the European project and remains the driving force behind integration. German cooperation with Britain on the building of a different Europe is certainly an imaginative idea, perhaps even fantastical.

Mutual self-interest can however make for strange bedfellows. With Britain's cheque book withdrawn Germany will have to pay even more to the EU. The theory is that they will support anything that stops them being left at the mercy of French farmers. The actuality is somewhat different, the requirement for any extra funds will hardly compare to the spoils taken during the 1923-25 French and Belgium occupation of the Ruhr. What is more, the sums involved pale in insignificance to the costs of supporting the Single Currency. The German taxpayer is guaranteeing loans to the Mediterranean-Rim states worth a total of €122 billion and more, much more, will have to be produced ad infinitum if the euro is to survive. In comparison additional agricultural payments are little more than a minor rounding error when looked at in proportion to German GDP.

Will Germany prove to be a useful ally? Well, an analysis of the British and German voting record in the Council of Ministers shows that the two countries remain at loggerheads in the EU and are far from allies. From July 2009 to June 2012 the UK and Germany voted against each other on more occasions than any other two states. The German position is diametrically opposed to the British national interest and is therefore unlikely to support British demands for a reform of the EU and a repatriation of powers.

Beyond financial considerations are there other reasons why Germany should support British demands? Germany may need the UK's agreement to have yet more political union. This, however, has not proved a problem in the past. On 1st January 2013 the Eurozone's Fiscal Compact entered force despite David Cameron's alleged veto. Moreover, the British Chancellor of the Exchequer, George Osborne, has already conceded that there needs to be more centralisation in the Eurozone. The Government has therefore abandoned the moral right to oppose further EU financial control and given away a negotiating position.

Nevertheless, the position for reform has been set out by the British Prime Minister in his Bloomberg speech of 23rd January 2013. Here David Cameron called for a reformed European Union focussing on the five principles of; competitiveness, flexibility, power must flow back to Member States, democratic accountability and finally fairness. If this alternative vision is unattainable then the return, via a renegotiation, of some as yet undefined powers to national control will be sought. How was this received on the continent?

The proposal by the British Prime Minister David Cameron received a swift rebuke from the French. The Socialist President François Hollande of France ruled out the possibility of an "à la carte" Europe; that is one cannot renegotiate the foundation of the EU to pick and choose which rules apply. The French Foreign Minister, Laurent Fabius, reiterated the President's position when he stated on the same day as David Cameron "Let's imagine Europe is a football club and you join, but once you're in it you can't say let's play rugby." The following day after Cameron's speech, Guido Westerwelle, German Foreign Minister dismissed the idea that terms can be significantly changed. He warned that "cherry-picking is not an option."

The cool reaction is continuing…

On 11th September 2013 the President of the European Commission, José Manuel Barroso, used his State of the European Union speech to the European Parliament, to launch a thinly veiled attack on David Cameron's belated suggestion for renegotiation. The Portuguese apparatchik said,

"Let me say to all those who rejoice in Europe's difficulties and who want to roll back our integration and go back to isolation: the pre-integrated Europe of the divisions, the war, the trenches, is not what people desire and deserve." The President's answers to the EU's problems in this address did not include flexible variable geometry as advocated by the British Prime Minister. The head of the Commission used his position to push for the surrender of more national sovereignty calling on member states to "rise above national or parochial interests". The President was referring to his perceived need for countries to comply with Commission proposals for banking union.

Yet even if the reaction to the Prime Minister's proposals was more positive, through what process can the EU change?

The EU's history of reform

Reform is often spoken of but the EU has a chequered, at best, history of restructuring itself in any way that leads to real change other than to suggest further centralisation.

Whereas voting in national democracies can at times result in radical policy changes. European elections can have little effect, or conversely they can lead to an outcome that is the polar opposite of what the message from the electorate intended. The 1999 elections to the European Parliament were a shock for the left of centre European political establishment. Not only did the UK Independence Party make a breakthrough in Britain, taking three seats, which then joined the

EU-critical Europe of Democracies and Diversities group in the European Parliament, the socialists also fared badly. The Social Democrat grouping lost seats to the centrist/centre-right European Peoples Party who won 233 seats as opposed to just the 180 held by the European Socialists. This was by European standards a lurch to the right. The result was that instead of listening to what the people of Europe said the EU decided to circumvent the will of its citizens by making sure that the rights contained within the article of a charter that was in being could not be undone at either national or European level. In 2000 the incorporation of the flamboyant Jorg Haider's quasi-Fascist, and camp, Freedom Party into a coalition government in Austria caused much consternation in the EU. The break from the political consensus led to political sanctions being imposed on Austria and acted as a further catalyst for the convention drawing up the charter to lock in place policies regardless of the whims of the voters and even the politicians.

The European Council had established a convention to draw up a charter that would details the rights of its citizens. This resulted in the Charter of Fundamental Rights of the European Union. It was proclaimed at the Nice Summit on 7th December 2000 and is incorporated in the EU via Article 6 of the Treaty of Lisbon. António Vitarino, the then EU Commissioner for Justice and Home Affairs, said in Lisbon on 13th May 2000 that the Charter "will mark a definitive change in the Community, which will move away from the essentially economic raison d'être of its origins to become a full political Union."

The task of drawing up the Charter was given to a convention chaired by Roman Herzog, the former President of the Federal Republic of Germany and the German Constitutional Court. The task of interpreting the provisions of the Charter rests with the European Court of Justice. Herr Herzog was later to criticise the ECJ, the very body whose power he had helped expand. He later wrote in a paper titled Stop the European Court of Justice that the,

'ECJ deliberately and systematically ignores fundamental principles of the Western interpretation of law, that its decisions are based on sloppy argumentation, that it ignores the will of the legislator, or even turns it into its opposite, and invents legal principles serving as grounds for later judgements. They show that the ECJ undermines the competences of the Member States even in the core fields of national powers. The conclusion one comes to is clear: The ECJ is not suitable as a subsidiarity controller inthe last instance and a protector of the Member States' interests.'

The implementation of the Charter is essentially a coup, not only by the federalists, but also by the socialists who were in power at the time and intent on making sure that their vision of the EU will continue to prevail regardless of who will be elected in the future. The Charter serves the goal of permanently enshrining into law left of centre anti-business measures such as; Articles 27 and 28 which enshrines trade union influence and Articles 31 and 34 which are intended to preserve and enhance rules which limit working hours, and lock in continental European social security systems. Article 29 which relates to the right of access to placement services simply states that 'Everyone has the right of access to a free placement service.' The EU's version of rights does not favourably compare to the documents of other comparable unions, such as those inspired by the English political theorist John Locke. The American Declaration of Independence which heavily relies on his beliefs states that people have the unalienable right to 'life, liberty and the pursuit of happiness.'

The Charter does offer the 'right to life', however, not all aspects of the Charter affirm positive rights. Under the final article, number 54, its rights will not extend to those who seek to change the the Charter's provisions. This prohibits what it describes as the abuse of the rights in the Charter. It goes on to state that, 'Nothing in this Charter shall be interpreted as implying any right to engage in any activity or to perform any act aimed at the destruction of any of the rights and freedoms recognised in this Charter or at their limitation to a greater extent than is provided for herein.' Free speech is allowed so long as it confirms to the principles of the EU and what the EU grants it can take away. This is very different to the tradition which believes that liberty is always freedom from the government.

The EU also established a Fundamental Rights Agency to oversee the implementation of the Charter of Fundamental Rights and the European Commission, the main source of law in the EU, are bound to apply its principles when making rules and regulations.

Whilst the direction of the EU had not changed the rhetoric did. The continuing financial scandals and the success of EU-critical parties as well as the low turnout in the 1999 European elections proved that there was an emerging disconnection between the European institutions and the people they govern. As the powers of the EU grew the popularity of its institutions declined. It was the reverse of what was expected. Jean Monnet, the intellectual driving force behind the process of European centralisation, had hoped that as the powers of the supranational EU system of government grew the public's loyalties would switch from the nation-state and its institutions to those of the European Union. The increasingly apparent disenchantment of the population led to a subtle change in the rhetoric coming from the EU institutions. Instead of "integration", the language of the EU incorporated calls for "reform". As will be shown this was to become just another word for centralisation.

Whereas the project of European centralisation was always intended to have as its capstone a constitution its immediate genesis was the Laeken declaration. Following the Irish rejection of the Nice Treaty, the European Council meeting in Laeken, a suburb of the Belgium capital Brussels, issued a declaration on 15th December 2001. It recognised that a divide had emerged between the EU's ruling class and the peoples of its member states. The declaration committed the Union to becoming more democratic, transparent and effective. Two paragraphs accurately assess the myriad of problems with European governance; it states that the European Union, '...is behaving too bureaucratically... In coordinating the economic, financial and fiscal environment, the basic issue should continue to be proper operation of the internal market and the single currency, without this jeopardising Member States' individuality. National and regional differences frequently stem from history or tradition. They can be enriching. In other words, what citizens understand by "good governance" is opening up fresh opportunities, not imposing further red tape. What they expect is more results, better responses to practical issues and not a European superstate or European institutions inveigling their way into every nook and cranny of life.

'In short, citizens are calling for a clear, open, effective, democratically controlled Community approach, developing a Europe which points the way ahead for the world. An approach that provides concrete results in terms of more jobs, better quality of life, less crime, decent education and better health care. There can be no doubt that this will require Europe to undergo renewal and reform.'

To deliver the reform the European Council established the Convention on the Future of Europe. It was presided over by former French President Valéry Giscard d'Estaing. The outcome of this was the draft EU Constitution. Whereas the mandate for the convention stated that the EU was as 'behaving too bureaucratically'. The resulting constitution proposed handed yet more power to the unelected fonctionnaires based in Brussels. It also locked in place decision making based on the Charter of Fundamental Rights.

Laeken also stated that 'the Union must be brought closer to its citizens.' The Constitution proposed to expand on its already existing ability to demand that criminal sanctions be applied to breaches of EU law and can rule; what constitutes a crime, what the penalty should be and disturbingly, what else should be done about it, and demand that member states comply with its rulings. The hand of Brussels can reach out across Europe.

The full text of the declaration mentions democracy and democratic no fewer than 12 times. The root of the work democracy comes from the Greek dêmos meaning people and kratos which translates as power. It appears, however, that the EU has reformed to only adopt half the concept, kratos.

The Laeken declaration also highlighted the importance of national parliaments. The result however, was that Constitution seized 63 areas of decision making from one where a national veto existed or was the preserve of the nation state to qualified majority voting. The result of the Laeken Declaration was that it became little more than the tombstone of effective parliamentary democracy in the European Union.

Asking the EU to reform clearly carries risks for both the UK and other EU member states. Despite the EU Constitution being rejected in the French and Dutch referenda, its text was finally put into place under the guise of the Treaty of Lisbon. This episode shows that the EU is capable of spotting problems and even voicing back to the public the concerns that they have. Yet, the use of the word reform appears to be simply the creation of a political pretext for the seizure of more power.

With such a history of incorporating and taking control of the language of the EU's critics, occupying EU-critical messages and then echoing it back to the peoples of Europe it is difficult to trust the intentions of the EU. Reform is centralisation; and the language of Brussels becomes little more than doublespeak; a deception to prevent discussion on the EU reaching its logical conclusions.

José Manuel Durão Barroso, President of the European Commission, has seized the gauntlet of the EU's 'reformist' agenda. Despite being a leader of Portugal's Moaist/Communist student revolutionary movement Barroso has called for reform of the EU. In particular within less than a year of his inauguration as President he even announced grandiose proposals for the deregulation of the economy stating that one third of screened proposals were to be withdrawn. On 27th September 2005, the European Commission announced that to achieve growth and creation of jobs,

'the "acquis communautaire", the existing stock of legislation, needs to be simplified... The Commission has also decided that better regulation needs to be integrated in the design of policy and that new legislative proposals presented by the Commission must seek to promote better regulation and contribute to competitiveness.'

Despite the fine words the reality was very different. No directives and regulations have been scrapped. It simply meant that 68 of the latest 183 draft laws were not to be proceeded with. The reason behind not going ahead with them was not a desire to free businesses from the burden of excessive regulation, rather it was many of proposals were withdrawn because they were no longer relevant for instance those that related to the enlargement of the EU the year before.

There was no bonfire of EU red tape which at the time amounted to more than 102,000 pages of rules and regulations. The fact remains that half of Britain's new laws are made in Brussels.

What is more, the announcement of the alleged 'reform' of the EU masked the fact that just two weeks before the European Court of Justice made a landmark ruling. In Case C-176/03 Commission of the European Communities v Council of the European Union the ECJ confirmed the right of the Commission to mandate areas that should be subject to criminal sanctions if EU law is breached.

A Commission press release welcomed this recognition of the bureaucrats power stating that the 'Commission welcomes Court of Justice judgment recognising the exclusive competence of the Community to adopt criminal law measures to ensure the effectiveness of Community law.' And without any hint of irony they stated that the decision of the ECJ was 'beyond all doubt an important step forward for European democracy.'

Throughout his tenure as the chief bureaucrat in Brussels, the main source of EU law has not stopped the flood of EU law. Such is the political dominance of a man that is in effect a civil servant that in a 2006 BBC poll he was voted the most powerful man in Britain. He received more than three times the votes than the then British Prime Minister, Tony Blair.

Some in the UK have mistaken the policies of the European Commission for the liberalisation of the economy throughout the EU. Perceiving the Brussels bureaucracy as a force for economic reform; implementing the British vision of Europe. EU rules do outlaw the subsidisation of industry, unless the Commission approves this, and that it has broken-up the dominance of national champions by enabling market access to companies from other countries this does not constitute liberalisation. Those who believe that the European Union is coming Britain's way are actually just observing in the EU what they wish to see; it is largely wishful thinking.

The real aim is to emasculate the nation-state; eliminating nationalised industries and ending the dominance of national regulators. The result of the EU policies is that the management of economic affairs has been handed to the European Commission. Whilst the European Union does not seek to own the means of production it does aim to dominate all aspects of economic life and govern it according to its whims and wishes. The restrictive practices that some European countries followed have been replaced with restrictive rules imposed from Brussels. Arguably this has made the European market less free than before and certainly less competitive. Where only big businesses can afford to absorb the costs placed on them by the Commission, steadily the market share of national companies will be replaced by an oligarchy of European corporations operating under EU law. The European Commission's concept of reform is to impose yet more regulation.

The attempts at reforming the markets of its member states has developed a new problem, that of excessive EU interference.

It has long been recognised that the overregulation is a drag on economic growth. There have been publically stated attempts to reform the economic situation that has emerged in the EU. In March 2000 the European Union launched in the Portuguese capital its so-called Lisbon Agenda. Its aim was to make the EU 'the most competitive and dynamic knowledge-based economy in the world, capable of sustainable economic growth with more and better jobs and greater social cohesion.' It recognised that as there was little growth in Europe with North America and Asia forging ahead that 'Time is running out and there can be no room for complacency.' The outcome is best described by the Swedish Prime Minister Fredrik Reinfeldt on 2nd June 2009 that it 'has been a failure,' Unemployment is now at crisis proportions in parts of the EU, the economy of the EU has stagnated and become sclerotic and its share of world trade significantly decreasing.

The failure of two of the EU's landmark policies, the Common Agricultural Policy (CAP) and the Common Fisheries Policy (CFP), illustrate the rigidity of the EU's system of governance. Like the Single Currency these policies once set in place remain locked in and despite being modified significant reform has been largely unobtainable. The CFP has simultaneously managed to deprive British fisherman of their livelihoods whilst at the same time deplete fish stocks. Under the UN's law of the sea the waters stretching out for 200 miles around a nation are the responsibility of that country. However, as a condition of entry into the EEC these were made a common resource. The EU opened up the North Sea, which once ranked amongst the most abundant fishing grounds in the world, to industrial scale fishing from other member states and even sells the right to fish there to businesses based in Morocco. In an attempt to stop overfishing by the multitude of fleets exploiting what were once British waters the EU introduced a quota system limiting the amount each vessel can catch. If the quota was exceeded or the wrong fish were caught then by law they would have to be disposed of by discarding them overboard – dead. Bringing back to port more than what is allowed resulted in criminal prosecutions.

The result of this policy was as much as two thirds of fish that have been caught have had to be thrown back to the sea even though they would have already succumbed to the nets and being hauled from the water. This just further depleted fish stocks and exacerbated the on-going environmental catastrophe.

Despite the clear damage done by this policy, and the example of Norway which banned the discarding of fish overboard in 1987 the EU was unable to reform its economically harmful and even unethical fishing policies. This is despite the fact that the Norwegian example proved that banning fisherman from throwing wrongly caught fish back actually led to the once declining stocks recovering.

Why, despite the evidence, was the EU unwilling to reform its harmful Common Fisheries Policy? The answer is because some large scale industrial vessels were able to manipulate the system by throwing back the less valuable part of the catch whilst retaining the most profitable fish. When the EU listens it is usually to those that have access to power.

After more than forty years, and much of lobbying from environmentalists and the crews of smaller vessels, the harmful practice of fish discarded will finally be phased out from 2016. Yet not before decades of damage were done. The opening up of access to excessive exploitation of the marine environment will however continue. Sustainable fishing under national and regional control by those who understand the precious resource of the sea is still unobtainable. The once prime fishing waters will remain poorly managed for years to come.

The Common Agricultural Policy though declining as a percentage of EU expenditure from as much as 87% in 1970 to around 40% it still represents a serious misallocation of resources when agriculture accounts for less than 3% of gross domestic product in the EU.

The waste at the heart of the CAP is not the only area of financial abuse in the EU. Fraud, mismanagement and waste have always been endemic within all aspects of the European Union.

How has the EU dealt with this issue?
One approach was to give the former British politician Neil Kinnock the task of reforming the system. He was appointed European Commissioner for Administrative Reform. A role that included responsibility for auditing and anti-fraud efforts. Neil, now Lord, Kinnock's performance in reforming the EU was far from stellar.

The problem of EU corruption was far from reformed under Lord Kinnock. In fact whistle-blowers were persecuted. A Marta Andreasen was given the role of Chief Accountant. She produced proposals to reform EU spending which were ignored. When she raised concerns she was removed from her post and finally dismissed on 13th October 2004 for 'breaching the principles of loyalty and discretion laid down in Articles 11 and 12 of Staff Regulations.'

Marta Andreasen said the changes that the former Labour leader brought in as purely cosmetic. Paul Van Buitenen, who was also victimised for speaking out, also commented on Kinnock's reforms on 30th September 2004 that "the whistleblowing facilitation procedures put in place by Commissioner Kinnock were "almost a criminal offence" as they were "fundamentally wrong and deliberately did not work." Van Buitenen exposed the scandals that led to the resignation of the Santer Commission, including that of Neil Kinnock in 1999. Kinnock, however, then the Transport Commissioner kept his position as a Commissioner and was given the role of cleaning Brussels up. For his public service Van Buitenen faced disciplinary action, was suspended and had his salary cut in half.

Even those who do not work for the EU have been persecuted. The German journalist, Hans-Martin Tillack who had been exposing EU corruption was seized by Belgian police in the early hours of 19th March 2004. This was on the orders of the European Anti-Fraud Office (OLAF). In an attempt to identify his sources Herr Tillack was arrested and had his personal papers, computer and archives confiscated.

The failure to reform corruption within the EU is hardly surprising. It is the glue which binds bureaucrats from different nations together. Corruption is at the heart of this process to drive forward European centralisation. According to the academic Dr Cris Shore, the son of the former Labour Party Cabinet Minister the late Peter Shore, corruption and the resulting,

'collusion between EU officials, MEPs and politicians suggests that a sense of common purpose is developing, not only within the institutions, but also between them. In short, what we see is the consolidation of an increasingly self-serving and detached classe politique with its own peculiar interests and agendas.'

Apart from Neil Kinnock Britain has been at the forefront of wanting to bring the concept of financial propriety to the European Union. The House of Commons Public Accounts Committee made recommendations to the EU as long ago as 2005 and again in 2009.

Even before that the UK was perceived in the EU as a force for proper financial propriety in Brussels. Indeed in 1999 when Édith Cresson, the former French Prime Minister had to resign her post as Commissioner for Research, Science and Technology she blamed it on a 'conspiracy' which had in part begun in Britain. Other bureaucrats in Brussels actually agreed that Cresson had been a victim of an 'Anglo-Saxon political crusade' against the Southern European civil service culture. Cressen further defended her actions by saying that she was 'guilty of no behaviour that is not standard in French administrative culture.'

The reality is that she had to resign for failing to report massive amounts of missing funds from her department and her highly irregular appointment of her close personal friend and dentist, Monsieur Philippe Berthelot, as a 'Visiting Scientist'. A role for which he was not qualified and he produced no work for the Commission.

The European Court of Auditors has, since 1994, been required to inspect the EU's accounts and provide an annual declaration of assurance that the funds have been spent legally, correctly and with sound management. They have never been able to give this assurance.

In 2006 the President of the Commission, José Manuel Barroso, set the EU the target of making sure that the auditors gave the accounts a clean bill of health by 2009. Yet, the court has still found cases of fraud for every budget year since then and has been unable to approve the accounts.

The response of Brussels is still to shoot the messenger. The President of the European Council, Herman Van Rompuy, on 13th September 2013 criticised the European Court of Auditors for shining a light on continuing cases of corruption in the EU. He accused it of producing reports that 'generate headlines that 'yet again the EU's accounts have not been signed off', with deceptive allegations of fraud and mismanagement.' Instead according to the President the Court of Auditors analysis should focus on the positive aspects of EU spending and thus create favourable headlines for the EU.

There have been improvements. In 2003 the Court of Auditors could only certify that just 5% of EU expenditure had been spent legally and that the accounts were reliable. By 2009 that figure was 45%. That means that more than half of the spending was flawed and perhaps even fraudulent. It rose still further. By 2010 64% of EU spending was without 'material error.' However, in the 2011 EU financial year, running from 1st January to 31st December, the figure again worsened and fell back by 8% so that only 56% was without material error as the Court of Auditors refers to potential EU fraud. Despite decades of mismanagement EU spending is still open to abuse because the controls over a staggering 86% the EU budget are only partially effective.

Despite the limited improvement it still cannot be said that British taxpayer's money is being spent efficiently and appropriately in the EU. Are there any examples of the European Union adjusting to suit British needs?

British success and failure
From the start of Britain's membership of EEC, later to be known as the EU, British negotiations have not been fruitful. The Common Fisheries Policy is a prime example. Geoffrey Rippon, the MP for Hexham and Chancellor of the Duchy of Lancaster under Prime Minister Edward Heath, had responsibility for the UK's accession EEC negotiations. He warned Heath about the seemingly excessive demand that the UK allow its valuable and well managed finishing waters to become an EU resource. However, Edward Heath told him to give way. According to the diplomat and Foreign Office British Civil Servant who was the head of the negotiating team, Sir Con O'Neill, the UK's position was to "swallow the lot and swallow it now."

The UK's negotiations have fared little better ever since. Harold Wilson's Labour Government was elected in 1974 with the manifesto commitment to 'a fundamental renegotiation' of the terms of EEC membership. Discussions to improve the terms of membership were attempted. Despite the very real threat of the UK leaving the EEC as it was then in 1975, the opinion polls at the start of the campaign favoured withdrawal, the Wilson renegotiation achieved little. The agreement that was reached on 11th March 1975 was lauded by the Government in official publications as 'Britain's New Deal in Europe.' However, it proved to be a sham as nothing significant could be achieved and this was firmly understood by the Wilson administration.

The myth that Britain's relationship with the EU had been improved was a major factor in the referendum of 1975. However the truth remains that nothing significant had changed. The reality was that there were only minimal adjustments on ancillary issues such as contributions to the budget, a mechanism was introduced that would try and limit Britain's payments to the EU. However, this was unworkable and the UK has been a net contributor to the EU for every year since. There was also a 'promise' of future reform of the Common Agricultural Policy. The same empty words were to be repeated 30 years later in 2005. The most notable success of the Wilson renegotiation was that the terms of trade relating to New Zealand butter were changed.

The government booklet that extoled the success of the 'renegotiation' also dismissed the idea that there may be a move towards Economic and Monetary Union and fixed exchange rates. It claimed that 'this threat has been removed.' This was another false claim. The Exchange Rate Mechanism which fixed exchange rates and was the precursor to monetary union was introduced in 1979. Britain's two year membership from 1990 to 1992 was an economic disaster.

On 26th June 1984 British Prime Minister, Margaret Thatcher, wins the famous rebate on taxpayer's money paying for the EU's overblown agricultural payments at a meeting in Fontainebleau. The rebate on payments to the EU, officially known as the abatement, is not a shining example of how Britain can make the EU see sense and reform. In 1984 discussions on the budget represented a very different situation to treaty negotiation where the balance of power is reversed against the UK. In 1984 Margaret Thatcher had a veto over agreeing to a new budget. If a British government proposes changes to the EU's treaties any other state can reject them. What is more, the rebate was thoroughly justified. At the time Britain was the largest net contributor towards the EU whilst being one of the least well off. Britain also imported more food from outside of the European Union than other EEC members and thus incurred more costs from the protectionist agricultural policies. Britain also raised more money for the EU as it imported more from outside of the EEC than other member states. The UK's agricultural sector was also relatively smaller than in other EU member states so Britain derived less benefit from payments to farmers. Despite the iniquitous funding arrangements of the EEC it still took nearly five years for Margaret Thatcher to achieve a permanent rebate mechanism. The then Prime Minister not only had to persuade the EU but also had to push British civil servants to fight for the UK's financial national interest.

The Thatcher rebate was also not that radical. There were examples of previous agreements. Harold Wilson had achieved one in 1975, though this proved to be ineffectual, and Margaret Thatcher had already achieved prior agreements whereby one off annual payments were made to the UK in 1980, 81 and 82. In 1980 £710 million was returned and in 1981 the considerable at the time total of £860 million was refunded to offset the imbalance Britain's contributions to the budget. It was also generally agreed that a permanent solution needed to be found. There is however no precedent for powers to be returned to the nation states. Whereas, the rebate was justified other European Union members have little moral compulsion to allow the UK to have a competitive advantage over their own economies by giving Britain opt-outs from EU rules. The scenario of powers being handed back to the UK is an unlikely one.

The rebate never was a complete return on funds paid to the EU. It involves the UK getting refunded $2/3$ of the difference on how much the UK pays towards supporting the 15 pre-2004 accession states and how much the UK receives back. Therefore the less that the UK claims for its farmers the greater the rebate will prove to be. Only a small proportion of the payments towards the new accession states predominantly in Eastern Europe are taken into account. The UK does not get money back on its contributions towards the EU's administration or on its payments to regeneration funds.

The British rebate is effectively paid for by the other member states in the EU whose contributions are higher as a result. However, Austria, Germany, the Netherlands and Sweden had a rebate on the British rebate paying 25% of what they would otherwise have been liable for. The so-called British rebate is made four years after the budget year it applies to. The arrears are taken off from what the total level of payments would otherwise be. The abatement is fixed in place and will need unanimity to be abolished.

The establishment of the Single Market has been presented as a uniquely British success. Proponents of the EU find that using the example of the Single Market as a tool to neuter predominantly Thatcherite Eurosceptics. It was originally conceived during the Premiership of Margaret Thatcher and put into law by her government asking Parliament to approve the Single European Act 1986. The creation of the Single Market is used as to illustrate the argument that the UK can win in the EU, but is this so?

Whereas it is true that Margaret Thatcher wanted to eliminate tariff barriers on intra-EC trade the British Prime Minister did not envisage that a new treaty would be required to do this. Indeed the elimination of customs duties could have been achieved without an inter-governmental conference agreeing to hand more power to the European Commission. Nevertheless, Margaret Thatcher was manoeuvred into accepting a transfer of power to Brussels by both Jacques Delors, the President of the European Commission, and the UK's own European Commissioner, the gone native, Lord Cockfield. The desire of Margaret Thatcher to reform trade between the members of the EEC, as it was then, was used as a pretext to persuade her to agree to a system that would, despite assurances, hand more power to Brussels. Twelve areas were moved from the national veto or were introduced under qualified majority voting. What is more, some of these areas did not relate directly to trade barriers, such as; environmental policy, health and safety, maritime transport and aviation.

On 17th February 1986 the Single Market was signed, Denmark, Italy and Greece added their approval on 28th February that same year. This came into force on 1st July 1987 and it called for the creation of an internal market, what is known in Britain as the Single Market. This gave the institutions of what became the EU the power to create a regulation red-tape area in all member states. It set the date for completion of the internal market, with standardised rules by 31st December 1992. The immediate level of legislation that came from the Commission included 280 laws to standardise rules and requirements across the European Community. The door to further integration had been opened and the flood has continued ever since.

What did Margaret Thatcher think of the 'great' achievement that has been attributed to her? Thatcher came to regret agreeing to the Single European Act.

The former British Prime Minister considered that the supposed economic benefits had proved to be illusory. Handing power to the Brussels bureaucracy to impose new regulations that affect the entirety of the British economy when only a relatively small proportion is involved with cross border trade with other EU states added more costs with little gain. Margaret Thatcher was to state in her famous Bruges Speech that "We have not successfully rolled back the frontiers of the state in Britain, only to see them reimposed at a European level, with a European super-state exercising a new dominance from Brussels."

Thatcher admits to making the mistake of believing that the Commission's legislative drive to establish the EU's internal market would come to an end. Another error was to trust the assertions that the Single European Act would not excessively intrude on the rights of member states. The result according to Margaret Thatcher was that,

'The European Commission and the European Court of Justice worked together to explore, exploit and widen every loophole... Thus the provisions of the Single European Act were abused in order to push corporatist social legislation upon Britain by the back door.' This has not only undermined competition between the countries in the EU, making them less agile and unable to compete globally especially as all European businesses must bare additional costs. Towards the end of Thatcher's Premiership the UK's battle to decentralise and liberalise what was to become known as the EU was alone in fighting an 'unwinnable battle.'

Ultimately, the much vaunted internal market created by the Single European Act does not so much resemble a British negotiating coup but it appears to be a prime example of the UK, hoping to improve the EU, in fact walking into a federalist ambush. This should have been obvious, the clue is in the name, but successive politicians have been bested by the Brussels bureaucracy.

The former British Prime Minister, John Major, claimed that the Maastricht Treaty was an achievement for Britain in Europe as it enshrined the principle of subsidiarity. This is meant to make sure that decision making is devolved to the member states unless there is a reason why the EU should make the relevant laws.

It is outlined in Article 5 3. of the Treaty on European Union and reads, 'Under the principle of subsidiarity, in areas which do not fall within its exclusive competence, the Union shall act only if and in so far as the objectives of the proposed action cannot be sufficiently achieved by the Member States, either at central level or at regional and local level, but can rather, by reason of the scale or effects of the proposed action, be better achieved at Union level.'

The final arbiters, however, of what is the appropriate level for a decision to be made rests with the institutions of the EU. Unsurprisingly it did not change the European Union. What is relevant is not so much what the rules say but who interprets them.

Lord Mackenzie Stuart, who served as President of the European Court of Justice, writing in the Times newspaper on 15th June 1992 described subsidiarity as 'a rich and prime example of gobbledygook.' Indeed the effectiveness of this principle fell at almost the first hurdle. The British Government challenged the EU's decision to apply the working time directive to the UK. Britain had secured an opt-out from this legislation when Margaret Thatcher agreed to the Single European Act. However, the EU merely applied the rules under health and safety legislation. John Major's government appealed this to the European Court of Justice. The Court's Advocate General on 12th March 1996 in his opinion on Britain's attempt to annul the Working Time Directive saying that "In view of the fact that the objective provided for in Article 118A is harmonization, there is no doubt that the aim of the contested objective can be better achieved by action at Community level than by action at national level." If the EU has a policy goal it will impose it regardless of the legal justification.

The Speaker of the House of Commons, John Bercow MP, described subsidiarity as, 'a cloak which seeks to disguise the ever increasing arrogation of powers to the institutions of the European Union.'

Subsidiarity is not only a policy failure its parentage is also disputed. It was not a British initiative but was actually conceived by the Italian Communist, Altiero Spinelli, who was also a Commissioner with responsibility for Industrial Policy and a Member of the European Parliament. Altiero Spinelli, after which one of the European Parliament's buildings is named, saw the principle of subsidiarity as a tool to keep national governments quiet and would thus help the 'transition to a higher level of union.' Spinelli is considered one of the so-called 'founding fathers' of the European Union who developed a plan for a federal EU.

Indeed in the 18th Report on Better Law Making (2010) the European Commission in its assessment on the working of subsidiarity and proportionality after it had been in operation for nearly 17 years stated that the European Court of Justice 'has yet to annul a measure for breach of subsidiarity.'

It did introduce a system whereby national parliaments will be directly informed of European Commission proposals and the opportunity for them to submit their opinion to the EU. This includes the so-called 'yellow card' system. Included in the protocols of the

Lisbon Treaty is the opportunity for national parliaments to object to a proposal from the Commission on the grounds of subsidiarity. This is contained in Article 6 of the Protocol on the application of the principles of subsidiarity and proportionality. Article 7 establishes a system whereby if a third of national parliaments object to a proposal, one quarter if it relates to the area of freedom, security and justice, the institution that issued the draft European legislative act 'may decide to maintain, amend or withdraw the draft. Reasons must be given for this decision.'

The yellow card does not stop it being implemented; it is essentially meaningless because there is no red card which can follow. How does the yellow card system work in practice? According a report by the House of Commons the threshold for even asking the Commission to reconsider has never come close to being reached. This reform is therefore just a small sop to national democracy and little more than a fig leaf to hide the Lisbon Treaty's real political intentions.

In matters pertaining to subsidiarity Article 8 of the protocol establishes the European Court of Justice as the arbiter of whether or not the principle has been breached. The European Court of Justice cannot be considered a neutral mediator between national democracies and the EU.

The Presidency of the European Commission is an important position that has, and continues to, drive forward the policies of the European Union and the process of integration. From the late-1980s to the mid-1990s successive British Prime Ministers became deeply dissatisfied with the direction and the speed of centralisation under the leadership of the French Socialist Jacques Delors. The division between what Britain wanted from the EU and the policies it was forcing on the UK had to be ended. It was hoped that a decapitation policy would deliver a man that was more amenable to the UK's interests. The British Prime Minister, John Major, in 1995 vetoed the Franco-German favourite for the post, the French born Belgian Jean-Luc Dehaene. The result was that a political compromise between the UK, France and Germany led to the appointment of the Prime Minister of Luxembourg, Jacques Santer, as the new and ninth President of the European Commission. The pace of centralisation did not however cease which continued unabated.

The 1997 Treaty of Amsterdam which took more power from

member states and passed 24 areas over to qualified majority voting is a prime example of how the EU carried on regardless of the changes at the top. This was an EU that was moving further away from the declared vision of the UK's government. British standards of financial propriety, long a source of divergence between what the UK expected from the EU and how it worked in practice, also reached a new low under the stewardship of the man that John Major had placed in power. Institutional corruption in the Commission led to the en masse resignation of the Santer Commission on 15th March 1999. British attempts to negate the less palatable aspects of EU membership from within had resulted in failure.

The UK did achieve an opt-out to the final state of Economic and Monetary Union, the euro, thus keeping Britain out of the Single Currency. However, this was when Britain's consent was needed for the Maastricht Treaty to go ahead. Yet, Britain has not always had positive results in negotiations in EU treaties.

The Charter of Fundamental Rights is a prime example and was to all intents and purposes brought in via the back door. It was originally proclaimed at a meeting of the European Council in December 2000. The British government's reaction was not favourable. On 11th December 2000 the then Prime Minister Tony Blair said to the House of Commons, "Our case is that it should not have legal status, and we do not intend it to. We will have to fight that case." On 13th October of that same year the Europe Minister Keith Vaz stated that the Charter would be no more binding in the EU than a copy of "the Beano or the Sun." The principles enshrined within the EU's charter were, however, being applied in Commission legal proposals and the enforcement of its rules were being monitored by the EU's Fundamental Rights Agency before it was ratified. It was eventually introduced via the Lisbon Treaty.

The UK, along with Poland, did succeed in having a protocol added to the treaty to make it clear that the Charter of Fundamental Rights does not concern national law. This is largely cosmetic as the purpose of the Charter is to apply to EU legislation and guide both the Commission's production of law and the ECJ's interpretation of it as well as the enforcement of the rights in EU areas of competence. The Swedish Foreign Minister at the time Lisbon was agreed, Fredrik Reinfeldt, said in a speech to the Swedish Parliament on 26th June

2007 that, "It should be stressed that the UK was given a clarification, not an opt-out." As the EU's power expands into new areas such as policing and security it becomes ever more relevant.

The protocol is of little use as the British legal system can be, and is being, interfered with by the European Court of Human Rights (ECHR). Despite this court being a non-EU institution Article 6 2. of the Lisbon Treaty binds the EU to'accede to the European Convention for the Protection of Human Rights and Fundamental Freedoms.' This compels the UK to accept the jurisdiction of the Strasbourg based ECHR. What is more, its rulings according to Article 6 3. 'shall constitute general principles of the Union's law.' Other areas of the Charter of Fundamental Rights already apply through the European Social Charter 1961.

There have been other inglorious episodes where the UK has sought to protect its sovereignty only to be outmanoeuvred by the European Union. The government of Tony Blair had the initial short lived success of having energy policy, which would force Britain to share its reserves in a time of crisis, removed from the final draft of the proposed EU Constitution. This was taken out from the constitution after concerns were raised by Britain's oil and gas industry about the implications of the handing this important sector which at the time was paying £5 billion in taxes and employing around 265,000 people in 2004. However, after political sleight of hand in negotiations to revive the EU Constitution first under the title of the Reform Treaty and finally as the Lisbon Treaty it was reintroduced as Article 100 1. This was presented to Britain as a fait accompli and it became Article 122 of the Treaty on the Functioning of the European Union.

More matters concerning energy policy were also introduced becoming part of the Treaty on the Functioning of the European Union. Article 194 a handed Brussels the power to decide where and how the oil and gas are sold. Article 194 b means that the UK must supply energy to another member-state if they are having problems with their network. Article 194 c will make much of the debate in Britain about how energy is produced irrelevant as Brussels will be influencing those decisions. Article 194 d gives the EU a key role as the system guarantor, thus threatening British control over the North Sea reserves. Whilst fiscal issues relating to energy have to be decided unanimously it does meant that Brussels can decide issues relating to the taxation of the energy without Britain's Parliament having a veto.

Regarding the interpretation of EU law there have been challenges to the European Court claiming that draft EU laws are technically illegal as they are incompatible with the treaties going beyond the legally defined principles of the European Union. The Advocate General has on a number of occasions advised the Court that the ban on short selling was illegal. As is the financial transaction tax; which undermined national control of tax and was 'discriminatory.'

Despite these successes this is not reform merely preventing the expansion of EU power in limited areas. What is more, it does not bode well for the national sovereignty. There are other examples of the European Union operating beyond its powers; that is ultra vires. One of the main examples of this is in the area surrounding the Eurozone bailout.

It has been claimed that the British Prime Minister David Cameron has been successful in negotiating Britain out of the EU's bailouts; persuading the other EU leaders to release the UK from being liable for the debts of other EU states. Yet is this actually true? Certainly Cameron told the House of Commons on 20th December 2010 that, "we should not have any liability for bailing out the eurozone when the new permanent arrangements come into effect in 2013... Crucially, we have also ensured that the current emergency arrangements are closed off when the new mechanism comes into effect in 2013."

The temporary European Financial Stabilisation Mechanism (EFSM) has been superseded with by the permanent European Stability Mechanism (ESM); yet the two will continue to exist in parallel. The UK is omitted from any liability arising from the new ESM scheme. However, contrary to the assurance given to Parliament by the PM the ESFM continues to exist until the debt has been repaid. This means that a €6 billion liability, 12.5% of the total loaned out, still exists from the scheme that the Prime Minister stated does not apply to Britain. Cameron continues to maintain the fiction that the UK has been excused from the debt.

What is more, if the loans cannot be repaid and the other EU states are unable to meet the liability the whole debt will fall upon the British taxpayer who will become exposed to the full €48.5 billion that makes up the EFSM. The risks are joint and several. What is more, it can be increased to €60 billion and this can be decided by qualified majority voting where Britain does not have a veto. The UK's continuing responsibility to underwrite the EFSM will continue until 2042. As the eventual collapse of the euro over the long term remains a probability therefore the exposure to the EU's bailout scheme remains more than just a hypothetical risk.

It is noteworthy that the original bailout scheme has Article 122 2. of the Treaty on the Functioning of the European Union as its legal base. This was intended for emergency measures in the event of a 'natural disaster'. To use this for the very man-made euro crisis is in essence illegal, but that did not deter the EU from putting it in place.

The fact that a new scheme has come into being which does not include the UK is less than gracious. The limited achievement of not signing up to a new mechanism does not constitute the return of powers, nor is it even evidence of the success of renegotiation. The UK along with eleven other states, were not included in the ESM because the new scheme was not intended to apply to euro-out state. It is a financial mechanism dedicated to the Single Currency.

The EFSM is not the only scheme the places risks on the British taxpayer. The UK is also part of the Balance of Payments Facility which exists to bailout states in Eastern Europe that have not adopted the euro. This is yet more costs that may add as much as a further €50 billion onto the British taxpayer. The parlous state of the Romanian and Hungarian economies, who have already received loans, means that some degree of liability will potentially fall on Britain.

The political culture of Brussels, its need for conformity and the deeply ingrained belief in the core principles of the European Union do not create an environment that is conducive to resist further centralisation. Yes does that mean that there is no method by which radical change in the EU can be achieved with powers returned to the nation states?

Renegotiation
If British governments can perform so poorly in negotiations and ultimately find itself agreeing to clauses it had originally rejected, even when a veto could be theoretically used, what chance is there of persuading the EU to perform a complete volte face? To assess the chances of changing the terms of membership the constitutional workings of the EU need to be analysed.

Leaving aside a cataclysmic geopolitical event, for instance successful en masse civil disobedience, not impossible when considering the persistent crisis levels of unemployment in the EU; there are only two ways by which a state can limit the power of the EU. One is to seek to change the main text of the treaties and the other is to have protocols, annexes to the treaties, added to the rules which govern the European Union. That is the treaties. These protocols can just relate to the UK. These can be used to clarify the British position in relation to specific aspects of EU law.

However, when the European Court of Justice comes to interpreting the rules of the European Union protocols take secondary importance to the main text of the treaties. Whilst being a useful tool to influence the application of EU rules and despite whatever good intentions they may have they cannot significantly reverse the drift towards ever closer union.

What is more, the adding of a specific protocol as an annex to the EU treaties can only relate to areas of limited importance and as such they are not an effective legal instrument to extensively return power to the nation state. To achieve a major change there will have to be a whole series of protocols introduced. This will not be tolerated; other states will have little reason to agree to a measure that gives the UK a competitive advantage over rivals on the continent. What is more, any change including the addition, alteration or subtraction of a protocol will need to be approved by both the governments and parliaments of every other member state. This will be through the process of treaty change which is set out in Article 48 of the Treaty on European Union.

As changing the protocols annexed to the treaties will not be sufficient to support a substantial renegotiation the main text of the treaties will have to be changed. Regardless of whether protocols are changed or the main text the systems for altering the rules of the EU involve the same convoluted process.

There are two methods by which the treaties of the European can be changed. One is the so-called 'Ordinary revision procedure' which deals with major changes to the treaties and the other is known as the 'Simplified revision procedures.' The latter is used for small changes to the EU that deal with Part Three of the Treaty on the Functioning of the European Union. These are areas to do with the 'internal policies and actions' of the EU. These areas are for instance those that relate to the internal market, the customs union and the free movement of goods and capital. Any proposal for change to these areas can come from the Commission, the European Parliament, or a member states government. The proposals will then be submitted to the European Council who will then discuss them and seek to come to an arrangement. If a proposal for change can be developed the European Council, after it has consulted both the European Parliament and the Commission, will vote on whether the changes are made. There will have to be unanimous agreement in the European Council before any changes are agreed. They will only finally come into force when they are 'approved by the Member States in accordance with their respective constitutional requirements.' This will mean no less than the approval of each and every national parliament. What is more, they cannot be radical alterations to the treaties.

It may even be difficult to reach the state final proposals that are suitable to the British get voted on. There is the necessity to discuss with other states and for a census to be reached. What is more, the discussions will not be managed by the UK. The work of driving forward the EU's agenda lies with the country that holds the rotating Presidency. From January to June 2014 Greece will hold this role. It is unlikely that with their continuing need for a financial 'fix' that their politicians and civil servants will wish to aid the UK's non communautaire agenda. Italy succeeds them in July whose Presidency will run until the end of December 2014. From the start of 2015 the Baltic state of Latvia assumes the role until June of 2015; with Luxembourg taking over in July. Incidentally this will approximately coincide with formation of a new government following the British general election scheduled for 7th May 2015. So far none of those states will offer the UK a particular advantage in the quest to change the EU and the UK's conditions of membership.

The British government does hope that the Netherlands can be a potential ally. The Dutch begin their six monthly presidency of the EU in January 2016. Will Dutch leadership in Europe change the situation and help create an agenda for reform of the EU?

Whilst the Dutch government has concluded after its own balance of competences review that 'The Netherlands is convinced that the time of an 'ever closer union' in every possible policy area is behind us.' Its findings as to what areas of decision making should or should not remain with the EU are not radical enough to appease British

Eurosceptics. So far they have called for the European Commission to cease intervening in areas such as 'forest policy, national flood management, or in rules governing air quality, school milk, tunnel safety or olive oil jugs. The Dutch Prime Minister, Mark Rutte, has also dismissed the idea of opting out from EU policies and repatriating powers back to the nation state. What is more, he has also ruled out the possibility of treaty change. The Dutch Foreign Minister, Frans Timmermans, also stated in an official press release that, 'The government emphasises that it is not aiming at treaty change. The Netherlands fully accepts the existing distribution of competences. It is the division of tasks that it is aiming to discuss: is everything that the EU currently does really necessary?' The substantive conclusion from the Dutch

Testing European legislation for subsidiarity and proportionality – Dutch list of points for action argues that the principle of subsidiarity, contained within the EU's 1992 Maastricht Treaty, should be applied better. It even states that, 'consultations have confirmed that in many fields there is broad support for European legislation.' As there is not an appetite, even amongst the Dutch, for a full-scale repatriation of powers from the EU the chances of David Cameron finding allies anywhere in the EU are slim.

Slovakia then holds the Presidency from July to December 2016 and Malta takes over from January 2017. Interestingly the UK takes on the Presidency for the final half of 2017. However, as the date for the referendum on the revised terms of EU membership is scheduled for that year the British presidency will simply be too late to make a difference. The conclusion of Britain's leadership of the European Council will not take place until December of 2017. Whilst Britain can get limited proposals onto the table it is unlikely that the UK will have an opportunity to effectively influence the agenda to get them turned into changes to the treaties that work for the UK.

This sole remaining realistic route is to alter the terms of membership through seeking a wholesale change to the text of the treaties themselves. This will be through the 'Ordinary revision procedure.' Here, just as in the simplified system, any member state's government, the European Parliament or the Commission may submit proposals to either expand or decrease the power of the EU. They will then be submitted to the European Council and national parliaments will be informed.

The European Council will then consult both the European Parliament and the Commission. Following that it will then decide after taking a vote on whether or not to further examine the proposals. A majority will be needed, otherwise the proposals fall at this stage. If they are agreed then the President of the European Council convenes a convention to consider the proposed amendments to the treaties. It will consist of representatives from: national parliaments, heads of state or government, the European Parliament and representatives from the Commission. The convention will then according to Article 48 3. 'adopt by consensus a recommendation to a conference of representatives of the governments of the member states... ' The requirement of consensus is a further bar to Britain being able to push its unique agenda forward.

If the proposed changes are not considered to warrant a convention then the European Council can decide by a majority, with the agreement of the Parliament, to decide for itself the conferences terms of reference. Here the European Council will be setting the structure and how the conference will work. However, if the proposed changes are not minimal then it will be the President of the Council, Herman Van Rompuy, who shall convene a conference of representatives of the governments of the member states. The proposed amendments to the treaties will have to be determined by common accord. The proposals even if they reach as far as this intergovernmental conference can be vetoed by just one other member state. here is every likelihood that the European Council, Commission or the European Parliament will, in the spring of 2015, call a convention to develop a new treaty. This however is currently opposed by some countries, in particular the Netherlands. Quite simply a British Prime Minister does not have the ability to control the agenda of treaty change let alone demand that a new one comes into force. If there is no appetite to give the UK opt-outs from EU law and have the UK still voting inside its institutions as a member then there will be no return of powers back to Westminster and Britain's democratic institutions.

The requirement for unanimity does not just extend to the leaders of the European Union member states, the intergovernmental conference and the European Council. Ultimately any new treaty will need to be ratified by each and every Parliament of the member states before it can be deemed to apply. This process can in itself take years especially as any controversy will cause delays in ratification. Václav

Klaus, as President of the Czech Republic, delayed formally adding his consent to the Lisbon Treaty despite the Czech approving it. The Treaty was already delayed by the Irish 'No' vote. If the hypothetical treaty that returns powers back to the UK also transfers more authority to the EU over the eurozone states, as there is every chance that it will, then there will constitutionally have to be a referendum in Ireland and possibly politically in other member states.

Even if the other EU leaders are minded to accommodate Britain's unique and extraordinary demands for special treatment the opinions of their own voters will need to be taken into consideration. This introduces another unfavourable variable into the equation.

The timing of a referendum, set for 2017, is not scheduled at a time when the renegotiation that precedes it will have the greatest chance of success. Any strength that the British may have in the negotiations will potentially be negated by the French Presidential elections scheduled for April and May of that same year.

Considering the firmly ingrained Euroscepticism amongst the general population in France it is unlikely that Hollande will want to grant concessions to les Anglais. There is little to no incentive to grant to the UK opt-outs and advantages which he and the French political elite, the graduates of the École nationale d'administration, the so-called ENARCs, will not want to award to their own citizens.

It is fanciful that a significant change in Britain terms of membership can be achieved through negotiation. As persuasion is an unrealistic route to achieving significant changes to the governing treaties of the European Union anytime soon; are there other methods by which an understanding can be reached?

Bargaining for reform
This process of negotiating in the Europe Union often descends into what is described as horse trading; this is a political term where someone votes either for or against a measure in exchange for another voting a certain way on another item. In the committees of the EU it becomes one country agreeing to do something bad for them being offered in exchange for the other representative agreeing to do something bad for their country. This has been at the heart of the European project since it began. The German desire for free trade in industrial goods, something which was anathema to French tradition

of protectionism, had to be paid for by the establishment of a system by which the French could subsidise their agriculture. This was primarily at the expense of the German taxpayer.

There is little that the EU can surrender in exchange for reform in the EU. The budget rebate is reducing in value and is therefore less of a bargaining chip; and increasing the financial costs of the EU still further in exchange for opt-outs on various policies is not an attractive proposition. It has been tried before. At the meeting of the European Council from 15th – 16th December 2005 the then British Prime Minister Tony Blair agreed to the 2007 – 2013 EU budget known as the Multiannual Financial Framework. The budget negotiations were dominated by two main points of controversy. One was the British rebate, raised primarily by the French, and the other was the disproportionate amount of money spent on the Common Agricultural Policy, Blair championed the cutting back of the CAP. Ultimately Blair agreed to give up £7 billion from the rebate in return for a promise to review all EU spending including funds spent on the Common Agricultural Policy. However, in the agreement for the 2007 – 2013 budget CAP spending remained fixed until at least 2020. The French veto over any cut backs to agricultural payments, from which they derive the most benefit also remained in place. At the time Tony Blair was being touted as a possible President of Europe.

Some countries have opened up access to their markets in exchange for one country reforming restrictive practices in its own. As the EU advances the creation of a single regulatory regime across the EU with voting by qualified majority voting the opportunities for this tactic come to an end. What is more, it has traditionally not been a strength possessed by the UK. Britain has one of the freest economies in the European Union. According to the Heritage Foundation's 2013 Index of Economic Freedom the UK is the 14th freest economy in the world and the fourth most open in the EU. The UK's markets are open to all within the EU and restrictive practices are kept to a minimum. There is little that Britain can give up in exchange for economic reform by the other member-states and the EU itself. It is not the UK but in fact other European states that have not as yet fully implemented the services directive. Legal and administrative barriers to the sale of services across the EU are still in place in some sectors on the continent; but not in the UK.

If enticement cannot lead to change; can coercion coax the EU into reform?

Forcing change

Charles de Gaulle, as President of France in the 1960s paralysed EEC institutions by boycotting them from 1965-66. This resulted in the Luxembourg Compromise which was a convention that gave nation states the right to veto legislation, even if unanimity in the Council was not required, if it concerned a matter that was a very important. The understanding has not been in practice since the early 1980s. As the majority of EU law is now decided by qualified majority voting there is virtually nothing that can be achieved by such a strategy; all that will happen is influence will be further diminished.

Preventing a new EU treaty coming into force and stopping further centralisation unless there is a corresponding return of power to the UK is another idea by which it is hoped that the UK can gain leverage. However, when it comes to the culture of the European Union there is one rule regarding the return of powers and another for their capture. Whilst it is true that treaty change requires the agreement of all centralisation does not necessarily require the consent of all.

At a meeting of the European Council from 8th – 9th December 2011 David Cameron did try just such an approach. He refused to acquiesce to further controls over the budgets of the Eurozone states, yet the willing members of the EU choose to go ahead regardless claiming they were making a compact that was an extra EU arrangement. Interesting the price of the Prime Minister's approval would have required the other EU states allowing for the regulation of financial services to be moved from qualified majority voting back to unanimity, restoring the veto. It was an attempt at a renegotiation of just a small part of the UK's terms of membership and it ended in abject failure. What hope for an even more significant change? What is more, this is not the only example of the EU progressing with integration without the need for a treaty.

There are other examples of integration taking place between the states of the European Union when there is no consensus though an agreement that operates outside of its official architecture. The Schengen Agreement, which abolished border controls between its signatories, was only originally signed by half of the EEC, as it was then, just Belgium, France, Luxembourg, the Netherlands and West Germany. The Schengen borderless zone was eventually officially incorporated into the EU via the Amsterdam Treaty with both the UK and Ireland having an opt-out. The Schengen area has since expanded beyond the EU to include; Iceland, Lichtenstein, Norway and Switzerland. These four non-EU states chose to join voluntarily.

There are also other ways by which the EU can create further centralisation by amending the treaties without the need for an intergovernmental conference. Again this does not apply to devolving power to the EU only taking it from member states. Article 48 7 of the Treaty on European Union gives the European Council the power to move an area where unanimity, and therefore the national veto applies, to one that can be decided by the Council under qualified majority voting. This does not apply to defence or military matters. The European Council will have to unanimously approve this action after a majority of the members of the European Parliament have given their consent. National Parliaments will also need to be notified and if one makes its objections to this known within six months then the move to QMV from national veto will not be able to proceed.

There are, however, areas where there are little to no checks and balances on the EU expanding its power. Article 352 of the Treaty on the Functioning of the European Union allows the European Commission to bring forward proposals to take control over new areas of law making. After gaining the approval of all the heads of government and the European Parliament a new area of law-making will become an occupied field of the EU. This is without the necessity of requiring a vote in national parliaments who must merely have their attention drawn to the proposals. These new measures that will have been introduced under Article 352 procedure will however have to be decided by unanimity and cannot be moved for qualified majority voting. Yet, unlike moving items from one where a veto can be used to QMV the national parliaments do not have the power to stop this power grab. The following article, 353, clearly states that the measures contained in Article 48 7. of the Treaty on European Union do not apply to 352 so neither does the national parliaments veto. The rules of the EU are self-amending and allow for the Commission to seek the expansion of its power into new areas without first getting the consent of the people governed by the European Union. All that is needed is the consent of the European Council.

So the EU can reform, but only in one direction...

Parliament and the government can refuse to incorporate new EU directives into British Law. However, the European Court of Justice and the British legal system will, considering that EU law takes precedence, rule that any existing legislation that contradicts Brussels instructions should be struck down. Such a strategy does not keep pace with developments in Brussels. The European Commission has been steadily moving away from legislating via directives. Most new EU law is passed as what is known as a regulations. These take effect instantly; they do not have to pass through national parliaments before becoming law and cannot be stopped by national institutions. The EU's reach will not be stopped through parliamentary stubbornness.

Other ideas are that the UK should withhold payments to the EU; surely depriving Brussels of £53 million per day will force reform. Even if this was legally possible the political consequences may just be counter-productive and will not win the friends that are needed, all 27 Presidents and Prime Ministers, in the EU. The effect that it can have, even if tolerated by the British courts, is to stop the expansion of EU projects, subsidies and grants in Eastern Europe. Many of those countries like most EU states are still wedded to the idea of financial support and any reduction of funds towards them will not only alienate Old Europe but Eastern European states as well. Saving one currency, pounds sterling, will just lead to costs in another, the currency of goodwill.

Refusing to agree to a future financial framework, EU budget, is even less ineffectual which is why it was not persuade by both Blair and Cameron in their disputes with the nature of the European Union. The powers to stop a budget being agreed is limited and even if not agreed it till not result not stop a single EU law being implemented by the Commissions subordinates in the national civil services or in the EU agencies. The previous budget would just carry over with a 2% increase. However, this again will only prevent the expansion of new EU schemes thus losing more friends and alienating people.

The option of unilateral action is also another untenable alternative. Britain is legally obliged to honour its treaty commitments by both European institutions. Without a specific act of Parliament the UK's domestic courts will not acknowledge a government's enforced disavowing of the demands of membership.

The point was, and is, that if an organisation is set up in a certain way, its behaviour is pre-ordained. Both the structure and the history of the European Union show that it was set up to take power from national democracies handing decision making to higher authorities. It embodies at its core the supranational Commission and a Council operating away from national democratic institutions. All the other institutions were designed in such a way that they would either present no challenge to the supremacy of the concept of ever-closer Union. The European Parliament, which apart from a few limited exemptions, does actively favour the further centralisation of authority in Europe away from national institutions. The European Court of Justice also actively works towards the mutual goal shared with the European Commission. The EU can only act in an interfering, bureaucratic and anti-democratic manner which it was designed to do in the first place; and not to return power to national institutions.

What is more, the European Commission, like bureaucrats operating in any system seek to expand their budgets and their power. Brussels is bound together by a culture of collective self –interest which will stymie reform at every stage. The bureaucracy has no incentive to give away the power which has been steadily amassed since the late-1950s.

If the UK cannot significantly change the EU, or change Britain's terms of membership, from inside then logic dictates that the UK should look towards establishing a new relationship with the EU and other European states from a new position outside the EU. As Roy Jenkins recognised there are but two logical paths. Either to try and marshal the influence the UK has to produce policies that favour Britain or seek an amicable separation.

Yet is this feasible; can Britain really leave the institution that has been the cornerstone, or perhaps millstone, of Britain's economic policy for more than four decades? And can divorce ever be cordial?

Chapter 5

Which Way Out?

"If any state in the Union will declare that it prefers separation to a continuance in the union I have no hesitation in saying, 'let us separate'."
Thomas Jefferson, statesman and third President of the United States of America

Opposition to the European Union draws on many different strands of thought and often widely differing political traditions; seeking numerous different solutions to the problem of Britain and the European Union. The issue of whether Britain should leave the EU is contentious; yet this question is not the only provocative topic. How the UK can leave the European Union is also a controversial subject; especially amongst those who actually agree that Britain is better off out.

A Referendum

Despite the prospect of a referendum dominating the debate about leaving the EU it is the case however that in the British political system the monumental decision to leave the EU does not come through a public vote. It can only come about via one of two ways; either through an Act of Parliament that expressly repeals the European Communities Act 1972; or through following a specific exit clause in the Treaty on the Functioning of the European Union.

The referendum may be seen as politically, even morally, necessary but it is not required constitutionally. At the very least it sends a powerful message and in the event of a vote to leave the British people's exercising of their self-determination should be recognised internationally. However, other nations have rejected further EU centralisation, notably Ireland which rejected both the Nice and Lisbon

Treaties but were made to think again as was Denmark when it rejected the Maastricht Treaty. When both the French and the Dutch voted 'Non' and 'Nee' to the EU Constitution its provisions and transfers of power from the nation-state to the EU were brought in via the Lisbon Treaty, this time without making the mistake of asking the people.

An Act of Parliament can make a referendum binding, unless the result has been expressly repealed by another Act, yet the issue of leaving the EU is much more complex.

A role for the courts?
It has also been claimed that EU membership, and its handing of authority of law making to a body outside the realm of the UK, is unconstitutional. Therefore, under this minority school of thought all that is required is to legally recognise this and use the courts to strike down both EU membership and the rules that follow from this. Regardless of whether or not there is merit in this view is immaterial as cases have been brought to court making such claims. However, as membership has the consent of Parliament the courts will never make such a ruling. The British system of government holds statutes, law coming from Parliament, above all else – bar of course legislation from the European Union. Under such circumstances similar legal approaches will remain cul-de-sacs that do not offer a way out of the European Union.

The will of Parliament
One commonly advocated idea is that Britain should just leave; this is often qualified with the statement that the UK should just have a free trade with the EU. A unilateral withdrawal from the European Union is permissible under Britain's constitution. According to the constitutional theorist Albert Venn Dicey in his work Introduction to the Study of the Law of the Constitution Parliament has 'the right to make or unmake any law whatever: and, further, that no person or body is recognised by the law of England as having a right to override or set aside the legislation of Parliament.'

It was once recognised that repealing a law can be done simply by passing another law which if it contradicts the earlier legislation the latter rule will apply. This concept is known as 'implied repeal'. This once sacred principle has been challenged by exponents of the EU and human rights lawyers who have sought to put the European Communities Act and the Human Rights Act, amongst others, on a pedestal above other legislation classing those laws as 'constitutional acts' of parliament. This recent innovation means that those statutes cannot just be abolished by a later piece of legislation unless it is expressly stated that the new legislation cancels the previous law. This is known as 'express repeal.'

Both the views surrounding statute law do ultimately give sovereignty to the United Kingdom Parliament which has the supremacy to make and unmake any law that it sees fit. There is a difference of opinion amongst scholars as to how EU law fits into Britain's constitutional system and quite clearly Parliament is voluntarily bound by legislation emanating from Brussels and rulings made by the European Court of Justice in Luxembourg. Yet it remains the case that Parliament – that is the House of Commons, the House of Lords and the Monarch with the granting of the Royal Assent – can pass legislation that expressly repeals the 1972 European Communities Act. This is constitutionally still possible. As the commitments of membership as laid down in the various EU treaties have been established by an Act of Parliament the repealing of that act will mean that as far as domestic law is concerned they will cease to have legal force in the UK. The decision to repeal the Act will according to Britain's own political system take the UK out of the European Union. It will also strike down the amendments to the European Communities Act which originally took us into the EEC as it was then. Consequently the later treaties that have further entangled Britain into the EU system of governance will also therefore no longer apply as their base is built upon the original 1972 Act.

However, the unilateral abrogation of the treaties by the UK will still leave many important issues unresolved. The matter of the international treaty commitments that Britain has voluntarily made since 1973 will not be cancelled so easily. The EU, and its remaining member states may claim that Britain is still beholden to some of them. Furthermore, as the EU has been a source of law for more than forty years the status of the regulations and directives which governed life in the UK will need to be resolved.

EU law

Section 18 of the European Union Act 2011 reaffirms the view that EU law is only directly applicable through the European Communities Act. Thus repealing the ECA will end the dominance of the EU over British political life but from now on until that time the British Courts will consider that EU law takes precedence over national law.

As a member of the European Union its laws are also the laws of Britain and so much of national life is, for good or ill, governed according to those requirements. It is impractical to strike down all EU law. Some may find it as liberating for the economy as it would be for the nation. Others would point out that it would leave black holes in many aspects of our law from environmental legislation to rules on consumer protection and even aspects relating to the design of motor vehicles.

Britain has become so entangled in the web of EU law that for it to fall overnight will create a void. This would no doubt require the complete incorporation of EU legislation, the entire acquis communautaire, via an Act of Parliament. Then the monumental task of repealing the unwelcome rules whilst retaining the necessary and acceptable could begin. It will also be possible to modify these rules, which are in excess of one hundred thousand pages, so that they better suit Britain's needs.

To review the mass of adopted EU legislation would require a Grand Committee consisting of both Houses of Parliament, the Lords and the Commons. This wold debate and review each major field of law. Proposals from each civil service department for the abolition or alteration of legislation originating from the EU will be submitted to them to decide what should be retained, repealed or revised. This process will receive evidence from professional organisations, businesses, academic experts, think tanks and all generally interested parties in each field of law making. The proposals will then need to be voted on in Parliament. This process will take at least several years and will be a major national endeavour.

The EU's assumption of power has made Parliament redundant in many areas and has led it to enter a legislative slumber where MPs have been allowed to focus too much of their time on how to optimise their expense claims and not enough on matters of state. The caffeine of independence will come as a real shock to the system.

The international dimension

The issue of the European Union is of course not just a matter of domestic law. The arrangements that make Britain an EU member also carry with them rights and obligations to the other states as well as to the European institutions. The field of international relations is much more complex and requires considerable consideration.

Repealing the European Communities Act 1972 will just create the possibility of an international dispute. The issues at stake will not just be arcane questions of Britain's constitutional status but mammon will dictate that real tangible issues such as access to the UK's fishing waters will arise. The UK made these once rich waters available as an EU resource as part of its treaty obligations with the EU. Exiting the EU will take them back under national control to the chagrin of Spain's fishing fleet. Other areas of dispute will also appear and in some case the transnational Olympians of international law may judge the UK to be in the wrong; a perverse twist in Britain's quest for democratic self-government. It has been claimed that the UK can, under the provisions of the 1969 Vienna Convention on the Law of Treaties, the international rules which govern the application of agreements between sovereign states, exit the provisions of a treaty at will. However, is this the case; can the UK annul its numerous treaties with the other EU states at will?

Articles 56, 65, 66 and 67 of the Vienna Convention do indeed recognise that a state may withdraw from the obligations of a treaty. That is as long as a minimum of 12 months' notice is given. The Convention also sets a procedure whereby in the event of a dispute each of the parties has one year in which they can attempt to negotiate a resolution to the dispute that has arisen causing the schism in the international agreement. The states, in the circumstances considered here the members of the EU, can also ask for arbitration or transfer it to the International Court of Justice. If no agreement is forthcoming then the obligations on the departing member state cease so long as the other parties are notified. So far so good; but withdrawal under the Vienna Convention only applies under certain circumstances. It will need to be proved that 'the parties intended to admit the possibility of denunciation or withdrawal.' This, however, is a concept that is not readily accepted in treaty law.

The European Union is an organisation that has been created by treaty and once agreed much of the law of treaties seeks to make sure that they are not undone. It has not only become customary in international law to regard that a treaty obligation must be honoured but this convention is made compulsory by internationally accepted agreements. These agreements were voluntarily signed up to by the UK on 23rd May 1969. The United Nations have considered them to be binding since 27th January 1980. Its text places law enacted by transnational agreement on a pedestal above national law. It reads 'Recognizing the ever-increasing importance of treaties as a source of international law and as a means of developing peaceful cooperation among nations, whatever their constitutional and social systems... ' It then states the stipulations which govern international treaties.

Again the Vienna Convention offers further bad news for those that advocate abrogating the treaties. Article 26 of the Vienna Convention affirms that 'Every treaty in force is binding upon the parties to it and must be performed by them in good faith.' Article 27 states that 'A party may not invoke the provisions of its internal law as justification for its failure to perform a treaty.' This is unless according to Article 46 the domestic legal issue is of 'fundamental importance.' However, the test is an objective, not subjective, one. Any supposed incompatibility of the EU with Britain's constitution has not been proved in a court of law as yet and remains unlikely to be established as legal fact.

Article 42 goes further. It forbids the denunciation of a treaty. In its section on the validity and continuance in force of treaties it states that 'The validity of a treaty or of the consent of a State to be bound by a treaty may be impeached only through the application of the present Convention.' It also states that 'The termination of a treaty, its denunciation or the withdrawal of a party, may take place only as a result of the application of the provisions of the treaty or of the present Convention. The same rule applies to suspension of the operation of a treaty.'

However, if a fundamental change of circumstances has occurred the provisions of a treaty can be judged to have lapsed but only if the new circumstances were not anticipated when the international agreement was struck. Article 62 of the same convention allows for unilateral withdrawal from a treaty and its obligations. It states in those terms of the Vienna Convention 'a party may invoke a fundamental change of circumstances as a ground for terminating or withdrawing from a treaty it may also invoke the change as a ground for suspending the operation of the treaty.'

Does this mean that the UK can use this to exit the treaties that have entwined Britain into the EU without any international disputes? The right to leave the terms of a treaty is guaranteed if there is the 'fundamental change of circumstances' can be claimed but what would the change be? A major difference that has emerged in Britain is the lack of public consent for the EU that now exists. Another change is the expansion of the EU which has further diminished Britain's influence coupled with the fact that if the member states of the eurozone act as a caucus they can continually out vote the UK in the Council of Ministers. Can these reasons be considered sufficient justification to denounce the UK's international commitments? The EU has certainly been awarded many more powers than some would have liked. However, the fact remains that EU membership and the handing of many powers to that growing monolith has been agreed to by Britain's nationally elected representatives. EU dominance has not been imposed from without. It has been accepted via the signing of new treaties and ratified from within the UK's political system and accepted as constitutionally sound by the legal branch of the British state; the courts. In addition until recently it was heresy to even suggest that Britain should leave the European Union. Article 45 establishes that a country cannot cite reasons for 'invalidating, terminating, withdrawing from or suspending the operation of a treaty' if it has 'expressly agreed that the treaty is valid or remains in force or continues in operation'. A state cannot also withdraw if it can 'by reason of its conduct be considered as having acquiesced in the validity of the treaty or in its maintenance in force or in operation.'

Abrogating the treaties will therefore be questionable under the Vienna Convention. It would certainly cause consternation internationally, which may not be helpful when the UK wants to assume the free trade agreements with other states around the globe that the EU has negotiated on behalf of Britain and the other EU members. In time the UK would be able to negotiate itself back into them, but it will take time and in an economically and politically inter-connected world this may prove to be less than practicable.

What is more, the UK has a long tradition of reverence towards international treaty obligations that have also been underpinned by Parliament viewing them as binding upon the signatories and almost infallible. This was the case in 1914 when Britain honoured the 1839 Treaty of London to maintain and defend Belgian independence. This attitude remains and has led the situation that has allowed the European Court of Human Rights, established by Article 19 in Section II of the European Convention on Human Rights, to interfere with Britain's judicial process. The long running saga surrounding Abu Qatada, who was known as Osama Bin Laden's right-hand man in Europe, is a particular exemplar of this interference. Here the British courts stopped his deportation to Jordan on human rights grounds which were originally established by international treaty.

Furthermore, the provisions in the Vienna Convention for governing the rules of international organisations, Article 5, give precedence to the internal rules of that intergovernmental group. It states that 'The present Convention applies to any treaty which is the constituent instrument of an international organization and to any treaty adopted within an international organization without prejudice to any relevant rules of the organization.' Article 54 maintains that a party can withdraw from or terminate a treaty when its actions doing so are 'in conformity with the provisions of the treaty' or 'at any time by consent of all the parties after consultation with the other contracting States.'

Therefore, as the international treaties that form the basis of EU governance do, as will be shown later, offer a precise procedure for renouncing EU membership then it is the treaties own conditions that should be followed. Not the infrequent grounds set out in the Vienna Convention. There is an explicit exit clause that is expressly laid out in the rules governing the European Union. It is known as Article 50 of the Treaty on European Union. If there was no specific right to repudiate the terms of the EU's founding treaties then the Vienna Convention can be explored for possibilities. However, as there is a clearly identifiable alternative it is to the EU's own rule book that Britain must look to extricate the UK from the EU.

As far as international law is concerned; the rules governing the functioning and cancellation of treaties contained within the Vienna Convention do not offer a process by which the UK can withdraw from international commitments that have arisen through European Union membership. Therefore, another solution will have to be found.

A voidable agreement

Perhaps the British legal establishment should take a different view to the treaties that establish trans-national governance across Europe. Here the views of one of the prominent Founding Fathers of the USA, Thomas Jefferson, a noted statesman and third president of the United States, are of use. He saw such agreements between states not as binding treaties creating an insoluble union but as compacts between sovereign entities that can be dissolved under certain circumstances.

Any domestic and international tension that may emerge through the UK abrogating the treaties can be dealt with through recognising that instead of their being hallowed texts that sit above and out of reach of national democracies free to impose from above they are in fact compacts between sovereign states. Despite the treaty establishing another system of government that sits above the nation-states Compact Theory argues that the national institutions remain supreme.

Arguably, the agreement that has brought the European Union into being is a compact between sovereign states. This has the potential for a profound impact. Despite the EU's ability to sign international agreements and regardless of the recognition that the laws passed by the EU institutions have supremacy over national law, a member state has the right to reject, or repeal, laws that originate from the supranational body if a state believes that it has exceeded its authority in making them. The member state also has the right to decide that the agreement is void if the terms of the compact are broken by another signatory or the Union has evolved beyond what was originally intended.

Does Britain's present state of affairs vis-à-vis the EU justify nullifying EU membership?

A reasoned analysis of current developments in the EU paint an interesting picture of an organisation which has breached its own rules and the limitations placed upon its power. There are ample breaches of jurisdiction which can be used to make the case that the European Union is not an organisation which should continue to have authority on these shores. Not only have the British people firmly moved against ever closer union, but also because the EU's actions breach its own rules.

Precedents have been set for an expansion of power and responsibility that clearly go against the EU's own rules. Taxation is meant to remain a power that belongs to the nation state which can exercise its national veto over any proposals emanating from the European Commission. However, the European Court of Justice has ruled that if the stated main goal of the law is to achieve another end, such as in the case of environmental legislation, then the taxation which is introduced to enforce the rules by pricing out behaviour that the EU deems to be unacceptable will be subject to Qualified Majority Voting and cannot be stopped by one state alone. This contravenes the principle of no taxation without representation.

States were allowed to join the euro without meeting the necessary criteria. This does not just involve the irresponsible and even corrupt economies of Southern Europe but also the two main drivers behind European integration, Germany and France. Despite the fact that Germany had insisted on the rules in the first instance these two nations were allowed to breach the Stability and Growth Pact and treat the principle of fiscal responsibility with contempt. This gave a green light to other delinquent nations who were then free to flout the rules.

This amounts to gross misconduct that has damaged economic growth in those states and recklessly risked the economies of the other member states in the EU which have to deal with the drag created by this folly and can be held liable by the European Central Bank for losses that it incurs in the eventually vain attempt to hold the political project of monetary union together.

Yet the illegality in the EU does not just concern the turning of blind eyes to the rules it also involves overcompensation by the creation of new legal requirements which have no base in the treaties which establish the EU and in fact run contrary to its principles.

The bailout of the indebted member states also runs contrary to European rules. The original legal justification for the bailouts came through an article designed to assist a member state in the event of a natural disaster. Article 122 2. reads;

'Where a Member State is in difficulties or is seriously threatened with severe difficulties caused by natural disasters or exceptional occurrences beyond its control, the Council, on a proposal from the Commission, may grant, under certain conditions, Union financial assistance to the Member State concerned. The President of the Council shall inform the European Parliament of the decision taken.'

The debt crisis however was a manmade debacle that most certainly could have been avoided if honesty prevailed and the indebted nations were kept out of the Single Currency.

The bond buying programme of the European Central Bank is also contrary to EU rules. Article 123 1. states,

'Overdraft facilities or any other type of credit facility with the European Central Bank or with the central banks of the Member States (hereinafter referred to as 'national central banks') in favour of Union institutions, bodies, offices or agencies, central governments, regional, local or other public authorities, other bodies governed by public law, or public undertakings of Member States shall be prohibited, as shall the purchase directly from them by the European Central Bank or national central banks of debt instruments.'

The ECB has been indirectly buying government debt from the banks. This, however, is also against Council Regulation EC No 3603/93 which makes it clear that, 'purchases made on the secondary market must not be used to circumvent the objective of that Article.'

The European Union and the European Central Bank, have along with the International Monetary Fund, imposed conditions on the recipients of the financial support which include tax rises and budget cuts including reducing welfare, social service and pensions. These austerity measures have brought nothing but harm to all those who have to live under them. However, the EU does not have the legal authority to impose those stringent financial policies.

Article 125 1. of the Treaty on the Functioning of the European Union reads;

'The Union shall not be liable for or assume the commitments of central governments, regional, local or other public authorities, other bodies governed by public law, or public undertakings of any Member State... A Member State shall not be liable for or assume the commitments of central governments, regional, local or other public authorities, other bodies governed by public law, or public undertakings of another Member State... '

However, the bailouts have led to the debt risk being spread to the European Central Bank and other member states.

Furthermore the Fiscal Compact, 'the treaty that never was' for which the British Prime Minister David Cameron won plaudits for vetoing in December 2011, should also not be in force. This agreement seeks to manage the budgets according to EU rules of most of the EU member states that have signed it. Britain and the Czech Republic have refused to do so. The agreement of all member states is required for a treaty change so this agreement is considered to be outside of the EU framework, however, to all intents and purposes it is part of the EU's rules. The Fiscal Compact uses the already established EU premises and rules. Failure to comply can lead to the European Court of Justice fining a state that contravenes its rules.

As such it is against the spirit of the European Union's principle of unanimity. Furthermore, bringing it into force is an affront to Britain whose Prime Minster was opposed to its provisions without safeguards to allow the British government to veto EU financial services legislation. Despite the slight to the UK the British negotiating position was met with incredulity and invective from the unelected President of the European Commission José Manual Barroso.

Instead of reducing unemployment and resolving the problems within the eurozone these laws of dubious legality will only store up more trouble for the future and create further tension between the member states. A more realistic solution may be to go back to national currencies and recognise that the building of the house of Europe on fraudulent foundations was always going to end in disaster.

It is however clear that the deeper the union becomes the more breaches that follow. Far from Britain changing the EU from within, thus reconciling the British people to membership, as had been hoped by some, the result of European governance has been the opposite. Centralisation has continued and expanded unabated; this gives the UK a powerful constitutional justification to leave. The case can be made that the UK is not so much leaving the EU, the situation is also one of the European Union leaving Britain.

What is more, a powerful justification for Brexit can be made on the grounds of the repeated cases of fraud, mismanagement and waste that is endemic within EU spending. Other parties may, however, claim that the canons of the Vienna Convention deal with breaches of the rules and therefore override compact theory. Article 60 2. maintains that there must be unanimous agreement to terminate or suspend the treaty. Or the complaining country must be especially affected. What is more, this can only be followed if the breach is materially relevant to the execution of the terms of the treaty. Any action relating to a breach of the rules must therefore be very significant. What is more, section 4 of that article mandates that if the treaty has its own remedy to a violation then this route should take precedence. The EU does have its own resolution mechanism; a state can take a case to the European Court of Justice.

Self-determination
Ultimately, the right to secede from the EU remains because it is just the creature of the member states and ultimate authority rests with national institutions from which it derives its authority. Any attempt to place transnational European governance on a pedestal above the nation state is profoundly contrary to national sovereignty, independence and democracy.

Furthermore, according to international law self-determination for a once self-governing territory such as the United Kingdom is a right; indeed it is a founding principle of the United Nations (UN). Article 1.2 of the UN's Chapter 1: Purposes and Principles states that its aims are, 'To develop friendly relations among nations based on respect for the principle of equal rights and self-determination of peoples, and to take other appropriate measures to strengthen universal peace.' Both Part 1. Article 1. of the International Covenant on Civil and Political Rights and the International Covenant on Economic, Social and Cultural Rights state that, 'All peoples have the right of self-determination. By virtue of that right they freely determine their political status and freely pursue their economic, social and cultural development.'

The realpolitik of Britain as, for the time being, a prominent member of Nato, and still a significant economy with excellent global links be that via the Commonwealth or through the UK's permanent seat on the UN's Security Council is that it will have influence and be able to take back its independent position in the world again. Leaving aside the vagaries of international law and the internationally recognised national right to self-determination; authority, and the debate surrounding the EU is a question of where dominion should reside. Ultimately, regardless of what the international lawyers may claim, power comes from a source that is very different to a treaty. Joseph Stalin famously asked the rhetorical question "The Pope! How many divisions has he got?" Likewise the EU relies upon the institutions of its member states and their security services to enforce EU law. It does not have the ability to impose its writ on an unwilling state, that is not for the time being.

The difficulties of divorce

It is undoubtedly legally possible to unilaterally leave without agreement with the EU yet is it politically and economically practical? These two considerations are increasingly becoming one and the same. The business case for UK plc will be the key determinant in any referendum on this country's future.

Arguing the case that Britain can and should just exit the EU has the advantage that it's a simple message that can readily be understood and has so far succeeded in getting the issue of session from the EU firmly onto the political issue. The British establishment has certainly been shocked into having to engage with the issue further pushing it into the public consciousness. Yet, the withdrawalists' partial success in this phoney war has brought added scrutiny. Claiming that Britain should simply withdraw without detailing a feasible exit strategy is no longer feasible.

It fails to answer the questions that will be raised in a referendum. Such as what will the future terms of trade be between businesses in Britain and those in the remaining parts of the EU? It has been argued by Europhiles that this trade is important in its own right but also to attract inward investment to the UK. This will of course continue, and perhaps at a higher rate than before, but there is a tendency for the public to favour the status quo over a relative leap into the unknown. This is well documented. Those wishing to leave the EU will have to provide the British people with the answers that they require as to what independence means.

There will have to be negotiations on Britain's future trading relationship with whatever remains in the EU and the trade deals that have been signed up to on Britain's behalf. It is likely that an agreement can be reached and any problems will not be insurmountable. Yet it will be to the advantage of everyone if uncertainty can be avoided.

Yet there is a solution that can be used to compel the EU to not only consider Britain's terms of membership but can also be used to mandate the EU to complete a post-membership agreement to guarantee trade without obstacles being placed before us. This is to invoke Article 50 of the Treaty on European Union.

Controversy surrounding the European Union encompasses not only whether Britain should remain a member or not but also how the UK should leave. Currently there is a debate amongst Eurosceptics on the merits or demerits of using the exit clause which exists in EU law – Article 50.

The EU's prescribed method of withdrawal
Article 50 is the EU's stated and approved mechanism and process for a member state wishing to leave the European Union.

This makes it clear that a member state can leave the European Union '1. Any Member State may decide to withdraw from the Union in accordance with its own constitutional requirements.' In terms of the UK this can be done via two methods and a referendum is not one of them. The first process by which the British government can invoke the withdrawal clause is to pass an Act of Parliament. This will require legislation being approved by both the House of Commons and the House of Lords. The second, though more controversial method, will be to simply use the Royal Prerogative to give notice that the UK will leave the EU.

The Royal Prerogative is the power of the monarch, now exercised by the Prime Minister and Her Majesty's Government. They include the power to declare war, make peace, and specifically relevant to this case the power to conduct diplomacy and make and ratify treaties. This will include the power to invoke Article 50. Other EU treaties have been ratified by an Act of Parliament because they award powers to the European Union and require the British legal system to accept the supremacy of EU law in an increasing number of areas. Invoking Article 50 places no such obligation upon the UK. Furthermore, the original European Communities Act 1972 has been amended to incorporate the provisions of Article 50 and as it is part of the EU's rules it is also therefore a part of British law. This will be challenged and contentious but it will be a surer method than attempting to pass a bill through a potentially hostile House of Lords.

Article 50 also stipulates that, '2. A Member State which decides to withdraw shall notify the European Council of its intention... '

Section 2 of Article 50 goes on to decree that 'In the light of the guidelines provided by the European Council, the Union shall negotiate and conclude an agreement with that State, setting out the arrangements for its withdrawal, taking account of the framework for its future relationship with the Union.'

This compels the EU, initially with the European Commission and later with the European Council acting upon recommendations from the Commission, to begin negotiations with the country that wants to leave so as to reach an arrangement on the subsequent association between the EU and the exiting state. What form would this agreement take? The Treaty on European Union suggests an answer. Article 3 5. of the Treaty on European Union (TEU) states that amongst other things 'In its relations with the wider world, the Union shall uphold and promote... free and fair trade... ' This is the holy grail of what many in Britain want from the European Union. Furthermore, Article 8 1. (TEU) 'The Union shall develop a special relationship with neighbouring countries, aiming to establish an area of prosperity and good neighbourliness, founded on the values of the Union and characterised by close and peaceful relations based on cooperation.' This further mandates the EU to establish a mutually beneficial trade area with a post-EU Britain.

What form will the withdrawal agreement take? If one is indeed settled it will establish a relationship between Britain and with the EU and its member states that is primarily based on trade and issues that surround such economic activity. The agreement will also deal with issues relating to nationals being residents in other member states and the possible continued participation of the UK in continent wide student programs and other pan-European projects.

There are many complex issues that will need to be resolved. If the Article 50 procedure is followed the withdrawal agreement will be a document of considerable size. Even agreeing a new trade relationship alone will give the UK responsibilities as well as rights. The UK may wish to pass legislation allowing for the recognition of other country's goods and standards and agree to the elimination of tariffs on trade between Britain and the EU. This agreement will therefore need to be ratified by both Houses of Parliament and be given the Royal Assent. The UK's withdrawal will not be dependent upon making and then ratifying the agreement in Parliament, if it is not agreed or is rejected by Parliament then withdrawal, without resolving any outstanding issues, will take place. Ironically the UK will then be outside of the European Union not through the repudiation of the European

Communities Act (ECA) 1972 but by embracing one of its later amendments, the European Union (Amendment) Act 2008. This legislation forced into law, without there being a referendum in Britain, the Treaty of Lisbon which included for the first time the exit clause. Invoking these provisions can clearly lead to the EU considering Britain to be outside of its orbit.

The difficulties with Article 50 will most probably appear before there is an opportunity to vote on any agreement in Parliament. The negotiations with the EU may not be that straight forward... Article 50 2. goes on to state,

'That agreement shall be negotiated in accordance with Article 218(3) of the Treaty on the Functioning of the European Union. It shall be concluded on behalf of the Union by the Council, acting by a qualified majority, after obtaining the consent of the European Parliament.'

Therefore, the agreement under which a nation withdraws has to be approved by both the European Parliament and the Council and as such can be voted down. Negotiations with the members of the Council, representing the nation states, will in all likelihood be cordial; as it will be in every counties interest to keep good relations after Brexit. Here the culture on consensus building can work in Britain's favour. The need to gain the consent of the European Parliament will be the stage that problems with the Article 50 withdrawal process will emerge. Whilst some MEPs may be glad to see Britain leave the EU, its membership is largely wedded to the principle of 'ever-closer union' and does not take kindly to set backs to the process of European integration. MEPs have previously rejected deals that have been painstakingly reached between the heads of government. On 13th May 2013 the European Parliament rejected their proposal to cut the EU's budget which the European Council had agreed to on 8th February of that year. Perhaps the withdrawal agreement with Britain will be another opportunity for it to show that it is not just there to rubber-stamp the Commission's proposals. Nevertheless, if an agreement is not reached then two years after the notice to withdraw is given the departing state will be outside of the European Union, yet it can be out as soon as the accord is in place.

Section 3 affirms that 'The Treaties shall cease to apply to the State in question from the date of entry into force of the withdrawal agreement or, failing that, two years after the notification referred to in paragraph 2, unless the European Council, in agreement with the Member State concerned, unanimously decides to extend this period.'

The fourth section reads 'For the purposes of paragraphs 2 and 3, the member of the European Council or of the Council representing the withdrawing Member State shall not participate in the discussions of the European Council or Council or in decisions concerning it.' This limits the UK's negotiating hand especially as the UK will not have a vote on the potential agreement. Such an exclusion will put the remaining EU members in the driving seat and give them a greater ability to set the terms of the divorce. However, paragraph 4 of Article 50 does not prevent British MEPs from taking part in the discussions and voting in the European Parliament. on the withdrawal agreement. This fourth section finishes by establishing that 'A qualified majority shall be defined in accordance with Article 238(3)(b) of the Treaty on the Functioning of the European Union.'

Finally, Article 50 concludes as follows '5. If a State which has withdrawn from the Union asks to rejoin, its request shall be subject to the procedure referred to in Article 49.'

That means that if the UK decides to re-join the EU it will have to re-apply as if it a new potential member joining the EU, in such an event it is unlikely that Britain would be offered the opt outs, such as those on the euro, which the UK currently enjoys. These are terms that the UK is unlikely to agree to. Furthermore, this procedure like all EU negotiations is long and not straight forward. Article 49 states 'The applicant State shall address its application to the Council, which shall act unanimously after consulting the Commission and after receiving the consent of the European Parliament, which shall act by a majority of its component members.' And 'This agreement shall be submitted for ratification by all the contracting States in accordance with their respective constitutional requirements.' It can therefore be vetoed at many different stages; once the UK is out it will remain out.

It needs to be noted that the process envisaged in Article 50 is not a means by which the UK can compel the EU into negotiations on renegotiated terms of EU membership. That can only be done via an Intergovernmental Conference (IGC). Any agreement that can come out of the Article 50 procedure will not have the legal force of an article in one of the treaties that governs the EU. However, a new settlement may emerge if the Commission, the Council and the Parliament realise that they do not want the member state in question to leave and promise to change that state's conditions of membership. Alternatively, a botched notification to withdraw will have thrown away the country's strongest negotiating position, the threat of exit, and will therefore have lost credibility and influence in future negotiations.

Once taking the decision to invoke Article 50 the countdown to a new role in the world begins.

The provisions in Article 50 not only shows that the European Union wants to perceive itself as a voluntary union but also that in the eventuality of a Brexit it will most probably want to negotiate a future post-EU relationship based mainly on trade and preserving the four freedoms. After all it is in the interests of the continentals to maintain with as little hindrance as possible the free movement of labour, goods, services and capital. However, some Eurosceptics reject out of hand the option of initiating discussions under the process of Article 50.

Which is the true path?

Some withdrawalists do not favour following the EU's approved modus operandi for leaving the union and instead argue that the European Communities Act 1972 (ECA) should unilaterally be repealed. Britain does not have to follow the rules for leaving set out by the EU; the UK is sovereign and repealing the ECA will also strike down the provisions of Article 50 thus nullifying this procedure. However, that will deny the UK an opportunity to talk to the other EU nations about what our relationship should be once out of the EU.

Those who favour unilateral withdrawal and object to the invocation of Article 50 not because they do not favour getting out but because it is feared that the EU's apparatchiks will tie up, perhaps willingly, the UK's negotiating team and delay the reaching of a conclusion and extend the discussions until there is political change at home. However, once the UK has submitted its notice to leave Britain will automatically withdraw unless those negotiations are extended. The European Council will have to unanimously agree to the extension, perhaps one or more of the UK's less reliable 'allies' on the continent will wish for Britain to just go and will therefore not extend the discussions thus forcing the withdrawal to take place regardless of whether or not there had been a change of heart at home. It is indeed interesting that there is no mechanism for cancelling the Article 50 notification, perhaps this scenario came to mind when the rules were being drafted…

The exclusion of the withdrawing state from the discussions concerning it is a concern and appears iniquitous. There are also fears that allowing the EU to set our terms of exit will be to invite our jilted partners to set the terms of our divorce. Leaving hurt feelings to one side there are concerns that the EU may decide that allowing one ex-partner to go its own way on reasonable conditions will set a precedent for others wishing to leave. However, this logic fails to recognise that the terms would have to be agreed by the UK and therefore cannot be excessively onerous otherwise there will be no trade agreement which will not be in any country's best interests. What is more, a unilateral declaration of British withdrawal would not deliver optimum results for British exports to continental markets. This mutually beneficial trade arrangement will only come when a free trade agreement has been finalised. And without initiating Article 50 such a settlement may take years to agree, if at all.

Even if there is no withdrawal agreement the EU will not be allowed to treat British exports to its markets in any way that it saw fit. Just like in any divorce, where a judge decides the terms if there is a conflict, the actions of the EU will have to conform to the rules of the World Trade Organisation, this will go some way to protecting British interests. Regardless of that the EU's Common External tariff on non-agricultural goods averages as little as 1%. What is more, Britain is a food importer. It has no food export market on the continent that is so significant that it would create ruin in the UK if it had to compete with the EU's protectionist agricultural policies.

Nevertheless, just exiting will not force the EU into negotiations where it is compelled by its own rules to consider a framework relationship whose cornerstone will be free and fair trade…

…Perhaps the two year cooling off period will be the best way forward.

On a less sceptical and more emotional level the opponents of the Article 50 option have moral objections to a sovereign nation having to negotiate over its right to independence. Furthermore, the advocates of an unconditional exit without a negotiated parting of the ways make the case that the UK has the right to withdraw at any time and to set a two year timetable after notice of wishing to leave has been submitted is an affront to Britain's inalienable sovereignty. Yet, what will be the fastest method of taking the UK out of the EU; giving notice under Article 50 which will take no more than two years, perhaps less, or through legislation passing through both the House of Commons and the House of Lords?

All EU related matters are highly contentious political issues. Given this and the strong support for membership in some sections of the British Parliament there will be serious and sustained opposition in both the House of Commons and the House of Lords to the repealing of the European Communities Act. The unilateral process of withdrawal will therefore take time to be achieved if at all. Following the EU's approved method may therefore be faster and more certain of delivering an agreed post-EU settlement that suits Britain's economic needs.

The different proponents of withdrawal are far from having a meeting of minds. Although they are agreed as to where Britain should go, they are yet to agree as to how best to get there. In 1939 as the forces of Fascist General Franco advanced on the Republican held stronghold of Barcelona the mainstream Communists and their socialist coreligionists known as the Anarcho-Syndicalists were fighting each other as to which exact road was the true path to their promised land...

...The ideology changes but the ideologues do not.

Unilateral withdrawal begs the question as to what would be the future relationship between Britain and the other states in Europe that remain members of the EU. Presumably that would be one of mutual cooperation rather than diktat; ultimately it is in the interests of businesses on the continent to continue trade with Britain. That view is certainly correct but we live in sceptical times and hoping that all will be well fails to answer the key questions which need to be addressed. If the British public are to be persuaded to vote for leaving the European Union they will need more than vague assurances.

However, there are alternatives to EU membership that address the concerns that some have relating to trade and ease the process of exiting. When it comes to the UK's options there are alternatives that solve the concerns that will inevitably be raised. To decide what the best alternative to membership of the EU is the implications of exiting the European Union need to be considered carefully.

Chapter 6

The Implications
of Withdrawal

*"The British are solely concerned about their economic
interests, nothing else. They could be offered a different form of
partnership... If the British cannot support the trend towards
more integration in Europe, we can nevertheless remain friends,
but on a different basis... I could imagine a form such as a
European Economic Area or a free trade agreement."*
Jacques Delors, Former President of the European Commission,
28th December 2012

*"Of course, Britain could survive outside the EU...We could
probably get access to the Single Market as Norway and
Switzerland do..."*
The Rt Hon. Tony Blair MP, UK Prime Minister, 23rd February
2000

There is concern that withdrawing from the European Union
will undermine Britain's ability to influence the rules of the
UK's most important export market. The anxiety is that
depriving the UK of influence to shape EU legislation will not only
mean that Britain will have less ability to make rules which suit British
businesses when exporting to the continent. Furthermore, it is also
feared that Britain may also suffer from rules which actually prejudice
the UK. However, it is clear that Britain, despite having a large
population and economy by European standards, is denied the right to
exert sufficient authority in the EU at present. With regards to leaving
the EU there is no question of Britain losing essential influence.

Outside of the European Union Britain will not be able to have

MEPs and therefore no representation in the European Parliament. This will create a saving of more than £130 million per year, each of the UK's 73 Member of the European Parliament costs £1.79 million per annum. Few MEPs, bar some exceptions, have real influence over the direction and development of the EU. Retaining them is not crucial to Britain's interests, some are more of an irrelevance than people of influence. Name your MEPs; quod erat demonstrandum.

The UK will also lose its right to have a Commissioner. The fact that a Commissioner may come from a certain member state does not mean that country's national interest is being protected in fact far from it. The UK outside of the EU will therefore not be losing a great deal of interest; their present effect is minimal. As the Commissioners are appointed to their precise role by the President of the Commission and are not delegates, being divorced from the nation state, the only time their loss will really matter to British influence is on rare occasions when chance combines to determine that the right person is appointed to the right position.

The MEPs and the Commissioner are not the only British citizens whose job security will be threatened by Brexit. People from the UK also work in the European Commission there position will be different. They will immediately lose their jobs. They not only have contracts that have to be honoured but will also be involved in projects that need to be brought to conclusion. However, once out new staff will not automatically be appointed from the departing member state unless there is a special exemption for a recognised expert in a particular field. However, if the influence was small before not having any British citizens in Brussels, many of whom will have originally come from the UK's civil service, will mean that there are less British ideas filtering through the EU system.

The institutions in Brussels are Strasbourg, the Commission and the various establishments of the Parliament, are not the only organisations that influence the rules of the Single Market. The quasi-independent agencies that help to both develop and enforce EU policies also employ British citizens, some are even based in the UK. In time the EU may wish to relocate these outside of the UK, but if Britain remains a member of the European Economic Area there will be less impetus to do so as Britain will still have a seat at the table in some areas of decision making. What is more, it is logical that the agencies will be based where the best expertise are available and continue to employ the most talented staff possible. Therefore, some British staff may well retain their posts. This is especially the case for those EU institutions involved with banking which benefit from being close to the leading financial centre – the City of London. And if Britain does remain in the European Economic Area then the legal considerations of employing British citizens will be resolved, however, less will be given posts via the system of secondment from the civil service. Yet, the competition from the remaining EU member states to host these high prestige organisations which are also lucrative employees may be enough for them to be relocated to the struggling economies of the eurozone sooner rather than later.

At the heart of the question, however, is influence. As the purpose of the agencies is to implement EU policy away from the influences of the member-states national government then the any loss will be limited. Therefore exiting the EU will not on its own especially damage British influence in the European Union.

A member of the European Court of Justice, based in Luxembourg, will also be lost. The British judge that sits on the European Court of Justice is not there to fight the UK's corner nor is it to introduce common law legal ideas and principles. The official role of the court and its judges is to interpret EU law, and it surreptitious function is to expand the writ of the EU institutions. As the UK has no tangible influence over the ECJ nothing can be lost by exiting it and the EU. The best guarantee of being free from the influence of the European Court of Justice is not to have a seat on it and be outside of its jurisdiction.

Outside of the European Union Britain can regain more influence over its domestic affairs but will lose the ability to vote on Commission proposals in the Council of Ministers as well as in the European Parliament. This is currently one of the most significant ways in which the UK influences the regulations of the internal market. Nevertheless, the UK's share of the vote in the Council is limited to just a little over 8%. As the UK is often isolated in the Council exiting it will not overly retard the UK's already restricted ability to shape the Single Market according to the UK's interests. Not having a say in the Council cannot, however, be considered to preserve and enhance the authority of the UK at the final point of when EU legislation is decided. Having a voice at the concluding stage where Single Market rules are voted on also means that there is upstream influence in the formulation of Commission proposals. In discussions on contentious matters that may not be passed there will be some requirement to take on board the views of the British negotiating team and their minister. Usually the ability of the UK to sway developments inside the internal market is confined to rare occasions.

The workings of the numerous committees are the main area where British involvement in the internal market matters most. There is a prima facie case that exiting the EU and losing all participation in these will harm Britain's ability to try and make the Single Market conform to British interests. The economies of the other EU states do contain some of Britain's most important customers. Yet the influence is already limited.

What is more, discussions between Britain and the EU will not cease altogether; they can still continue even if the UK is outside of the European Union. British civil servants are in touch with their counterparts in other jurisdictions but this will not be in the regular and formalised meetings of the EU working groups and with the representatives of the European Commission. However, contrary to the claims of some; non-EU member states can and do sit at the heart of discussions on the regulation of the Single Market and are valued contributors to the formulation of laws governing its operation. The European Countries that sit at the heart of decision making in Brussels are the members of the little known European Free Trade Association and European Economic Area (EEA) states. This has Norway, Liechtenstein and Iceland amongst its members; those three states are not in the European Union. The difference between them and the EU members is that the EFTA/EEA countries do not have a vote on the regulation or directive at its final stage in the Council of Ministers; but at that point much has already been decided. There are therefore other ways of having a saw on some EU affairs. At the crux of the issue is that fact that the weighting attached to the UK's vote inside the Council of ministers is small and is much closer to zero than some give it credit for.

The issue of influence in the rest of the world outside of the EU is another salient matter. Will exiting the European Union diminish or enhance Britain's role in the world? Outside of the European Union the UK will not have its foreign policy entangled in the EU's web of decision making. Britain will also be able to reclaim its seat and make its own case in international bodies such as the World Trade Organisation and form commercial alliances that better suit Britain. The UK can also have a say, unencumbered with having to present the political compromises reached with the other EU states, at specialised agencies such as the particularly important United Nations Economic Commission for Europe. Other organisations include; the International Organization for Standardization, the Universal Postal Union, the International Telecommunication Union, International Electrotechnical Commission, Intergovernmental Organisation for International Carriage by Rail, the World Intellectual Property Organisation, the World Meteorological Organisation, the United Nations Economic Commission for Europe, the International Bureau of Education, the International Organisation for Migration, the World Health Organisation, the Global Alliance for Improved Nutrition, the International Union for Conservation of Nature, the International Maritime Organisation and the Advisory Centre on WTO Law. The list goes on.

Britain will then be able to have greater influence in world affairs and a larger say in the technical and trade regulations that govern many aspects of life from economic to environmental affairs.

As the EU vision has adopted a system of high regulation, it has made its economy uncompetitive. To resolve this, rather than creating smarter regulation at home, it is seeking to export its costly rules. Having the UK within the EU just adds weight to its arguments. If the UK was disentangled from the Brussels culture of conformity then Britain, outside of the red tape zone, will have more of an interest to be a voice for growth.

Outside of the European Union the UK will not only be able to deal directly with those bodies, allowing for British democratic influence to be at the heart of their decision making but the UK will also be free from the EU's enforcement mechanisms. And will have greater freedom to either ignore certain flawed rules or withdraw from those organisations that Britain no longer considers as serving the national interest. This is not currently an option inside the EU.

Leaving the EU will enhance British influence abroad. Britain outside of the EU would gain influence in a number of areas, while maintaining our current links on the world stage. Rather than waiting for the EU to formulate a position; exiting the European Union will allow for influence even further upstream at the initial source of where many rules and regulations actually originate. This will allow Britain to show leadership in the United Nations specialised agencies and amongst the other nations that also take part in these international standard setting global bodies. Countries around the world are continually in touch with each other through these numerous international fora which are increasingly setting the rules by which we live. Unless Britain represents its own voice in these organisations then the UK cannot claim to have any real influence in world affairs.

Norway and Switzerland have a greater global influence in the international legislative agencies and in terms of trade policy from outside of the EU. Norway especially has a greater impact in terms of foreign policy by operating free of the EU and its CFSP. They are even more significant than similar sized states that are within the EU's inflexible structure then Britain can have an even greater global say by exiting the European Union. Furthermore, it will be a say that will ultimately be accountable to the British people, not an unelected commissioner. Exiting the EU would be an upgrade in Britain's voice in international organisations and the UK's influence in the world.

Influence in Britain

The question of influence cuts both ways. For all the influence that the UK has over the markets of the other states in the EU there are now as many as 27 other nations exerting influence, via the EU, over Britain. What is more, that does not include the power of the European Commission and its supporting agencies and its court of justice. Furthermore, the EU's ability to impose upon the UK the rules made by the international standard setting agencies, which are then rubber stamped by Brussels, will also be brought to an end. The European Union will no longer be able to act as a conduit for enforcing regulations from organisations that are even less open to democratic accountability and scrutiny than itself.

Any supposed loss of British influence in the EU will be maximised by expanding British influence within the UK. Exiting the EU will free Britain's democratically elected institutions to have more influence over matters internal to the UK's and perhaps in the world.

Even if the UK did exert sufficient influence in Brussels decision making any potential benefit to this is outweighed by the cost of compliance with EU regulation in Britain. Upon independence the British government will become responsible for areas ranging from; immigration from the EU to food safety, trade policy to foreign policy. The list goes on.

The EU will still seek, through negotiation rather than diktat, to export its regulations to Britain, just as Britain will be able to make the case for economic competitiveness. The UK cannot be forced to still accept EU rules. Switzerland, a small nation which is surrounded and whose economy is massively dependent upon trade with it is not compelled to accept all EU law. As much as 62% of Swiss exports go to the EU and 79% of its imports come from 'Europe.' Therefore, Britain with all its traditional strengths and global links will also not be coerced into accepting EU rules and regulations. Britain may for the sake of convenience voluntarily opt to keep some degree of synergy between what will become two different jurisdictions. The rationale for any collaboration will be that in the sectors of the British and European economies where there is a high degree of trade and mutual dependency having similar technical standards will prevent barriers to trade emerging. Another factor is that the British authorities have for more than forty years accepted an ever increasing amount of interference from the EU. To break this trend, even after leaving the EU, will require a major change in culture; one which many British civil servants may be unwilling to make.

At present, inside the European Union Britain has to accept 100% of EU law when just less than 10% of the British economy relates to trade with business and individuals in other EU member states. Considering the excessive costs of this regulation this is a high price to pay for accessing the Single Market. Exiting will allow for a substantial repatriation of powers to the UK's democratic institutions. The amount of symmetry that will exist between post-withdrawal British and EU regulation will largely depend upon the nature of the withdrawal and the alternative relationship with the other European countries that replaces membership. A unilateral exit, with no withdrawal agreement, will allow the British Parliament to establish the domestic laws that it sees fit, however, this will potentially create a disagreement with Brussels as to issues regarding market access and mutual recognition of goods and services. Establishing an accord with the EU on Britain's departure, or even establishing a free trade agreement on similar grounds to the Swiss model, may resolve some issues but have a requirement to keep some EU standards in a very limited number of areas. Remaining in the European Economic Area will require that some areas of EU law relevant to the internal market remain in place. However, whatever model is chosen influence over the UK's domestic affairs will inevitability increase after Britain leaves the EU. And even if the UK chooses to reach a consensus with Brussels which requires some degree of compliance with other EU states to keep trade links as open as possible this will be as an independent sovereign state rather than having no choice but to obey.

The impact on trade in goods and services
In terms of trade in both goods and services the UK has been running a deficit with the other states in the EU since 1984. It appears therefore that other EU states are benefiting from the 'pooling of sovereignty' more than Britain does. For instance from 2007 to 2011, the cumulated German surplus on its trade with the UK totalled a staggering €108 billion. A new trade framework between Britain and the EU will mean that a number of costs and practicalities will have to be overcome before barriers to trade are eliminated.

When exporting goods to another territory the host nation can stipulate a designated port of entry for the good's entry. At present Britain and the European Union are one trade zone the UK has free access to any and all established places where both people and produce can be admitted. The EU has the hypothetical ability in the short term to prescribe a port of entry, and terms, that are inconvenient for British exporters. However, this will be a serious breach of international trade law. Articles XI:1, XIII:1, V:2, V:6 and I:1 of the 1994 General Agreement on Tariffs and Trade now administered by the World Trade Organisation. Under these rules one country cannot be treated less favourably than any other state in the export and transit of goods. What is more, as both businesses and consumers on the continent depend upon British imports there is no reason to believe that such problems will arise. Regardless of how the UK leaves the EU it should be business as usual via the existing ports of entry.

Other potential repercussions are more subtle but can still have a negative impact. Without the UK's participation in the formal institutions of the internal market there will be less opportunity to lobby for the abolition of national protectionist measures and for the opening up of new commercial opportunities on the continent. However, it can be argued that the other EU member states have moved as far as they will already and that little more progress can be expected. The progress on the completion of the EU's single market in services, which should be of particular benefit to the UK, has been slow and is still not complete. The EU's services directive was passed in 2006, but is still not fully implemented.

If the British regulatory framework develops new rules outside of the European Union which are distinctly different to those in operation inside the EU then there will be a more difficult environment for service providers from Britain to make sales on the continent and take part in public procurement. In fact unless they conform to EU standards they may be disbarred from doing so. The high quality of Britain's renowned services sector, however, makes such a development unlikely. Furthermore, the UK can adapt its own regulatory regime to suit its export interests as it sees fit. What is more, multi-national companies can by definition and do establish themselves in different jurisdictions.

The principle of mutual recognition amongst European Union and European Economic Area member states is also important. Regulation EC 764/2008 of 9th July 2008 demands that all members allow goods that are legally sold in one country to be sold in another. For exporters this means that a product that has been cleared for sale in one EU or EEA nation should not have to pass another set of requirements in another member state to which the products are being exported. Whilst this may create risks for consumers who may be sold items that have been permitted in a member state which does not demand that adequate safety standards have been met, it is good for both competition and for businesses. If the UK was outside of this framework British exporters will have to submit to more tests and complete more red-tape. In areas where the harmonisation of standards has not yet taken place this will mean that permission will need to be obtained from every jurisdiction in the EU where it is sold.

There is also the fear that prejudicial legislation may queer the pitch against British sales to the continent. Arguably EU proposals can and are already beginning to act against the interests of the UK. The European Central Bank's location policy is a case in point. This policy will demand that large scale clearing, the system of delayed payments, in euros takes place in the eurozone under the direct regulation of the EU. It will therefore undermine the City of London by preventing the UK from taking part in this business, depriving Britain of some business and tax revenue. EU rules on establishment that would have deprive British financial service firms from operating inside the remaining EU states can be sidestepped by opening subsidiaries inside what is left of the European Union. The EU-out Swiss have shown that such a strategy does indeed work. A report into this found that 'Though extremely cumbersome this does give them full access to the EU market.'

Another scenario is that UK trade to the continent can face new taxes via the introduction of tariffs. These can have the potential to reduce the sale of British made products in the Single Market. Much will depend on the nature of Britain's withdrawal and the terms that the UK can secure. A successful withdrawal under the terms of Article 50 would ideally result in a free trade agreement, applying to all relevant sectors of the economy. Alternatively, the UK could remain as a member of the European Economic Area via re-joining the European Free Trade Association. Another option will be to stay as a member of the EU's customs union. There are no levies on goods traded inside the union, but those which come from outside will face a tax.

If there is no free trade deal then customs levies will have to be applied on goods imported from outside of the EU. These customs levies charge a percentage of the transaction value of the item in question. If the charges were not put against products from the UK then will become in World Trade Organisation terms the 'Most Favoured Nation'. This will mean that every other state on the globe that is a member of the WTO can lobby it to have the EU's tariffs against their products struck down. Free trade agreements and customs unions are not included in the WTO legal principle that the trading relationship of the 'Most Favoured Nation' must apply to all other countries. The EU is not politically ready yet to completely liberalise trade with the rest of the world, even though to its credit it has a proliferation of free and preferential trade agreements. And to those outside these arrangements the EU has reduced tariffs in many areas to where they have almost become meaningless. In many cases, such as pocket-sized cassette players and integrated electronic circuits as well as telephone answering machines, goods are actually zero rated. There is no charge. Yet in some areas tariffs still have relevance, despite having to overcome the common external tariff the United States and China still manage to export more to the other EU states than the UK.

Examples of some of the charges range from; steel imports being taxed at a rate of 2.7%, bananas 16%, toys and games 4.7%, sports shoes 17%, cheese 7.7%, wine 32%, ink-jet printers 2.2%, sewing machines 9.7% and microwave ovens 5%. The list goes on.

Another important area is the tariff on the importation of motor cars. This can have a maximum tariff of 10% placed on top of the cost of the product. As the UK's car industry may face a relatively high charge and as it is an important employer it is the often quoted area that is cited as an industry that will be damaged by a British withdrawal from the EU. In recent years this sector has been one of the few genuine success stories in the British economy. The UK now exports more cars than it actually imports. A tenth of all British exports are cars.

It has been stated that a British withdrawal from the EU will damage investment in the car industry primarily because the EU imposes an average 9.8% tariff on imports of cars from outside of the European Union's preferential trading partners, the EEA, and the customs union. This makes imports from outside less competitive when competing against the products free of this levy. There is the potential that this charge will be applied to cars made in Britain if the UK leaves the EU. However, at present it does not apply to those numerous states around the globe that have signed free trade agreements with the EU.

Naturally this tariff will not apply to the UK, even after Brexit, if a free trade agreement with the EU is establishes or if Britain remains in the customs union or if Britain chooses to continue as a member of the European Economic Area.

There are market factors which will protect investment in the British car industry after Brexit. The UK is not just a staging post for sales to be exported to continent. Car sales within the UK have recently seen a massive growth in sales. The Automobile Manufacturing Association stated that in 2013 Britain experienced a 13.4% increase in car sales.

This compares very favourably with the situation in, other EU states where there has been a significant decline in sales. France has experienced an 8.4% reduction in new car registrations. Italy is experiencing a 5.5% decrease and even Germany is suffering from a 4.7% contraction in sales. These problems can be accounted for by the poverty and high unemployment in the eurozone driven by the problems caused by the Single Currency and the austerity measures that are designed to underpin the euro.

Furthermore, car companies are based in the UK, not because of the UK's membership of a supra-national political organisation but because of its highly efficient car plants in Britain. These are amongst the most productive and cost-effective in the world. A car is produced in Britain on average every 20 seconds. It is unlikely that the car industry will wish to move away from this productive base let alone the UK's thriving and expanding domestic market for an uncertain future on the continent.

What is more, there are other markets for the British car industry. As the continental EU car market continues to decline, manufactures based in Britain offset the EU's 2012 9% fall in sales by selling an additional 19% in sales to the rest of the world outside of the European Union. Furthermore, there is no reason to believe that a trade deal on cars cannot be reached, despite the often cited danger to the car industry if the UK left the EU.

Presumably if a free trade agreement with the EU was not arranged and the tariff was imposed on cars made in the UK then under those circumstances the UK would be entitled to retaliate to protect its own domestic market. Britain would then impose a 9.8% customs duty on cars made in the states that remain in the EU. This will particularly harm German manufactures. They will then not only have their products made nearly 10% higher in the UK but, as the UK will no longer be forced to comply with the EU external tariff cars exported from outside of the European Union – such as those from Japan, China and South Korea – will be free from the customs duty and be almost 10% cheaper. Therefore, German costs are higher and must then compete with rivals whose costs have been lowered. It will also give British producers in their home market an advantage over exports from the continent.

The numbers of German exported to the UK is quite telling. For instance the Volkswagen Group has a 19% share of the UK market, which totalled 374,000 cars sent to Britain in 2011. BMW sent to Britain that same year 130,000 cars produced in Germany. What is more, BMW also produce the Mini in the UK and exported from Britain to the continent 156,000 cars; they also own Rolls-Royce which sends cars to the continent. UK car plants are so efficient that the Japanese car firm Toyota even exports cars back to Japan from its plant in Derbyshire; yet Japan is not in a union with the UK.

Those major corporations, which have been fundamentally important to Germany's economic growth, will put pressure on the German government to make sure that access to the UK's growing market is not jeopardised. It is highly unlikely that Germany, the highest financial contributor to the EU and the euro bailouts, will allow for tariffs to be placed on British car exports to the continent. Failure on Germany's part to prevent tariffs on goods such as motor vehicles will damage its access to the only significant growing car market in Western Europe and undermine the profits of the German owned British manufacturers who export back to the continent.

Therefore, it appears that the car industry, potentially one of the most vulnerable sector of the economy to a withdrawal, will in all probability be safe after Brexit. And if that is secure then other areas should also be confident of Single Market access after Britain's departure.

If a free trade agreement can be reached quickly then this will be to the benefit of all and thus any dislocation and uncertainty will be kept to a minimum. However such agreements can take years to complete especially in the case of the UK and other EU states which differ widely in economic outlook and philosophy. Any failure or delay in reaching a concord will have repercussions. Whilst the implications of failing to come to terms will not be a catastrophe it will be sub-optimal.

Whilst investment decisions are based on more important factors than belonging to a political union such as the host countries tax regime and the opportunity for economic growth in the investee state the ability to easily access as larger market as possible will undoubtedly be a consideration.

Whereas the break-up of the USSR and the resulting political dislocation which followed caused economic disruption to the communist command economy, and considerable hard-ship for many, the political break-up of the EU will not harm Europe's market economy. In Europe the interlinking of trade and mutual dependency will make sure that goods will be allowed to continue to flow across borders. An exit from the EU may well improve the conditions for investment in the UK but the economic potential of Britain will be maximised if tariff free and uninhibited trade with the EU's Single Market can continue.

When Lord Lawson, a former Chancellor of the Exchequer, announced that he favoured withdrawal from the EU he estimated that any loss of trade to the EU's Single Market can be made up for by increasing sales to the rest of the world. This is certainly true; the UK's trade with the rest of the EU has fallen, in goods and services, by over 13% since the year 2000. Over the same time frame it increased by 12% with the rest of the world. No doubt there are emerging markets around the globe that present new and exciting opportunities for British businesses. Yet should Britain expect that its share of continental markets will be reduced by Brexit?

If Britain chooses to remain as a member of the European Economic Area (EEA) then it will keep tariff free access to the Single Market. And there will be no change to the system which allows for the free movement of goods, services, capital and labour.

Naturally if an agreement is reached with the EU then there will be no impediment and even if one is not concluded then EU's external tariff is so low that it can hardly be considered ruinous. The potential benefits of leaving can more than compensate for the EU's customs duty to external goods. Under WTO rules that EU's tariffs that apply to the most favoured nation outside a free trade area must apply to all. This average levy is little more than 1%; therefore on a worst case scenario for the UK British exporters to the EU will in most cases face a minimal external tariff.

Nonetheless, will any ill feeling created by the UK leaving the EU damage British trade beyond the costs of the tariff to imports from outside the European Union? Again this is unlikely. Even without the World Trade Organisation (WTO) commerce will continue and economic self-interest will prevent the EU from overtly discriminating against British exporters.

For the avoidance of all reasonable doubt the UK should make sure that the parting will be as amicable as possible. The best way to ensure this is to resolve the trade issues at the start of the UK's withdrawal rather than having to resolve it later in what may still, despite the trade interdependency, be long drawn out discussions. The Article 50 procedure and the reaching of a post-EU relationship withdrawal agreement is still the most logical way forward.

What is more, Articles 3 and 8 of the Treaty on European Union legally requires the EU to negotiate free and fair trade with non-EU countries. It is not just a matter that the EU is mandated to pursue equitable trade agreements with its neighbours; at the heart of what will keep trade open is the simple fact that the UK is the single biggest purchaser of exports from the other 27 EU member-states. They sell far more to Britain than British businesses sell to them.

British exports are not just to the European Union, in fact 60% and rising goes to the rest of the world. However, the EU on the UK's behalf has negotiated preferential trade deals with more than forty countries outside of Europe stretching from Mexico to South Korea. A major part of the negotiation of these agreements will have included the promise of levy free access to the UK's domestic market. These other states around the world will want to keep privileged admission to this market open and therefore it is highly likely that, so long as the UK is inclined to keep them, these tariff free trade agreements will continue once Britain is out of the EU. However, this will need to be formally agreed with the states in question. The European Commission will also want to make sure that Britain keeps free trade with its partner countries in other continents. If an independent Britain raised custom duties against the produce of the states that have free trade agreements with the EU, costing them market access, then the European Union may have to pay them compensation. This gives the UK an unlikely ally in any discussions with these states on retaining the free trade agreements and extra leverage in any discussions with the EU on the terms of the UK's withdrawal.

Beyond potential customs levies; UK trade to the continent can be subject to costs that come from the need to overcome the administrative burden of .the EU's customs union. Anything that is already inside the customs union that has originated from a non-member will have been charged at its original port of entry and can therefore circulate freely. At present, as the UK is an EU customs union member, British exporters to the other 27 do not have to prove that they comply with the EU's rules of origin. However, even if the UK had a free trade agreement with the EU an exporter to the continent will have to prove that the goods have been produced, or predominantly worked on, in a state that has a free trade agreement with the EU. If not the goods will be charged at the applicable rate. Naturally if a preferential trade agreement was not in place then the importation charges would apply anyway. As value chains are becoming increasingly globalised the need to demonstrate an item's origins can be a complex burden.

The Trade Policy Research Centre argue that 'the process of adapting to rules of origin based duty-free trade under a new UK-EU free trade agreement would be tedious, costly and disruptive to trade.' However, some developments are making this concern less relevant. The reduction in tariffs where many goods are zero rated reduces the need to complete the administrative duties. The EU has extended the area in which origin can be accumulated to not only cover more states but also to allow for an item to be obtained and manufactured in a number of countries without the final product losing the benefit of being tariff free when it enters the EU. This system has already been in existence the EU and European Free Trade Association since 1997 and for Turkey since 1999. It will be allowed to claim origin for more goods and from 2017 the procedure for doing so will be simplified.

The effect on jobs
It has been claimed that exiting the European Union would put at risk the 3.5 million jobs, around 10% of the UK workforce, whose employment is connected with exports of goods and services to the other 27 EU member states. However, what truth is there in this assertion?

As has been shown it is nonsense to suggest that all trade will cease once the UK is outside of the European Union. Business can and do trade with other businesses and individuals in other countries regardless of whether or not they are in a political union. As the EU's own proliferation of free trade agreements shows there is no prerequisite to belong or remain in a supra-national bloc to have a trading relationship. For that reason employment should not be adversely affected; so where does this figure come from?

The misleading jobs statement first emerged in the year 2000 from the now defunct Britain in Europe group which unsuccessfully campaigned for Britain to join the euro. They apparently based this claim on research they commissioned into how many jobs were involved with the EU. The report originally stated that 3 million jobs were related to trade with the EU, this has since become inflated in rhetoric to 3.5 million jobs. However, Dr Martin Weale the Director of The National Institute for Economic and Social Research described Britain in Europe's spin as "pure Goebbels" and said, "in many years of academic research I cannot recall such a wilful distortion of the facts." The report had in reality came to the conclusion that the jobs would still exist regardless of whether the UK was a member of the EU or not.

The co-author of the report Professor Iain Begg, formerly of South Bank University, also stated that actually "three million jobs were associated with EU demand.' However, this number was,

'not the same as saying that these jobs would disappear if we left the EU. Many of the jobs would still be sustained because people in other European countries would continue to buy some British goods," he added. So it's always been a bit of a false perspective to say that three million jobs would be lost. It wouldn't mean overnight losses of jobs. It wouldn't mean there would be a loss of prosperity instantly, just the risks become greater.'

Using the same logic that underpins the 3.5 million jobs myth as Britain has a trade deficit with the European Union the UK is effectively exporting jobs to the continent. As many as 4.5 million in the 27 other EU states rely on selling goods and services to the UK. If all trade did cease, using Britain in Europe's own argument against them, a further 4.5 million jobs would be created in Britain servicing the UK's domestic needs alone. The same reasoning that underpins the still widely propagated 3.5 million jobs myth can show that instead of the UK's citizens effectively paying the wages of continental workers they can instead buy British. This will create a net benefit of 1 million more jobs in the UK.

However, in the event of the EU's external tariff applying to British exports then there will be a cost to jobs, however, this can be off-set against the savings to the taxpayer and through ending the EU's excessive regulation.

Another concern that opponents of Brexit have is the fear that British jobs will be harmed by the EU, still a significant market, will set the rules of the Single Market in such a way that the interests of British companies will be prejudiced. Anxiety over this would be justified if it were not the case that many of the EU's rules actually originate from the global standard setting bodies. Where harm does come from Single Market rules that originate in Brussels is usually through the strategy of raising competitor's costs by binding them into a highly regulated market. Exiting this red-tape area will free UK businesses.

Where harm can come would be through the EU embarking on a strategy of putting in place complex rules to increase costs so far that only large and established companies can afford to implement them and remain in business. For instance employing lawyers to make sure they comply with the regulations. This creates a barrier that stops new companies entering the market; stopping competition. This will deprive British businesses to export services to the states that remain in the EU. An example can be banking regulation mandating that certain services need to be based in the eurozone. A requirement that demands a high-standard of quality for meat imports from outside the Union is another instance which compares with the EU laissez-faire system of self-regulation is another instance. However, the areas for protectionist regulation are limited; and as they cannot be targeted against individual states they will risk alienating other trade partners who will also be affected.

Creating obstacles to new entrants into the market through placing excessive burdens on businesses will also harm entrepreneurship on the continent. Undermining what little economic dynamism is left in the EU. However, having input into the development of the EU's Single Market will still be preferable to having none; that is unless the club's membership fees are extortionate.

The impact on the economy
Ever since the 2008 financial crash and the ensuing great recession one of the great questions of British politics has been how to get growth back into the system. Exiting the European Union presents a number of risks and potential rewards that can either help or hamper economic growth. Although there is good reason to believe that trade links, and the jobs that depend upon both exporting and importing,

will be retained there are also other factors that can impact on the wealth of the nation.

Unilaterally curtailing tariffs can help the economy. The UK, if so minded can decide to cancel or cut the tariff rates charged on imports. Being outside of the EU's common external customs levy will enable prices of many consumer goods to be cheaper. It will also mean that home grown producers of for instance wine will now face more competition from new world wines which will then be 32% cheaper. The UK will also have the right to retain the existing tariff system, which the European Union negotiated at the World Trade Organisation on behalf of the UK, and currently applies to Britain. The EU's common external tariff will be in place upon exit until abolished. In such circumstances Britain will be able to charge the French 32% of the transaction value of their wine imported in Britain.

Generally reducing or even eliminating tariffs will be good for the consumer and the retail industry. As a political act it will generate good will with the rest of the world, particularly in future trade negotiations. Assessing the value of this commodity is difficult; but it may prove to be priceless.

So far so good; however, customs levies are not the only means by which the EU manipulates the price of goods in the internal market. Outside of the European Union the EU may feel free to apply what are known as anti-dumping measures on selected UK exports. Dumping is an aggressive pricing policy where exports to a foreign market are being sold not only cheaper than the price in the domestic market but on occasions actually below the cost of production. This predatory pricing policy damages the market opportunities of domestic producers and where it is taking place, or merely suspected of taking place, the EU threatens to impose taxes on the imports to off-set the perceived damage that is being caused.

Is there a danger that the EU will threaten anti-dumping action against British exports to the continent? The EU's pattern of behaviour has been to take action against the economies of the far-east. Threats against Chinese made solar panels are a case in point. It is unlikely, that anti-dumping action will be threatened against UK producers; but the possibility will still remain. One way of reducing, though not entirely eliminating this risk, is to make sure that businesses are subsidised and follow a level playing field across Europe. This should not be a problem as the UK as it fits into the economic ethos of succeeding British governments; especially in their approach to the Single Market.

Anti-dumping measures are a double-edged sword. One the hand they protect home grown businesses but as the modern corner-stone of an aggressive trade policy they also risk a trade war with the state whose business suffers from their imposition. They raise the costs of imports making prices for consumers more expensive. Even the fear of them being imposed can encourage an importer to increase its prices. Professor Patrick Minford CBE, of Cardiff Business School, estimates that this aggressive strategy amounts to a 'Common Manufacturing Policy' which is an attack on competition; and allows for the creation home-grown EU cartels which further increase prices. The cost to the UK may be according to Professor Minford as much as £30 billion per year. Outside of the EU the UK can still have the option of imposing anti-dumping measures if it so wishes but it will give Britain a choice and create a consumer market with more competitive pricing.

The UK is the leading destination for Foreign Direct Investment (FDI) in the European Union. According to the Office for National Statistics (ONS) FDI stocks by the close of 2011 totalled £766 billion, which is an increase of 5% on 2010. This is giving the impression of increasing at a geometric rate. The most recent data for 2012 from the United Nations Conference on Trade and Development (UNSTAD) shows that the annual figure is now £867 billion, an increase of more than 11.5%.

This is clearly very important to the British economy; but how will Brexit affect this investment?

According to a survey by the multinational accountants Ernst & Young opinion of investors in the UK; 56% of those from Western Europe thought that less integration will there is still a significant, but smaller, proportion business that believe that less integration would harm investment into the UK and only 38% thought that it would make Britain more attractive. However '72% of companies interviewed in North America thought reduced integration into the EU would make the UK more attractive as an FDI location.' Whilst just 23% thought that Britain will become less attractive.

The views of investors from Asia were even more telling and add weight to the opinions of those from North America. According to the Survey "Fully two-thirds (66%) of Asian respondents say a lower degree of EU integration would make the UK a more attractive location for FDI, against 25% who think it would make the UK less attractive."

Therefore it is clear that European integration may actually be retarding economic activity in the UK. It is perhaps even conceivable that investment in Britain will increase if the UK leaves the EU. Those Asian and North American investors must recognise that the hidden costs of excessive European Union regulation lead to a lower rate of return on investments.

It is claimed that the UK's position within the EU is a major factor behind those investment decisions. However, according to the Ernst & Young European Attractiveness Survey 2011 the UK remains a popular destination because;

'The UK maintained its leadership in FDI projects and FDI jobs, which grew by 7% and 6% respectively. Investors came to the UK for its strength in services and increasingly its industry, investing in business services (14% of the projects received), machinery and equipment (11%), computers (7%) and software (7%). The UK remains a highly attractive destination given its position as a global player in the world economy and its capacity to reform a difficult economic situation. Furthermore, the weaker pound has enticed investors already considering the UK for service sector investments to evaluate its industrial potential as well.'

There is no mention of the EU as a positive factor. UK Trade & Investment, a government department that seeks to encourage overseas companies to invest in Britain, mention the relevance of the UK as a gateway to the Single Market. Yet they rank it in their list of what makes the UK an attractive destination below other factors such as; the highly cost effective environment and that fact that according to the 2011 World Bank report Doing Business the UK is the easiest place to set up and run a business in Europe. Tax is another important issue. FDI also comes to the UK because Britain is a competitive location for tax. And corporation tax is low according to standards of the main EU economies, tax allowances are generous and individual rates are competitive. Arguably these are far more relevant to potential return than the UK's membership of a supranational political union.

Nevertheless, is admission to a large base of consumers pertinent to the encouragement of FDI? There is research which suggested that it is. Nigel Pain of the Organisation for Economic Co-operation and Development and Garry Young of the Bank of England theoretical study concluded that exit could cost the UK as much as 2¼% of GDP primarily from lost FDI. Does this mean that nations in the EU exponentially benefit from foreign investment and nations outside suffer from a dearth of FDI?

The evidence from UNSTAD of what is really happening shows that it is the EU that is suffering from a shortage of FDI. In terms of FDI counted in US dollar ($) per capita it is clear that membership of the European Free Trade Association benefits its members far more than belonging to the EU.

Foreign Direct Investment flows per capita per year (US $)

YEAR	2001	2002	2003	2004	2005	2006	2007	2008	2009	2010	2011	2012
EFTA	926	591	1,666	342	348	4,657	3,754	2,072	3,562	3,845	2,397	1,294
EU27	796	647	584	464	1,019	1,182	1,730	1,093	717	755	876	512
Euro	922	792	738	420	795	1,055	1,691	1,103	734	942	1,004	438
UK	906	422	458	950	2,944	2,570	3,272	1,447	1,233	813	816	989

Access to a large market, as the EFTA states have, will undoubtedly still have some degree of relevance but it is clear that belonging to the EU's political union may be detrimental. Other factors such as not being subject to excessive regulation and an efficient tax regime are the prime positive determinants of Foreign Direct Investment. Naturally it will be preferable to retain the right to trade with the EU's internal market so long as intrusion from Brussels can be limited.

The cost of excessive EU regulation has been well documented and analysed at as much as 5% of economic output or approximately £75 billion per year. Can the UK maximise that sum if it left the European Union?

As previously discussed cancelling the complete body of EU law will create a legal vacuum, the costs of which may far outweigh the cost of excessive regulation. For example EU rules relating to pollution may well add a burden onto British businesses and in fact drive jobs to other jurisdictions where the laws are less onerous and in global terms therefore have no positive net effect on the environment. However, a paucity of regulation will only lead to more costs in the long term resolving the damage to people's health and the environment. So although there may be a case for a review of how the legislation works in practice and even a case for it to be modified, cancelling all anti-pollution legislation that emanated from the EU may be impractical. A gradual and thoughtful assessment of what laws should be repealed will be the more logical way forward.

If just ²/5 of the EU's red tape can be disposed of then economic output will increase by 2% giving a benefit to the economy of as much as £30 billion. In European terms this is a considerable figure that will not only lead to lower unemployment but also have a number of positive affects as well, particularly on both private and public wealth.

The effect on taxation
If the UK no longer had to pay the financial contributions to the EU then there will be a clear benefit to the British taxpayer.

In 2012 the British taxpayer had to pay Brussels £16.6 billion; £3.1 billion being taken off at source. This is the annual rebate, otherwise known as abatement, originally negotiated by Margaret Thatcher but whittled down by succeeding governments. Over time the rebate will be further reduced and on current trends it will be effectively eliminated in future budget negotiations – there is a great deal of opposition to its existence. As such Britain will be paying close to £20 billion to the EU each year and receiving as little as £1 back for each £5 handed over. Influence has a price.

The return on the 2012 expenditure was just £6.9 billion. Yet, even the money that the UK receives from the EU has costs associated with it. The spending of the EU's structural funds in the UK come with strings attached and require the British authorities to match fund any spending; incurring further costs on the taxpayer on projects which may or may not be of an immediate priority. In the world of the EU even the benefits have costs.

Ending the requirement to pay the European Union the net 2012 total of payments, excluding the strings attached benefits, will produce a saving of £13.5 billion per year. Making a saving of that amount will allow for 3.65p in the pound to be taken off the basic rate of income tax. Each percentage point, or penny in the pound, generates £3.7 billion. On average nearly 3.65p of every pound of income tax you pay goes to Brussels.

Alternatively, saving these payments will enable the Personal Allowance to be increased by £2,673 so that you would earn £2,673 more than you currently do before paying tax – freeing millions of lower paid workers from having to pay income tax which they can little afford. The advantages of this will not only help alleviate poverty but will also help make work pay encouraging people back into employment. Personal Allowance for people born after 5th April 1948 is just £9,440. Outside of the EU it could become as much as £12,113.

If it is correct that the British economy will benefit from an exit then this will show in an increase in the key indicator of economic activity – Gross Domestic Product – and this will result in more tax revenue for the treasury.

On 24th June 2013 the UK's GDP, the total of the country's economic output, was £1,484.1 billion. There are different measurers of this measure of the economy and figures are revised but for the immediate future it will remain at around an approximate figure of £1,500 billion per year. Whilst there may be some small increase in GDP in the near future; on current trends the prospect of a significant upturn in economic activity is considered unlikely. That is unless the UK left the European Union. Excessive regulation is holding the economy back by as much as 5% of GDP. Economic growth cannot immediately increase by 5% on exit as it will take time to repeal all the excessive and unnecessary regulation but it is reasonable to presume that some can be abolished relatively quickly. Removing just over a third of those regulations will rapidly benefit the economy and it is reasonable to believe that the economy can increase by 2%. Considering the poor economic performance over recent years such economic growth will be a major fillip to the UK.

How will that impact upon taxation? Presuming, as the EU do, that Britain's tax to GDP ratio is approximately 36.1% then increasing GDP will increase tax revenue. If GDP increases by 2% after Brexit, a modest and conservative estimate, then the UK's total economic output will rise to approximately £1,530 billion per annum. This will result in the Treasury receiving approximately £10.83 billion more tax every year. The combined benefit of £10.83 billion in larger tax revenues and the saving of the £13.5 billion in payments to the EU coffers would enable the basic rate of income tax to be cut by a total of more than £24.3 billion. This figure corresponds to allowing nearly

6.58p in the pound to be cut from the basic rate. The same amount will alternatively enable an increase in the personal allowance by nearly £4,818 to a total of £14,258 of earned income before tax becomes liable.

The increase in the proceeds from greater economic activity combined with the savings can either result in higher public spending on social services or allow for a lowering of the tax burden. Both of which will be of further benefit. Alternatively a higher paying down of the public debt will be possible.

The clear savings to the Treasury and ultimately the UK taxpayer would, however, not be as absolute if the UK chooses to exit the EU but remain within the European Economic Area. Membership of which does require a contribution to various EU programmes and to off-set the large disparities of wealth that exist in Europe. Yet the most expenses option for the UK taxpayer is to remain in the European Union. The highest costs are applicable to EU members.

A lowering to various degrees of the basic rate of income tax is not the only benefit that withdrawing from the EU will have. Outside if the European Union the UK would have freedom to determine its own indirect taxation policy and have the right and the ability to decide which areas will be subject to Value Added Tax and at what rate. If the UK did not have to comply with the EU's flawed system of VAT, which has traditionally been open to fraud, then the treasury would have already been saved billions each year. The system was known to be open to abuse by criminals who claimed back VAT on fake transactions known as carousel, or missing trader, fraud.

The taxation of multi-national businesses can also be reformed. The EU has dominion over large areas of business taxation, such as transfer pricing, which is used by companies that trade in different jurisdictions to off-set tax the profits in one member state against supposed costs incurred in another. Outside of the EU the UK would have more latitude to address this issue.

The impact on immigration and emigration
Immigration is a major political issue and will be a central plank on both sides of the referendum campaign.

Eurosceptics will cite the uncontrolled numbers arriving from Eastern Europe and the resulting effects changing the face of some communities are important issues. Another issue is the economic impact of immigration which has been to lower the mean average wage, particular of those on low incomes. The creation of joblessness amongst the indigenous unskilled population which resulted from importing a highly motivated new unskilled workforce is also a social and economic problem that be raided. However, will exiting the European Union resolve those issues? The pro-EU campaign will argue that the UK benefits from immigration but also that exiting leaving the EU will endanger the status of British citizens who live and work in other EU states; but is that correct.

The different sides of the EU and immigration debate have very different options on the same topic. One side warns of the danger to UK nations having to leave the remaining EU state in which they reside and the other side claiming that it will resolve the problem of immigration from the East. Both are in fact wrong.

The free movement of peoples is a right that has arisen from obligations contained in the treaties that establish the European Union. Those that have established a residency, which will include both living and owning property, in an EU member state will have their rights protected. Their entitlement to continue living in another state is known as an 'executed right'. Article 70 b. of the Vienna Convention states that the withdrawal from a treaty 'Does not affect any right, obligation or legal situation of the parties created through the execution of the treaty prior to its termination.' This view is supported by the constitutional expert Lord McNair. He concluded that such rights established by a treaty will remain in force even if the agreement is terminated by Britain's exit. In law they are considered to be executed by the treaty and "have an existence independent of it; the termination cannot touch them." Their status will be guaranteed as a result of the "well-recognised principle of respect for acquired [vested] rights."

Therefore the impact of Britain exiting the EU will not be that great for those who already reside in the UK from other member states, nor will it be for the British citizens that live abroad. The difference will be felt amongst those who may want to move to a different state after the UK's withdrawal.

Separate legislation will be required to cancel the residency status of those who have arrived in the UK though taking advantage of the

EU's freedom movement. Any such move will be an internationally controversial act angering the governments of the remaining EU member states.

Yet cancelling the right to live and work of French and German citizens in the UK will prove to be diplomatically contentious. As such a future government may be unwilling to impose measures that cancel their residency status. It will be iniquitous to take action against the citizens of some European states, presumably those from the East, whilst not imposing measures against another. It is unlikely that stringent tests on these recent European immigrants will be applied, especially if there may be reciprocal action against British citizens living, working and or owning property on the continent.

However, at times British immigration policy has granted preferential treatment to some EU states. Traditionally the UK has positively discriminated in favour of citizens from the Republic of Ireland over continental European states even granting Irish citizens the right to vote in UK general elections.

What is more, workers from Western Europe will be more likely to be employed in high-productivity areas and will be a benefit to the British economy. The more recent arrivals from Eastern Europe have on the main found employment in low productivity sectors of the British economy and therefore in comparison to other workers they contribute less thus effectively taking out more from the economy than they put in. Whilst also undercutting their British counterparts.

Preventing future influxes of immigrants whilst allowing for some of those that have already came to the UK to leave on their own fruition will reduce the potential labour force. This will have a positive effect on the mean wage, driving up the pay of those at the lower end of the income scale. An effective and intelligent points based immigration system will be required to make sure that the economy receives the workers it needs from Europe without prejudicing the opportunities of British citizens in their own land.

Again much does depend upon the terms by which Britain leaves the European Union. The UK may negotiate a treaty that continues to allow for the continued free movement of peoples. Furthermore, if Britain stays within the European Economic Area (EEA) then there will be no change in the ebb and flow of individuals across borders. The EEA, to which Britain already belongs, guarantees the four freedoms that many associate with EU membership; the free movement of goods, services, capital and labour. For those that favour the free movement of Europeans across borders then they can rest assured that EEA membership will protect this; yet that does undermine a major argument for exiting the EU.

The issue of the UK leaving the EU does not just have implications for Britain; there will also be repercussions for the other states that remain in the European Union. These effects are not a side issue; they too will affect political and economic life in the United Kingdom.

The implications for Europe

If the UK is outside of the EU's single market and tariffs are placed on British exports then there is every justification for the UK, acting under the rules of the World Trade Organisation, to impose similar levies. If so then the harm to the fragile economies of the eurozone will be sizeable and will only add to their growing unemployment lines.

Initially continental Europe will be rocked by Britain departing the union. Nevertheless, there is also potential for the EU to benefit from a UK outside of the European Union. As long as Britain does not impose tariffs on goods originating from inside the EU then markets will remain open. What is more, the potential benefits to the UK's economy of a Brexit, less money having to be ceded to Brussels and less harmful regulation, will give British consumers more spending power to purchase continental imports. However, cheaper prices from outside of the EU's common external tariff and the potential for a less aggressive anti-dumping policy will mean that imports from developing nations will be more competitive than European produce.

The UK's independence endeavour will mean a substantial reduction in revenue for the European Union. This will either mean a reduction in subsidies for the less well-off states in the EU, or more likely, it will lead to the few economically successful states led by Germany having to pay more to keep afloat southern and eastern Europe.

Finland, one of the few fiscally responsible nations in Europe, already has a significant and growing Eurosceptic political party. The wildcard in the European equation may in fact turn out to be Germany. The industrial powerhouse of the EU is the biggest contributor to the EU budget and it is this state that has the greatest potential liability for the debts of the once profligate nations of southern Europe. It is to Germany that they look to pay off their bills and this is not without controversy. Germany citizens may realise that the people who end up paying for an empire are the working classes of the imperial power. The shock of having to shoulder yet more of the burden may cause a sea change in German politics.

It is not only a question of money. Without the balancing influence of Britain Germany may find that it is at the mercy of France and southern Europe working together to exploit the German taxpayer. Far from extending Teutonic efficiency into the parts of Europe that have not been touched by it for several generations the building of the house of Europe may lead to the withering of German financial resources. The voting in the Council of Ministers and the European Parliament will then grant power towards the impoverished many rather than have it resting in the hands of the wealthy few. The changes will be incremental and small but their sum may prove to be remarkable.

There is a prima facie case that a British exit will lead to a further centralisation of the European Union. What is more, it will then develop along lines that differ from the British vision of an economically liberalised political union.

This initial supposition does largely depend upon the belief that the UK has in some way slowed the march towards further centralisation and has shaped the nature of the union according to British standards. Evidence for this is, however, lacking. Nevertheless, it is a common belief not just in the UK but also on the continent.

This fear that certain malign influences will grow is certainly real. According to the BBC Anders Borg, who serves as the Swedish Finance Minister from the, by Swedish standards, centre-right Moderate Party, is concerned about British withdrawal because ending Britain's role in the EU would lead to Sweden becoming "more exposed and less able to punch above its weight" when negotiating with France and Germany. The Swedish Finance Minister also feared that the EU will become "more continental, more dirigiste and less flexible and open, so we need a strong British voice in these discussions."

Areas where the EU may miss a British influence will include the UK's steadfast links to Nato, the US dominated North Atlantic Treaty Organisation military alliance. However, the EU is already developing its own military systems, such as the Galileo satellite programme that is not only independent of the American GPS system but is actually a rival to it. The UK, in particular the British Parliament's House of Commons Public Accounts Committee, has also continually pushed Brussels to reform its financial practices and end the waste, mismanagement and fraud. This has led to some reforms; however the EU's accounts have still not been given a clean bill of health for over 17 years. One area where Britain has arguably had an influence is in the liberalisation of the markets of the other member states. Yet, the free market doctrine in the EU may have already reached its zenith regardless of whether or not the UK stays as a member. The EU's Single Market rules mandating competition, privatisation and an end to subsidies have already gone as far as they can in many areas. In others the UK has only managed token reforms such as in the case of the Common Agricultural Policy. What is more, current thinking in many EU states blames the 2008 financial crisis and its aftermath on Anglo-Saxon economic liberalism. There is now less desire to listen to British laissez-faire economic solutions. Another area is the pursuit of free trade agreements with countries outside of the EU, even outside of Europe itself. The EU, however, is now fully wedded to the concept of such trading agreements so long as French agriculture and the French film industry are protected and not open to competition.

The biggest loss will be financial; which will turn net beneficiaries of EU funds into contributors.

The UK does have a theoretical check on further integration such as in the ability to block future changes to the EU's governing rules and its power vis-à-vis the other member states. However, as was shown over the alleged vetoing of the fiscal compact this balance on the EU is largely academic. Nevertheless, the absence of an unwilling partner presents opportunities for the more fundamentalist federalists in the EU to push for greater integration. There will be less need for them to factor into their plans potential British resistance.

At present a future EU treaty can not only be vetoed by a British Prime Minister but also by Parliament and even by a referendum. An important factor that federalists have to consider is the so-called 'referendum lock'. This Act of Parliament mandates that if a further significant transfer of power from Britain to the EU is proposed this must be put to a referendum of the British people for approval. Which is unlikely to be given.

In the present political climate it is improbable that any future British government will seek to cede significant powers to the EU. However, it does create additional pressure for a referendum by adding to the expectations that one should be held on any future EU treaty. Furthermore, it will be argued in the UK that even if a new treaty is proposed that creates further centralisation for the eurozone, whilst not taking power from Britain, this should still be put to a referendum as it will fundamentally change Britain's relationship with the other member states. Those that follow the path of more centralisation will then become more likely to act as a caucus thus further diminishing Britain's already limited influence in the Council of Ministers and the European Parliament. As such the demands for a referendum on a treaty can become overwhelming. Depending upon if and when this new treaty emerges there may well have to be a referendum on both the UK's membership of the EU and if Britain stays in on any later treaty that may emerge.

In these circumstances it is likely that any new EU treaty that does not include a significant transfer of powers back to the UK will possibly be voted by the British electorate in a referendum. This is perhaps even a probability. Whilst the present British government has explicitly supported fiscal centralisation to support the euro the UK's membership may still prove to be a break on this. A new EU treaty may well be held up if the UK remains in the European Union. Therefore, Britain out of the EU will be a gain for those who want further centralisation; but this is not the end of the story.

It is a matter of debate whether further European integration is to the benefit of the people who live within the borders of the EU. Whereas many see the answer to the Eurozone's economic crisis as further political union; the imposition of EU policies has so far proved to be far from beneficial. What is more, the effect of an even greater level of centralisation will not only have economic costs but it will also exacerbate the political pressures caused by an ever widening democratic deficit. In time this has the potential to undo the process of ever closer union.

In the short term there will be a push for greater centralisation of the EU after Brexit but the longer term consequences may well be very different. Much will depend on the nature of Britain's withdrawal, the

UK's post-EU experience and a future British government's foreign policy towards other European states. This will determine whether or not other EU nations will seek to replicate Britain's strategy.

A unilateral withdrawal which makes an exit trade agreement less probable may lead in the short term to the UK lacking the trade links that Britain's economy depends upon. The confusion for other states that have less global links than the UK will quash any thoughts that they may have of leaving the union. However, if the UK follows the Article 50 procedure and manages to secure a free trade or remains a member of the European Economic Area or the customs union then other nations may start to consider such an arrangement for themselves.

Furthermore, if life outside the EU proves to be viable then any threats to leave the union will need to be taken seriously and this may lead to there being a break on further powers being handed to Brussels. An example of this process is Canada; this is amongst the most decentralised countries in the world largely because the state of Quebec has on occasions threatened to withdraw from the union.

Furthermore, Britain may once again lead by example and show that there are alternatives available. The UK led in the formation of the European Free Trade Association in 1960 as an alternative to the European Economic Community, which was to become in time the European Union. If the UK can actively promote different options to EU membership and make them a success then other countries may wish to join the UK in a more successful confederation. Or at the very least threaten to do so.

So far the EU has continued because its member states have been blocked from seeking a return of powers. Some member states will then have a bargaining chip for change. Competition between the nation states of the EU may then increase as its members seek to decentralise power away from the EU institutions back to national control regardless of whether or not the European Commission and the European Court of Justice agree. Once under way this process can only accelerate.

The potential for decentralisation of the political union upon a member states exit is a very real one. According to the German academic, Professor Roland Vaubel, it will encourage other states to seek a return of powers. This will re-create competition between member states whose civil servants and politicians begin to seek their own solutions to problems and search for innovative ways to achieve a competitive advantage over their rivals. This may include reducing the level of both taxation and regulation. Arguably these are the two main negative effects of the EU's system of government. The EU not only imposes high regulation but also seeks to limit tax competition and sets minimum, not maximum, levels of taxation in areas such as Value Added Tax and opposes levels of corporation tax that it deems to be too low.

At the very least it will give the citizens of the member states the opportunity to compare and contrast their neighbour's policies with those in their own country. Giving them a yardstick by which they can compete and learn best practice through studying diverse alternatives to the challenges they face. This will have a positive effect as the monolithic one-size-fits-all philosophy of the EU which will be put under pressure. What is more, politicians will be able to become more responses to their citizen's needs; instead of answering to the EU their accountability to their own electorates will become paramount. According to Nicholas Sambanis, a professor of Political Science at Yale University, democracy will also be enhanced. Professor Sambanis studied 125 examples of states becoming independent and he found that there is a substantial improvement in the level of democracy.

Therefore, far from the fears expressed by the Swedish Finance Minister the situation after the UK's withdrawal may well prove to be beneficial for those who want less powerful EU institutions and less interference from Brussels operating at the behest of the Franco-German axis.

Nevertheless, much depends on how Britain is perceived to manage outside of the EU. It is imperative that Britain negotiates the best deal possible. If the UK appears to not only survive but indeed thrive then others may follow Britain's example. Or at least use it as a negotiating tool. EU discussion will then have a whole new edge to them.

Nevertheless, this scenario depends upon whether or not Britain successfully uses its still considerable potential influence in world affairs and makes the case to the other EU member states that a clean divorce is in their's as much as the UK's economic interests. If so then the UK's future outside of the EU will be assured and it may just help to retard or even unravel centralisation from the outside thus realising

Britain's original approach. Stopping the process of centralisation from within has clearly failed; perhaps it will succeed from without.

What is more, a major state in European terms such as Britain exiting the EU will also bolster the political position of Eurosceptics in countries such as Norway, Iceland and Switzerland. Some amongst their political elites favour joining the EU whereas their citizens remain opposed. So long as the UK is seen to be prospering then their country's case against membership will be weakened. To guarantee this an amicable divorce will be required.

If Britain remains in the EEA and re-joins EFTA, achieving the same status as Norway, Iceland and Liechtenstein (Switzerland is also an EFTA member) then both these two alternatives to EU membership will have their influence advanced. It will add weight to those organisations, expanding their ability to reach preferential trade deals with emerging markets around the globe. And if Britain agrees with the other states then there will also be another voice beside them in the World Trade Organisation.

Together Britain and its new EFTA/EEA partners will be able to combine the good will that the European Free Trade Association has developed with the EU over decades of co-operation and combine this with Britain's diplomatic and economic might. This will then increase the economic and political influence of the EFTA/EEA members; this rise in power will then change the dynamic between them and the EU further towards the out states favour.

Brexit can dramatically change the status quo in Europe and perhaps end the drift towards ever closer union for some and enhance it for others.

The implications of staying in the European Union

There are on-going costs to European Union membership that have been documented. Staying in the European Union will mean that the regulatory costs will grow as will the financial burden; especially as the rebate is whittled away. There are also financial risks that remain at large whilst Britain stays in the European Union.

Should the crisis in the Eurozone worsen to the point that the Single Currency collapses this will bring into question the viability of a number of European Union institutions. There is a €35.7 billion liability to the Luxembourg based European Investment Bank (EIB).

This organisation borrows money on the financial markets and loans this capital to predominantly public authorities to support the EU's projects and political goals. These funds, however, are focussed towards the vulnerable economies in the EU, notably; Portugal, Ireland, Italy, Greece and Spain. Should these states, with very vulnerable economies, and their contingent municipalities be unable to pay back their loans to the EIB it be forced to call upon the funds of those member states that are still financially viable. The liability to the EIB alone can total as much as £30 billion.

This is not the only risk that can face the UK should the euro finally enter meltdown. The European Central Bank, whose headquarters are in Frankfurt, has managed to establish its own massive portfolio of debt. Its maximum exposure to the economies of Ireland and the Mediterranean-Rim totals nearly €1 trillion. If the re-payments of the debt owed to the ECB from the banks and nations that it has loaned to cease the of the European Central Bank will be put at risk. Despite the UK being outside of the final stage of Economic and Monetary Union, the euro, the Bank of England is still a shareholder in the European Central Bank. In addition to that the BoE is part of what is known as the European System of Central Banks (the Eurosystem). This was established by the 1997 Amsterdam Treaty.

The ECB is entitled under EU law to call upon the Central Banks of the Eurosystem for up to €50 billion of their currency reserves. In the event of a crash it may be attempted to project the exposure back onto the last few states left standing and in the case of the UK this will rest with the Bank of England. It is legally a grey area but the alternative to not taking on all or some of the liability will be to let the ECB, the European System of Central Banks and the Single Currency fail in catastrophic fashion. Despite the government claiming that it has extricated the UK from the EU's bailout schemes there is still a residual on-going liability to the European Financial Stabilisation Mechanism (EFSM) which totals €6bn.

The maximum exposure to the EIB, the ESFM and the ECB are absolute worst case scenarios yet as a member of the European Union there is the requirement to guarantee the risks on a joint and several basis. If there is to be continued difficulties in the eurozone then a proportion of the debt can find itself coming to the UK. With these risks inherent in the terms of EU membership leaving becomes not only financially advantageous but it also becomes the fiscally responsible and prudent course of action.

The emergence of growing markets outside of the European Union should also be an important factor that the UK should be cognitive of. The effect of staying in the EU

Although there is a price to staying in the European Union, including the opportunity cost of being tied to a market that has a declining share of global GDP, and clear benefits to leaving there may also be costs associated with Britain's withdrawal.

The reaction to Brexit in Brussels and the corridors of power in the EU's remaining member states will determine the fate of both the EU and Britain's success without it. There is a possibility that there will be recriminations towards the UK if Britain were to leave the EU. Herman van Rompuy, the President of the European Council, whilst recognising that the EU has a withdrawal clause and that exit is thus legally permissible, stated on 28th February 2013 in London that succession will, "be legally and politically a most complicated and unpractical affair. Just think of a divorce after forty years of marriage... But let us not dramatise. It is natural that all member countries can, and do, have particular requests and needs – and these are always taken into consideration."

So there is a possibility for synergy to exist between the UK and the EU member states on a new relationship. Interestingly the President of the Council did not state that there will be economic costs. However, in the same speech he also said that "Leaving is an act of free will, and perfectly legitimate, but it doesn't come for free."

Hubris on the part of MEPs, the other EU leaders and the European Commission may still be a factor that may impair the opportunities of exit. The Commission's advice to the European Council may include recommendations that do not favour the UK. In addition, a contrary and uncooperative European Council or Parliament can reject a reasonable withdrawal agreement or future free trade deal. Despite this being against the economic interests of the people's whose states remain part of the EU it will not be the first time that politics have been put before economic common sense. The Common Agricultural Policy, the euro and the austerity measures that underpin it are all fine examples of such callousness if it serves a political purpose. The most significant costs will be customs levies and a loss of influence in the committees of the EU that draft legislation.

So if there is to be a cost, a price to pay for leaving, then the question becomes how can the practicalities be smoothed? And how can any potential damage be mitigated whilst exploiting the potential benefits of a future outside of the EU? Following the Article 50 withdrawal procedure is the only way that the EU is not only obliged but legally mandated to enter into negotiations with the UK. However, Article 50 is just a means to an end towards restructuring the UK's relationship with other European countries. What post-EU membership alternative relationships, if any, are viable options that the UK can both explore and implement which will maximise advantages of leaving whilst minimising the costs?

Chapter 7

Alternatives to the EU

"We have no eternal allies, and we have no perpetual enemies. Our interests are eternal and perpetual, and those interests it is our duty to follow."
Lord Palmerstone, Statesman of the British Empire, 1st March 1848

Back to the future: The European Free Trade Association

Since the UK left EFTA the remaining member states have been prospering and handled financial crises much better than members of the European Union. With an average unemployment rate of just 4% the European Free Trade Association is in economic terms one of the most effective trade associations in the world. Despite EFTA consisting of the relatively small states of Iceland, Norway and Switzerland and the micro-state of Liechtenstein it still has considerable trade with the EU. EFTA's export trade in goods with the EU amounts to more than €189.2 billion. That is nearly as much as the USA which exported just over €190 billion worth of goods to the EU in 2011. In the same year EFTA states also sold more than €102 billion worth of service to the EU. More than China, Russia and Japan combined.

Arguably, the EFTA model of free trade without political interference and overregulation is beneficial. The rules of the European Free Trade Association, known as the EFTA Convention, is just 30 pages. The EU's combined Treaty on European Union and Treaty on the Functioning of the European Union totals 186 pages.

The balance sheet of costs to the taxpayer is also telling. Whereas the UK alone has to pay the EU tens of billions of pounds per year for the privilege of membership of the EU; EFTA's 2013 budget amounted to as little as £15.6 million; just 22,298,000 Swiss Francs. A token sum compared to the €7 billion spent by the EU on administration each year. What is more, whereas the EU's accounts do not receive the approval of the EU's very own Court of Auditors which concludes that they remain subject to waste, mismanagement and fraud; EFTA's accounts are approved and signed off each year. A taxpayer can rest assured that their money is being spent appropriately.

Whereas the European Commission, which is divorced from national democratic oversight, manages the EU's budget, EFTA's finances are administered by the Budget Committee which is part of the EFTA Council. The EFTA Board of Auditors, which sits alongside the Council inspects and appraises the accounts of the EFTA Secretariat as well as the EFTA Surveillance Authority and the EFTA Court.

The European Free Trade Association has its Head Office based in Geneva, Switzerland. One of its most important roles is the administration and negotiation of trade agreements with both non-EU and EU countries. EFTA's structure is simple and straight forward. It is an intergovernmental organisation seeking to foster trade cooperation between its members and beyond. Unlike the EU it is not a supra-national political bureaucracy and neither is it a customs union controlling its member states trade policy.

The EFTA Council, which usually meets twice per year, manages relations between the EFTA States under the terms of the EFTA Convention. Through this inter-governmental council the member states can; consult, negotiate and act together. As well as develop their links with other countries and trade groups around the world. The attendees at its meetings are usually relevant ministers from its member states. Extra meetings are usually attended by the member states' ambassadors to the European Free Trade Association.

It has special standing committees which monitor and develop trade relationships with other nations. These committees report to the Council. There is direct input from members of the national parliaments of its members who advise the Council. This exists under the EFTA Secretariat which has a Secretary-General based in Geneva; it also has representation in the Belgian capital. The Swiss based staff are primarily concerned with non-EU trade and supporting the Council. The representation in Brussels provides support for the running of relations with the European Union under what is known as the European Economic Area Agreement and assists member states to prepare for and to implement new legislation as part of EFTA's treaty with the EU. Both sections of EFTA work together on matters that relate to its own internal free trade agreement. The Secretariat also aides its member states input into EU decision making. There are around just 80 staff working in the Secretariat, the EU has as many as 30,000 working in its bureaucracy.

There is also an EFTA Statistical Office. This was established in 1991 through an agreement with the EU, it is now governed by the terms of the EEA Agreement. This Luxembourg based bureau contributes to Eurostat's information and the development of the European Statistical System. This does not sound exhilarating but it is another important mechanism by which EFTA, including Switzerland, can and does have influence over the development of EU rules by actively partaking in EU technical meetings and other EU committees. The opinions of experts from the EFTA countries do matter. As they come from states outside of the EU and its harmonisation they have a distinctive background of knowledge and research which they can bring to discussions.

EFTA and the EU have good working relations. The opinions of the representatives from the more prosperous EFTA countries are valued in discussions with their EU counterparts. EFTA is not only involved with discussing with the European Union but is also actively involved in negotiating with the UN sponsored standardisation agencies.

Unlike the EU, EFTA does not involve itself in countries' agriculture, fisheries, home affairs or justice policies. It is a trade association that not only establishes free trade between its members and guarantees membership of the European Economic Area, but also reaches free trade agreements with other states. It managed to conclude such an arrangement with South Korea long before the EU. EFTA's came into force on 1st September 2006 whilst the EU's accord with the democratic part of Korea finally entered into force nearly 5 years behind the one which Iceland, Liechtenstein, Norway and Switzerland were already benefitting from.

EFTA, not only has free trade between its constituent parts and access to the EU's Single Market but also, outside of the EU, it has free trade with a further 36 other countries. The EFTA states profit from this effective set of agreements. Over 80% of their trade in goods is with countries with which they have successfully negotiated preferential trade arrangements.

Its world-wide links are substantial. EFTA gives the businesses of each of its member's access to a market outside of the European Union that totals 680 million consumers. In Europe, beyond its arrangement with the EU, EFTA has agreements with; Albania, Bosnia and Herzegovina, Croatia, Macedonia, Montenegro, Serbia and the Ukraine. In the Americas formal trade relations exist with Canada, Central American States- which include Costa Rica and Panama – Chile, Colombia, Mexico and Peru. In Asia EFTA has arrangements with the Cooperation Council for the Arab States of the Gulf - which include Bahrain, Kuwait, Qatar, Saudi Arabia, Oman and the United Arab Emirates - Hong Kong, Israel, Jordan, The Republic of Korea (South Korea), Lebanon, the Palestinian Authority, Singapore and Turkey. In Africa the links include Egypt, Morocco, the Southern African Customs Union - which include Botswana, Lesotho, Namibia, South Africa and Swaziland – and Tunisia.

Yet unlike EU states EFTA members are still free to negotiate and conclude their own free trade agreements with any outside country. On 15th April 2013 Iceland signed a free trade agreement with China. The first FTA the Chinese have signed with a European country. Clearly it is a misconception that only large Orwellian blocs can reach such important agreements.

Reflecting the increasingly international supply chains in the production of both agricultural and industrial goods EFTA takes a liberal approach to the origins of imports. Its rules of origin state that as the item in question has been either "wholly obtained" or "sufficiently worked or processed" in a state that has signed a trade agreement with EFTA then it can be imported without difficulty. EFTA's general approach is a user-friendly one. It considers that it has a practical approach that does not inhibit trade. What is more, any disputes that arise in EFTA are resolved through a system of arbitration; not diktat from the European Commission or the European Court of Justice.

Advocating re-joining the European Free Trade Association does not just have an economic justification; on a number of levels it also makes sense politically. It keeps the UK a formal party in EU/EEA discussions but it will also be an alternative to EU membership that proves to be popular with the British public.

A recent Survation opinion poll, commissioned by the Bruges Group, found that 71% of respondents favoured the EFTA alternative with just 29% of those asked wanting to remain in the European Union. That is a significant margin of victory. This is not surprising as the European Free Trade Association (EFTA) is a working alternative with member states enjoying lower unemployment and higher standards of living than their counterparts in the EU. Polls have consistently shown that members of the public, when offered a 'looser' relationship with the EU have expressed support for such an option. Now we can see that there is such a relationship already available and support for this alternative to EU membership exists in very significant numbers.

If any future referendum was framed in the context, not of Britain leaving one trading bloc and system of governance for an as yet undefined and obscure future, or of joining and taking advantage of the benefits of an alternative to the EU then the chances of winning an out referendum increase exponentially. For those who want out of the European Union the debate needs to be shifted towards the opportunities that await Britain.

Whilst the almost endless listing of the disadvantages of the EU and its rules and regulations has been a gift to Eurosceptics that has just kept on giving and brought the problems of membership into the national consciousness the debate now needs to develop the positive alternatives to the EU which are available.

Those who will campaign for Britain to stay in the European Union will rest their campaign on the insecure future the UK may, according to them, have outside of the EU.

To combat this fear the outers need to embrace and promote the positive concept of hope. Making the case that the answer to Britain's ills; namely a sluggish economy and a political elite that only seems accountable to its own self-interest can begin to be cured by exiting the monolithic structure of the EU and embracing a new independent path. Euroscepticism will need to shift from simply highlighting the demerits of the EU and become the hope for a better future.

Throughout history national liberation movements have not just wanted to oust the occupying power but have embraced a philosophy, and at times even a theology, that offers not only national confidence but also positive change. Joining the rest of the world which is enjoying economic growth and aligning the UK politically with the independent European countries that have far greater democratic accountability is a winning strategy.

However, there is another potential alternative that guarantees access to the EU single market without the need for financial contributions and with less of an obligation to apply EU rules. In short EFTA offers trade without the loss of sovereignty that membership of the EU entails. Beyond guaranteeing free trade with many nations and territories around the planet membership of the European Free Trade Association has much more to offer. Through an agreement with the European Union EFTA members states can be included in the formulation of some EU law and they have full access to the internal market. Discussion of EFTA is therefore often synonymous with the European Economic Area (EEA) and the so-called Norway option.

The UK is considered to be a member of the EEA through its membership of the EU. The EEA's founding treaty states that a nation can be a part of the European Economic Area if it is a member of either the EU or the other European trade arrangement namely the European Free Trade Association. Belonging to one of those will enable the continuation, without let or hindrance, of the free movement of goods, services, capital and labour into the EU's Single Market.

Does exiting the EU mean that the UK leaves the European Economic Area? On the one hand to join the EEA there is the requirement to be in one of those two organisations. However, on the other there is no expulsion clause in the EEA treaty and nothing which affords any state or group of states or any other transnational organisation the power to cancel the membership of another country.

Arguably because the UK is a signatory to the European Economic Area treaty and is listed as such in its preamble a case can be made that Britain may have a secure future in the EEA. Under this line of reasoning there is little that can be done other than accept Britain's continued status as an EEA member with many of the rights and privileges that this entails. That is if Britain wants to retain it.

This case is supported by the prescribed terms of exiting the EEA. The EEA Agreement like the Treaty on the Functioning of the European Union sets out a path by which a member-state can withdraw from the European Economic Area. Article 127, which governs the rules of exit is much more straightforward than its counterpart in the

EU's rule book. The EEA Agreement states that 'Each Contracting Party may withdraw from this Agreement provided it gives at least twelve months' notice in writing to the other Contracting Parties.'

Article 127 not only means that the UK will remain in the EEA for 12 months until such notice is given it also makes no reference to a requirement of having to remain a member of the EU or EFTA. The paragraph's mention that notice must be given to the other plural 'parties' can also be read to imply that the contracting parties are each individual member states rather than the two international institutions.

This is the evidence that suggests that it may be feasible to conclude that the UK could automatically retain full access to the Single Market if it left the EU. However, it remains opaque. Article 2 (c) states that the meaning of the term 'contracting parties' is to be understood 'from the relevant provisions of this Agreement and from the respective competences of the Community and the EC Member States as they follow from the Treaty establishing the European Economic Community.' This suggests that Britain's membership of the EEA remains founded and dependent upon staying in the EU or becoming like Norway and re-joining EFTA.

There are also clear references in the EEA treaty which only make reference to EFTA and the EU; notably Article 28 1. This reads 'Freedom of movement for workers shall be secured among EC Member States and EFTA States.' This clear reference to the two groups means that key parts of the agreement can only function properly if all EEA members are either in EFTA or the EU. Otherwise the continued right to free movement will be undermined. What is more, many of the consultation and enforcement mechanisms that apply standard rules across the area are only workable through either EFTA or the EU. Much of the agreement therefore becomes nonsense if a member state decides to become a new group of one. Therefore, the EEA Agreement will at the very least need to be re-worked to adapt to an independent UK. This is not onerous. The EEA Agreement is flexible. Unlike the convoluted process of treaty change in the EU it remains easy and incumbent upon the EEA Council to amend the agreement. Article 89 says that the EEA Council 'shall assess the overall functioning and the development of the Agreement. It shall take the political decisions leading to amendments of the Agreement.' What is more the European Commission believes that the EEA is due for reform; the continued participation of an EU-out UK can provide the impetus for this.

Therefore, if the political will exists in both Britain and on the continent then the requirement to be either a member of the EU or EFTA can be managed in such a way as to keep the UK in the EEA. If this is indeed possible much will depend upon how Britain, along with the other members, and the EU choose to interpret the agreement; and if the other parties will be accommodating to the UK. This is especially important. It will after all have to overcome the established wisdom that has so far concluded that the continued membership and active participating in the operation of the internal market is only open to EU or EFTA states. Interestingly the European Commission has refused to address similar issues in European Parliamentary Questions that have been formally asked by British MEP Syed Kamall. The failure of the Commission to be forthcoming, despite its duty to respond is perhaps very revealing. The Commission stated it is 'not prepared to speculate on the legal consequences, including the consequences for international agreements to which the Union and the Member States are Parties, of the hypothetical situation of absence of such an agreement, while the treaty provides that such an agreement 'shall be concluded'. And that 'No Member State has decided to withdraw from the European Union.' That is yet.

The complexities and vagueness of international treaties and the armies of transnational lawyers and bureaucrats paid to interpret and then apply them have become the key factor in international relations. This has replaced the principle of Force majeure as the ultimate determinant of the fate of nations. The founders of the EU may think this preferable but at least in the past a nation knew where it stood.

If the UK has, in the eyes of the EU, not honoured its treaty commitments by unilaterally withdrawing and ignoring the Article 50 procedure then there will be little political incentive, and certainly no goodwill, to keep Britain in the European Economic Area. The European Union may feel inclined to ignore the creative interpretation of the EEA agreement and argue that Britain can only be a member of the European Economic Area if the UK is a member of the EU or EFTA.

In such circumstances Britain can take the matter to the International Court of Justice, an agency of the UN, for resolution. However, will another transnational body look kindly on a party to the case that has not followed the correct legal principles which it once agreed to in its binding contract with the other EU states? That is the prescribed procedure set-out in Article 50 of the Treaty on European Union.

Applying to re-join the European Free Trade Association will therefore be the surest way of maintaining the free movement of goods, services, capital and labour between Britain and the continent. It will also enable the UK to keep a permanent seat in many EU discussions sitting at the table as members of EFTA/EEA rather than EU/EEA.

Beyond guaranteeing full access to the Single Market, what else does continued membership of the EEA have to offer?

The Norway option: The European Economic Area

Britain is not only a member of the EU, it also belongs to another arrangement that carries with it rights and duties, this is the little known European Economic Area (EEA). This is essentially the association that guarantees access to the Single Market, the much vaunted trade relationship that allows for the free movement of goods, services, people and capital between all thirty-one participating European countries. These nations include 27 EU states (Croatia is not part of the EEA) and three of the four European Free Trade Association states; Iceland, Liechtenstein and Norway. Whilst belonging to the internal market they are not part of the EU's customs union and as such are free to negotiate their own free trade agreements with other states around the globe.

This is the so-called 'Norway option'. It is a formal understanding between the European Free Trade Association and the European Union. In 1992 three EFTA states, Iceland, Liechtenstein and Norway, elected to take part in the Single Market without becoming members of the EU. This agreement came into force on 1st January 1994 and since then those states have been an integral part of the EU's internal market. Switzerland, the other remaining EFTA member, chose a different path.

Whereas Britain is known as an EU/EEA state, a member of the European Union and the European Economic Area, a country such as Norway takes part in discussion with the EU as an EEA/EFTA state.

The EEA agreement was seen as a way of expanding access to the

Single Market to the EFTA members without having to dilute the goal of ever-closer union by permitting members into the union that did not want to take part in political centralisation. The agreement is straightforward and to the point. Its first article stipulates that, '... the association shall entail, in accordance with the provisions of this Agreement :

(a) the free movement of goods;

(b) the free movement of persons;

(c) the free movement of services;

(d) the free movement of capital;

(e) the setting up of a system ensuring that competition is not distorted and that the rules thereon are equally respected; as well as

(f) closer cooperation in other fields, such as research and development, the environment, education and social policy.'

These are many of the so-called benefits that belonging to the Single Market brings to a country and an economy. They are not just available to EU members but are clearly available to all states that are in the EEA.

Norway is clearly benefitting from its membership of the European Economic Area. Norway has become a major source for foreign direct investment from the EU; in fact 63% comes from EU member states. This coincides with the Ernst & Young survey into FDI. This found that less European integration will potentially increase investment flows in Britain. The EEA fulfils this by reducing costly integration by exiting the EU whilst retaining access to the still significant in size Single Market. It will fulfil this without the necessity for implausible renegotiation.

Tariff free trade with the EU's Single Market is not the only opportunity for access to a large market that the EEA states can have. If the much vaunted potential free trade deal between the USA and the EU, the Transatlantic Trade and Investment Partnership (TTIP), is agreed it will also cover the states of the European Economic Area. This will give Iceland, Liechtenstein and Norway tariff free access to the US economy. Britain can therefore benefit from this without the perceived need to remain in the European Union.

As a member of the European Economic Area the mutual recognition of standards will continue to apply to British exporters who want to sell their goods to other EU and EEA states. If approved in one member state the product can therefore be sold in another without having to undergo new testing to see if it complies with the regulations of the country it is being exported to and without having the administrative burden of seeking approval from other EU countries placed on it. This will remain the case even though a stricter regime may be in place in the other state to which the product is being exported.

Other advantages that are prescribed to EU membership, such as cheaper mobile phone roaming charges whilst abroad in another member state, are actually available to members of the European Economic Area. Incidentally, reduced costs of data and telephone use abroad will reduce mobile phone industry revenue by 2% which will result in increased charges for domestic use. This policy will benefit the best-off, who can afford to travel more frequently, the most. The European political class, who regularly travel between states, will especially benefit from the reduction in roaming costs.

The agreement that establishes the European Economic Area assures, for good or ill, 'equal rights and obligations within the Single Market for citizens and economic operators in the EEA.'

The obligations which come with EEA membership include the requirement to make payments to the EU's funds. The financial contributions will be made to the EEA programmes known as EEA and Norway Grants. These payments go towards reducing inequality between the 30 members that make up this bloc. They are targeted at the 15 less prosperous states in the European Economic Area. These are those 12 that have joined since 2004 as well as the existing impoverished members; Greece, Portugal and Spain.

Iceland, Liechtenstein and Norway also participate in numerous EU programmes ranging from culture to lifelong learning and from transport to the development of health policy in the European Union. This does give the EEA states influence but there is a financial cost. A report by the House of Commons found that in 2011 the total cost for Norway of these programmes and grants amounted to £524 million, which is £106 per head of population. The payments include £10 million towards EFTA's annual running costs. Norway's contribution to the so-called Norway and EEA grants, which are intended to equalise wealth disparities in the European Economic Area, amounted to £301 million per year. And £214 million towards the EU's running costs. Norway's payments to the EU are not scutage or Danegeld. A significant amount of the money goes towards paying for Norway's participation in pan European programmes from which they derive a utility most notably the Erasmus programme which allows for EEA students to study abroad. The Norwegians are coming as close as is possible in European terms to getting good value for their money. Of course inside the EU some other nations get good value from other people's money.

What is more, these payments compare very favourably with Britain's gross contributions in the same year. In 2011 Britain paid the EU more than £15.3 billion which is £243 per capita. This means that if the UK contributed to EU projects and EEA grants on the same basis as Norway, instead of as an EU member, then it will result in savings to the taxpayer of more than 55%. EU expenditure in the UK does reduce the total cost of the EU, but even when taking this into account the Norway option will still be financially advantageous especially as the British rebate declines. The UK should be able to negotiate a better financial deal than Norway making the potential savings even greater.

The benefits of the Norway option are not just financial. What is not part of the EEA agreement is just as important as what is included. Unlike the EU, membership of the European Economic Area preserves national sovereignty over policy in a number of important areas. These include; agriculture, they control their own fishing grounds, they are outside of the EU's customs union. Therefore exports from the EEA to the EU will have to comply with the bureaucratic requirement to complete Brussels rules of origin etiquette. The EEA/EFTA states are free to make their own trade agreements. EEA states also fully control their own tax policies, they are not part of the Common Foreign and Security Policy. They also control their own Justice and Home Affairs policies and are not part of Economic and Monetary Union.

This means that exiting the EU and remaining in the EEA will free the UK from any EU interference in those areas. Yet, it is not a regulation free alternative. However, whilst it is true that Iceland, Liechtenstein and Norway are obligated to implement some EU rules, these countries adopt 70% less regulations than those which are imposed on the European Union member states. The European Economic Area will therefore not only result in a tax cut for British citizens it will also mean a cut in the costs that businesses face. EU red-tape is thought to hold back economic growth by as much as 5% of GDP, costing businesses as much as £75 billion per year. Massively cutting back the amount of new regulations coupled with the eventual elimination of those EU rules that have now become redundant will effectively reduce business costs by more than $^2/_3$. That is the equivalent of giving businesses more than a £50 billion tax cut and should result in the UK's GDP rising by as much as 3.5%. If this growth continues it can result in unemployment falling to the low levels enjoyed in the EEA states; creating 1 million more jobs in the UK.

The, pro-EU membership, Norwegian government has described their participation in the EEA as 'fax democracy'. It is a way of describing their adoption of some EU law without any say in its composition. This, however, is a faux argument. It is correct to say that neither Norwegian ministers nor parliamentarians attend and therefore do not vote in the meetings of the Council of Ministers, or in the European Parliament. They are therefore not involved where EU laws are passed in the final stage of establishing the EU's rules. Yet this does not cause as serious a democratic deficit as supporters of centralisation suggest. In the final stages of the legislation much has already been finalised and all but formally agreed. The utility of having a small percentage of the vote is questionable especially as there is pressure for conformity, known in Brussels speak as solidarity. Moreover Norway and other EEA states have a formal system by which they can develop with the EU the Single Markets rules.

EEA/EFTA states have the right to not only be consulted about EU rules that may be relevant to the European Economic Area but can also shape EU decisions at the start. Representatives from the EEA take part in more than 500 EU committees and expert groups. Active involvement of nations such as Norway allows the EEA countries to have real influence over the European Union's process of comitology.

This is still less formal power over the rules of the single market than EU member states have, but the prosperity of the EEA nations adds to their prestige. The opinions of the Norwegian representatives are listened to and valued. The EEA countries, as independent sovereign states, contribute more to the development of the internal market than similar sized EU states. Those small European Union members are not expected to vocally take part in the EU decision making architecture; instead they merely align with one or more of the larger states.

There are other institutions which create cooperation between the EEA and the EU; and establish a system that is far removed from the alleged coercion of fax democracy. The management of the EEA agreement is also not top down from the European Union. It is undertaken by what is known as the EEA Joint Committee (EEA JC). This consists of Ambassadors from the European Economic Area states and the EU's European External Action Service. There is also an EEA Joint Parliamentary Committee. This scrutinises the decisions of the EEA JC and produces reports and recommendations about how the agreement can be improved. The EEA Joint Parliamentary Committee is made up of members from the national parliaments of the EEA/EFTA states and on the EU side by representatives from the European Parliament. There is also an EEA Consultative Committee. This consists of members of the EFTA Consultative Committee and the European Economic and Social Committee. This committee seeks to advise on and promote cooperation on the social and economic characteristics of the EEA. The EFTA Standing Committees also act as a forum for those states which are in the EEA where the EFTA members can establish a common position when negotiating with the EU.

Whereas, the European Commission and the European Court of Justice regulate the EU's compliance with the terms of the EEA agreement EFTAs side is managed by its own institutions. To make sure that the EFTA states that are in the EEA abide by the rules there is an EFTA Surveillance Authority. This monitors whether or not free competition is being followed and that markets are open to businesses from the EU members. Any contravention of the rules by a member state or company can be reported to the EFTA Court for resolution. The EFTA/EEA states are not subject to the European Court of Justice, There exists a separate EFTA Court, officially known as the Court of Justice of the European Free Trade Association States. It only has jurisdiction to interpret the EEA agreement and therefore does not apply to Switzerland which is in EFTA but not the European Economic Area.

An important factor that protects democracy in the EFTA/EEA states is that there are fewer mechanisms by which they can be forced to adopt an EU law. Iceland, Norway, and Liechtenstein are certainly freer than EU members. The laws, especially regulations, made by the institutions of the European Union are the law of the member states. With members of the EFTA members of the European Economic Area the situation is quite different. They are outside of the EU's system and independent of the European Court of Justice. The EEA states, when they choose to adopt EU rules, do not do so as countries that have transferred the making of legislation to the European Union like for instance Britain has. Nations like Norway establish EEA relevant rules at the national level. The legislation is not directly imposed on Iceland, Liechtenstein and Norway by the EU.

Furthermore, the EFTA states that have agreed to be part of the European Economic Area can opt out of areas of EEA where they feel that legislation does not serve their national interest. Inside the EU the UK does not have this right.

Norway has a rather nonchalant attitude to EU legislative instruments. Despite having the right to veto EU rules the UK's Nordic cousins still choose to flout the introduction of laws they do not like. A draft report from the European Commission from 12th December 2012 found that Norway had refused to incorporate into their own law 427 EU legislative acts. The commission bemoans the fact that 'the EEA EFTA side has been reluctant or even, outright opposed, to incorporate EU acts, which the EU legislator has indicated as EEA-relevant upon adoption of the latter (for example, the Norwegian government has publicly stated its refusal to incorporate the Third Postal Directive). EU postal rules were attempting to mandate the deregulation and part privatisation of postal services across the EU and the EEA/EFTA states.

What is more, the implementation of those acts that are not vetoed or ignored is often delayed. The custom of the EFTA states being responsible for drafting the decisions of the EEA Joint Committee often allows them to delay their implementation. The ruse of delaying the translation of the decisions is also regularly used by the Norwegians. The United Kingdom can use similar tactics and exploit the plethora of regional languages, such as Welsh, both Irish and Scottish Gaelic and perhaps even Ulster Scots. Those EEA relevant acts that are not delayed are often altered. The EFTA/EEA states demand that more than a third of the acts, and as many as 4 out of 10 of those which deal with services, are changed. This is not just an opportunity to tailor EEA rules to the EFTA states advantage, it is also in itself yet another source of delay. Negotiations then ensue; this does not speed up the process of implementation.

And because of those rules that are finally enacted by the EFTA members the situation becomes even more inequitable against the interests of the EU. As a result of the proliferation of executive agencies within the EU there is the potential for a higher level of enforcement of EEA relevant rules in the European Union than in EFTA. The states of Iceland, Liechtenstein and Norway have therefore managed to achieve a greater degree of autonomy from the EU than was originally intended by the EEA Agreement. This is certainly not fax democracy.

Whereas over 100,000 EU instructions apply to Britain as of December 2010 only 4,179 EEA relevant acts have been incorporated and are still in force. They are predominantly concerned with; technical regulations, standards, testing and certification (33.6%), veterinary and phytosanitary matters (28.0%), transport (8.6%), statistics (7.2%), Environment (4.8%), Cooperation in programmes and agencies (3.6%). A full list is available from the European Free Trade Association.

What is more, according to EU analyst Dr Richard North, 'more than eighty percent of EEA policy areas fall within the areas dealt with by international bodies.' And in these organisations Norway is often actively participating helping to propose and shape international law at its origin; whereas EU members are often passive recipients following their adoption by the EU. States that are in EFTA/EEA therefore not only have the opportunity to engage at a rule's conception but also modify it at its implementation that is if it hasn't been ignored.

There will not only be much less legislation if Britain leaves the EU and remains in the EEA like Norway but there will also be less legislative confusion. The quandary as to what regulations should apply after the exiting the EU is also resolved by EEA membership. All the EU rules that currently bind Britain that are also relevant to states such as Norway are clearly published as having 'EEA relevance'.

The requirement for financial contributions is a disadvantage of EEA membership even though the costs are not as ruinous as Britain's current ever-increasing EU membership bill. What is more, the costs of the EEA contributions can be off-set against the potential tariffs that may be placed on exports by the EU if the UK unilaterally withdrew. Customs levies will not help job and growth creation in the UK. And against any reciprocal tariffs that may be placed on goods from the states that remain in the EU which will just increase prices for consumers.

Clearly there are costs associated with the European Economic Area but with Britain as a member of both EFTA and the EEA there could be change in the paradigm between Brussels the two organisations. Presumably Britain, in partnership with the current EFTA states, will strive for a better deal that not only allows for lower payments to be made but also for more influence in the development of EU law and perhaps even fewer areas where EU standards apply. This may well be achievable. The European Commission itself acknowledges that if the European Economic Area agreement is updated membership of it 'would offer EEA EFTA countries a convenient "alternative EU Membership-status on an à la carte basis".' The option of leaving the EU and remaining in the EEA and re-joining EFTA therefore has the potential to form the basis for a flexible pick 'n' mix relationship with the EU. The route that has been set out by the British Prime Minister, David Cameron, in his Bloomberg Speech of 22nd January 2013 stated that he would use negotiation to reform the EU and Britain's terms of membership. This met with a cool response on the continent. Yet a flexible relationship can be achieved from outside through existing non-EU institutions.

Choosing to remain in the European Economic Area will also by-pass the risk that a satisfactory withdrawal agreement is not reached with the EU's Council and Parliament. It will strengthen the UK's hand in negotiations by showing that tariff free trade can continue regardless of whether the withdrawal agreement is in place. Alternatively, the UK can attempt to follow the path of another European state that has rejected the EEA model of pan-European economic cooperation. This nation is Switzerland.

The Swiss option
There is much that Switzerland can teach the UK, the Swiss enjoy many advantages that many Eurosceptics look upon with envy. It is a

confederation that successfully practices direct democracy; its citizens, not the European Court of Justice, are truly sovereign. It is time that the British government explored this alternative. It is working for the Swiss. Unemployment in the alpine dominated state is as little as 3%, nearly 10% lower than the EU average. Swiss GDP per head of population averages at €79,033. In terms of GDP according to purchasing power parity Switzerland has a rate of €39,300 whereas the EU has a corresponding average GDP per capita of just €25,200. The Swiss on average make €14,100 euros per year more than their counterparts in the EU. These figures demonstrate that even in real terms, taking into account prices, the Swiss have more than 60% greater purchasing power per capita above the average of the EU.

Switzerland is a member of the European Free Trade Association but stands apart from the other EFTA members as it is not a part of the European Economic Area. Yet they still have full access to the Single Market without being members of it. The Swiss achieve this through free trade agreements. Switzerland is by no means isolated. Whilst they are outside of the responsibilities imposed on EEA members the Swiss do have observer status in the formal EFTA/EEA structure. They actively take advantage of this and through it they can influence EU decision making.

On the face if it this alternative is the Holy Grail; the much talked about free trade agreement. However, Switzerland does not have one simple and straight forward arrangement with the EU it has a whole series of bi-lateral trade arrangements, in fact 120 of them, with the European Union. Together they cover each sector of the economy. The main body of the agreements between the EU and Switzerland were concluded in 1999. The Swiss refer to them as Bilaterals I. They liberalise trade in areas ranging from agriculture to air and land transport. To allow for easier trade they also standardise technical rules. The free movement of people between is also part of Bilaterals I as is access to the public procurement market. Through this 1999 agreement Switzerland also partakes in the EU's research programmes.

There is an FTA on industrial goods dating from 1972 which abolished quotas and customs duties, but not customs checks, between them. There was also a 1989 agreement on companies being able to establish insurance services in each other's territory.

The Swiss relationship is by no means one where they are

quarantined in their mountain republic. In 2004 Switzerland and the EU reached a further accord with Brussels known as Bilaterals II. They have chosen to enhance their co-operation with the EU in areas where they consider that mutual benefit can be obtained. Switzerland is a member of the Schengen agreement which eliminates border controls between the participating states. Britain and Ireland are not members of this, choosing to stay out. Whilst Switzerland is held up as the preferred model no Eurosceptic is advocating this part of their relationship. Through its agreement with the EU Swiss citizens do have the right to enter the UK along with those from the EU and EEA states, such as Norway.

The 2004 agreement also covers rights for asylum seekers. The Swiss ratified the so-called Dublin Regulation (2003/343/CE) on refugees in a referendum in 2005. It also covers pensions, information on the taxation of savings, measures to fight fraud, participation in the EU's media activities, and an agreement on the environment whereby Switzerland comes under the umbrella of the EU's Environment Agency. The participation in the EU's statistical programme is included in this agreement. The Swiss became involved with Europol and in 2008 they joined Eurojust; these two measures encourage police and judicial co-operation between the EU and Switzerland. In 2010 they opted to take part in European Union youth, educational and training programmes.

Whilst Swiss exports must comply with EU rules these trade agreements, apart from in the field of aviation, the FTAs do not involuntarily demand that Switzerland adopts EU law in the same way that Norway is obliged to do so as a member of the European Economic Area. Whereas Switzerland adopts fewer EU rules than EEA members such as Norway; the Norwegians, via the formal structure of the European Economic Area, have a greater input into the development of EU law.

Switzerland however is not totally without a voice. There are fifteen joint committees made up of representatives from the European Commission's directorate for trade with neighbouring countries and from Switzerland's government. They meet to not only discuss issues that arise out of their FTAs including rules of origin relating to products from outside the customs union coming into the EU via Switzerland, and vice-versa, but they also discuss the possibility of imposing EU rules on the confederation. There is meant to be parity between the two but in reality the EU is the first among equals. Whilst there does have to be mutual agreement before EU rules are applied the Commission does have the advantage in negotiations. The economic dominance of the EU's internal market and the common right to cancel the agreements in the event of non-compliance makes Switzerland the junior partner. In some ways it is beginning to almost resemble the relationship that Norway has via the EEA but without the formalised input mechanisms into developing EU law.

Yet many fewer rules are applied to Switzerland than to EU members. Since the start of 1993, when the Single Market came into being, the Swiss have adapted their legal code to bring it into line with just approximately two thousand EU legislative instruments. The UK, along with other EU members, has however had more than 20,000 imposed from above. What is more, there is a major constitutional difference between how EU legislation is enacted. Switzerland is a sovereign state that chooses to make its law in a number of areas compatible with that of the EU. It is not automatically imposed as it is in EU member states.

A significant disadvantage of the Swiss model is that since rejecting the EEA option in a 1992 referendum the bulk of these agreements took a staggering 7 years from then to negotiate before they could be agreed. What is more unlike the UK, Swiss EU relations have been built upon an already existing free trade agreement. Other than member ship of the EEA the UK does not have any existing arrangements that can form the basis of free trade with the EU.

Furthermore, the Brexit will be a geopolitical shock to the EU that may foster resentment and a fear that others will leave the fold. The democratic decision of the Swiss not to formally join the internal market was easily accepted if indeed it was really noticed.

The economic facts are that Swiss businesses are benefitting from the access to the Single Market that their government has negotiated for them. The sheer complexity of the agreements with Switzerland, along with the unsystematic process by which compliance with the EU's rulings are adopted, has created a relationship which the Swiss are mostly happy with but the EU is not. The EU would prefer a system where EU laws are adopted automatically through streamlined architecture rather than the proliferation of committees that can legally ignore the EU's wishes. Whilst the Swiss option is a model that many in Britain aspire to the EU's experience will make them reluctant to enter into precisely the same EEA-light arrangement. The European Union's desire to export its regulations to third countries will lead them to favour establishing with the UK a more formalised system for negotiating and possibly adopting EU law than that which Switzerland has at the moment.

Furthermore, whilst the European Union is mandated to reach trade agreements with its neighbours there is no guarantee that the complex issues surrounding post-EU membership trade with the UK will resolved, at least not in the short term. The clock will therefore dictate that the Swiss model of relations with the EU is therefore an aspiration that does not serve as a viable option that will not guarantee that there will be no economic dislocation in the event of the UK abrogating the treaties. Furthermore, business and the British electorate will not look favourably upon the uncertainty of having to wait until non-tariff trade and freedom of movement as well as capital and services are agreed. Despite this drawback of the so-called Swiss option it is still preferable to the UK's current terms of EU membership. It is also financially advantageous to the Swiss.

The Swiss Federal Council produced a report on Europe. It came to the conclusion that the most advantageous way forward for Swiss dealing with the European Union was not to submit to political integration with the EU but to continue developing the bilateral agreements. The cost comparison was telling. The Europe Report estimated that the cost to the Swiss taxpayer in the 2007 – 2013 period if they continued to follow the case-by-case two-sided negotiation approach was as little as 550 million Swiss Francs per year. This is Switzerland's contribution towards reducing inequality in the enlarged EU which the EEA states contribute to. If, however, Switzerland joined the European Economic Area (EEA) the costs to the taxpayer would have increased to 730 million Swiss Francs per annum. Full EU membership would financially be the worst option. Their gross contribution to the EU coffers would increase to 4.9 billion Swiss Francs, a nine fold increase. The net cost would have been 3.4 billion Swiss Francs per year. This excludes the cost of the inevitable increase in EU legislation.

In the long-term the UK should look towards achieving a free trade agreement(s) with the EU and the Swiss show what can be accomplished even by a small nation whose economy is far more dependent upon trade with the EU than the UK. Despite reticence from the EU, the UK should, in theory, be able to negotiate and conclude a more favourable relationship than that which the Swiss have at present.

The deep dependency that the Swiss have on trade with the EU, 60% of the Swiss economy compared to less than 10% of the UK's, shows what can be achieved even when the European Union has the stronger negotiating position. The Swiss need access to EU markets far more than European governments need theirs. And, the massively indebted EU member's, again did not benefit from a tax haven on their borders. Yet, the Swiss have achieved in under a decade of negotiation from without a relationship many in the UK would like but have so far been unable to deliver from within after more than 40 years of membership. For the time being they have free trade without surrendering formal political supremacy to the institutions in Brussels.

The Swiss manage to benefit from all that the four freedoms that are often associated with the EU have to offer without having to abandon their unique democracy and their self-government and political independence. The Swiss have jealously guarded their sovereignty for the past 700 years. In fact they have done so ever since a group of citizen soldiers drove out an army of Austrian Habsburg mounted knights at the point of their pikes and halberds at the Battle of Morgarten on 15th November 1315. The Austrians were serving one of the first incarnations of European unity – the Holy Roman Empire. At this battle the Swiss revolutionised mediaeval warfare, ending the hitherto superiority of cavalry at the same time as securing their confederacy's freedom. The Swiss are again facing pressure from the EU to change their relationship with Brussels so that they conform more automatically to EU judgements; this they are currently resisting.

Switzerland is not the only example of a country with a free trade agreement with the EU. There are 45 other nations that have preferential trade agreements with the European Union. Amongst some smaller territories these include countries as far afield as Colombia, Chile, Honduras, Mexico, Nicaragua, Panama, Peru, South Africa, South Korea and Zimbabwe. Perhaps they, with their limited economic dependency on trade with the EU, these are more like the UK and as such are better examples of what can and is being achieved.

And this is without the burden of EU membership being placed upon those states.

Clearly they are not neighbours of the EU and therefore Articles 3 and 8 of the Treaty on European Union, which legally requires the EU to negotiate free and fair trade with non-EU countries, do not apply. Yet the EU has done so. It has negotiated these FTAs because it recognises the economic importance of free trade. It is logical to conclude that in time the EU will make such an agreement with Britain.

Other countries have taken yet another course to gain access to the Single Market and have achieved this without having to belong to the EEA or negotiate a series of complex free trade agreements. This is the option of remaining in the EU's customs union.

The Turkey option: Remain in the customs union on a new basis

As a member of the European Union the UK has no choice but to remain in the EU's customs union. Whereas there are no tariffs between its members this customs union does produce costs for the UK; its external tariff means that imports are more expensive. As the UK is a trading nation this is particularly expensive for British consumers. Furthermore, the EU's focus on agricultural protection means that households are paying much more for their food than they otherwise should be. The UK imports a significant amount from outside of the EU and thus has to overcome these tariffs and the manipulation of prices caused by the Common Agricultural Policy. Remaining in the customs union also has an opportunity cost. Members cannot negotiate their own trade agreements with states outside of the EU; instead they have to accept what the EU provides for them.

However, being inside the customs union means that whilst tariffs apply the EU's aggressive anti-dumping policy on imports does not. Being free from this form of protectionism will mean that the higher prices that British consumers can face on selected imports that the EU thinks are priced too cheaply will not apply. This makes the option of remaining in the customs union more attractive. If continuing membership of the European Economic Area proves to be unobtainable or is considered undesirable by the powers that be then the option of remaining in the EU's customs should be considered.

This is the Turkey option.

The predominantly Muslim state is a growing power with a rapidly growing population. In 2011 its number began to approach 74 million. By 2023 it is expected to have more than 84 million residents. It will therefore have a larger population than the EU's most populous member state - Germany. Turkey did have pretentions of joining the European Union yet opposition from inside France and Germany to full membership has led to Turkey being offered membership of the customs union. This status was achieved on 31st December 1995. Along with EU members Turkey is part of the trade alliance that allows it to export to the EU with little let or hindrance with the EU's external tariff applying to imports into Turkey from states that are outside of the customs union. This access to the EU's Single Market applies for all produce bar non-processed agricultural goods. The European Union's public procurement and service markets have also not been opened up to Turkey.

Incidentally, Turkey's dealings with the European Free Trade Association have been straight forward. In 1991 a tree trade agreement was signed between EFTA and Turkey, this is still in force. It abolishes barriers to trade between Iceland, Liechtenstein, Norway, Switzerland and Turkey. They have not needed to establish complex customs unions to achieve a mutually beneficial goal.

Other states that are out of the EU's immediate orbit but belong to the customs union are San Marino, Monaco, and Andorra. The Principality of the Valleys of Andorra like Turkey has agricultural products excluded from the agreement whilst the other micro-states do not.

The exclusion of agricultural products will not be as negative for the UK as it is for Turkey which faces high tariffs of items such as olive oil which makes exporting these products to the Single Market deeply uncompetitive, especially when trying to compete with home grown EU produce. Though it will hurt the few sectors of the British economy that export food stuffs to the continent it will also have a beneficial effect. Presuming that Britain will not adopt a policy of agricultural protectionism and will re-open its markets to goods produced in developing nations perhaps those from the Commonwealth then there will be a benefit for British families. Food prices in Britain, especially those imported from outside of the EU, will be lower. Interestingly this may also prove popular with French farmers. They will appreciate the lack of competition from the UK allowing them to charge their customers more, whilst at the same time helping consumers in the UK. This is a deal that may be popular in both Paris and London.

The customs union does make sense for the Turkish economy as trade with the EU has a great deal of symmetry. According to the European Commission, 'Turkey's exports to the EU are mostly machinery and transport equipment, followed by manufactured goods... EU exports to Turkey are dominated by machinery and transport material, chemical products and manufactured goods.'

A similarity with Britain's trade relationship with the EU is that Turkey has a large annual trade deficit with the European Union member states. In 2012 this amounted to nearly €27.4 billion. However, much of this can be accounted for by the fact that the proceeds of sales to the European Union are re-invested in purchasing more industrial products from the EU for use in Turkey's development. What is more, as the Turkish economy establishes a more sizeable manufacturing base of its own the reliance on EU commodities will end.

Despite the imbalance in trade between Turkey and the EU membership of the customs union is working for Turkey. They have access to what is still the largest, in terms of GDP, internal market in the world without have to import the entire acquis communitaire, the massive body of EU rules and regulations. They just have to implement a proportion that relates to their main area of trade. No doubt this is a factor in Turkey's amazing economic growth which outshines levels within the EU. Turkey is also outside of the EU's VAT area which means that Brussels' version of a sales tax is not forced upon the Turkish Republic. This gives the near-eastern state control over its own indirect taxation policy.

Apart from the deficit there are, however, other aspects of the Turkey option that the UK will not want to emulate. Turkey has had to adopt aspects of EU law particularly in the area of industrial standards. Although Turkey is a member of the Euro-Mediterranean partnership and whereas an EU-Turkey Association exists there is in reality little effective input into the formulation of the rules which the EU asks Turkey to apply. Furthermore, Article 8 of the agreement which finalises the customs union gives the EU, via the association, influence over Turkish law. It states, 'Turkey shall incorporate into its internal legal order the Community instruments relating to the removal of technical barriers to trade.' This especially relates to EU 'instruments deemed to be of particular importance.' Furthermore, Article 66 mandates that the agreement must conform to the European Court of Justice's rulings. Yet Turkey does not have representation on this institution.

Whilst Britain is already in the customs union, exiting the EU would automatically mean leaving this trade arrangement. Therefore Britain will have to negotiate with the EU if it wishes to remain in the customs union. Presumably the other non-EU parties to trade agreements with the European Union will give their acquiescence as Britain was part of their deal with the EU when the trade links were established. However, even though EU policy mandates that such trade agreement should be reached it is by no means certain that the EU will consent to the UK remaining in the customs union after Brexit.

Whereas it will be in the EU's interest to keep trade open with the EU there may be considerable consternation at keeping continental markets open to British producers under such an agreement. As the UK will be able to repeal many EU and EEA relevant rules, which are acknowledged as a burden on industry, Britain will be able to become a low regulation and thus a low cost producer. This will give British manufacturers a competitive advantage. However, as such there will be less incentive for the EU to agree to this and negotiations to achieve it may prove to be drawn out if not another cul-de-sac. The EU may therefore demand that the UK adopts aspects of EU law as a price of remaining in the customs union.

If it does prove to be feasible then Britain, unlike Turkey, should be able to have the trade rules apply to all sectors of the EU Single Market. And likewise the EU will have access to all areas of the British economy. However, it will be difficult to escape from the EU's demands for a legislative level playing field.

There are benefits to the UK of staying in the customs union. Trade can continue unabated not just between Britain and remaining EU states but also between the UK and the many nations around the globe who have negotiated trade agreements with the European Union. The option of staying in the customs union will mean that the EU's external tariff will continue to apply to the UK, that prevents levies being imposed and stops rules of origin becoming a problem. However, under this alternative anti-dumping action can then be taken against British exporters as it can in theory against those from Turkey. Perhaps more importantly the European Commission will continue to negotiate the UK's trade policy subject to the agreement of the European Council – now with less British input. It will also mean that the UK will not be able to negotiate new trade agreements and take advantage of the opportunities in emerging markets around the globe. Nor will the UK be able to make alliances in the World Trade Organisation that better suit the UK's interests. If a future British government thinks that it can negotiate for the UK a trade deal that surpasses anything the EU can provide for Britain then the option of remaining just as a member of the customs union becomes less attractive.

As part of the positive case for leaving the EU is made on the grounds of exploiting the benefits of trade deals with the quickly developing nations, in particular those in Asia, staying in the customs union will undermine one of the main planks of the Eurosceptic campaign. However, it does solve the fears that Europhiles raise about losing trade links with the EU. Commerce with what will remain for the foreseeable future a vitally important market will be able to continue. Membership of the customs union also resolves rules of origin issues. In any free trade agreement with another state the EU is concerned that imports will be brought into its market from a third country which is not a signatory to the free trade area. This by-passes the customs duties. A common external tariff and trade policy eliminates this 'risk'.

Both the customs union and the European Economic Area offer undeniable access to the Single Market but what is best option? Leaving the EU and remaining in the customs union, also has the additional benefit of making the UK free from more regulations emanating from Brussels; an advantage that the EEA option cannot fully claim. However, just being in the customs union does not offer any formal process of influencing the rules of the EU's internal market. The EU and EEA members however retain this right.

To determine which option offers the UK the best option for the future, an evaluation of the costs of the limited number of regulations applying to the EEA members needs to be compared with the even more limited amount of EU laws that Britain may be asked to be subject to. The regulatory costs of the European Economic Area and the financial contribution that has to be made to it also needs to be compared with the charging of customs levies on goods destined for Britain from outside of the EU and the opportunity cost of not being able to reach our own trade agreements.

Perhaps Britain is better placed to exploit other alternative options. Arguably the UK's ability to explore new trade links with the rest of the world is being retarded by the EU's control over Britain's trade policy. Developing nations will open up their markets to goods from Europe if the EU ends its protection of agriculture. In such circumstances the UK may well be better off out of the customs union but only if the UK can have a free trade deal with the EU or access to the Single Market via the EEA.

There is also another consideration; before deciding which path to follow an assessment through preliminary informal discussions needs to be made as to which is the most likely to be achieved. Britain is already a member of the European Economic Area and can keep this status with little practical difficulty. Attaining just membership of the customs union will require a negotiation. The EEA is the safer option as such a status can be routinely achieved. What is more, the UK will be better able to predict which legislation the EU may wish for Britain to adopt.

However, what if Brussels refuses to play ball?

No agreement

There exists the possibility that there will not be an accord between Britain and the EU. A free trade deal may not be completed and either Britain's application to EFTA is rejected or the UK chooses not to join the European Economic Area .In this, unlikely but theoretical, scenario tariffs would have to be applied against British produce. Could the British economy survive if no agreement were reached as well as it could if one of the other alternatives were adopted?

The World Trade Organisation will protect Britain's right to export to the remaining EU states and go part of the way to safeguarding Britain's interests. Yet, even though the average tariff is little more than 1% placed on the cost of a product imported from a country outside of a trade arrangement there are still parts of the British economy that will be disadvantaged by levies placed on imports to the continent. Customs duties remain significant in some areas and not just the automotive industry. So can Britain mitigate those costs? Providing subsidies to businesses who export goods who are being hit by trade tariffs is not an option. Subsidies to meet export targets are prohibited under Word Trade Organisation rules. Such an approach merely runs the risk of provoking a complaint from the EU to the WTO allowing the EU to take counter-measures on British products sold into the Single Market.

Costs to exporters can be reduced in different ways. Exiting the European Union without an agreement does have one clear benefit. There will be little obligation on the UK to adopt further EU rules. Reducing the regulatory burden will be like offering some businesses a tax cut. Yet, existing legislation that has already been imposed will most probably be retained until it is reviewed and in some cases then repealed. Whilst EU tariff barriers to trade will apply instantly, the process of abolishing excessive red-tape will take years to complete. What is more, without an agreement there will be less of an opportunity for the UK have influence over the rules of the Single Market.

In time some of the harm can be off-set by the UK seeking to enhance economic competitiveness by embarking on a program of radical regulatory reform. What is more, a self-governing Britain will be able to reinvest the financial savings of leaving the EU in the economy. This can either be done through increasing spending on infrastructure and housing; or it can be achieved through tax cuts to the least well-off, which will then be spent in the local economy, boosting growth.

Off-setting harm is sub-optimal when compared to maximising potential. It seems that in the immediate future Britain is best served by reducing the level of regulations, and payments to the European structural funds at the same time as having tariff free trade with the Single Market. There is little doubt that such an agreement with the EU can be reached, one which offers tariff free access to the EU's internal market with much less regulation.

No agreement does have the benefit that the UK will be able to enter into future trade alliances with nations that better reflect Britain's interests and world outlook. Where nations have similar economic interests they are more likely to seek mutually beneficial trade policies.

This is a more rational approach to international trade relations than simply aligning with the nearest geopolitical bloc. However, forming new agreements will be a time consuming process. What is more, the no alternative agreement option ignores the fact that there are significant economies in an already existing association that have remarkable similarities to Britain. These are the two main states in EFTA, Norway and Switzerland. Both share with the UK a similar cultural liberal-democratic culture. Economically, they also correspond to the UK.

Norwegian economic success is built on; the production of chemicals, fishing and the extraction of both gas and oil. Norway also has a significant maritime industry. Switzerland has strengths that include; biotechnology, engineering, finance and pharmaceuticals. These are all strengths that the British economy benefits from. Once the UK is out of the EU the UK's fishing waters can be reclaimed and better managed like they are in Norway; rejuvenating an industry which has the potential to be worth in excess of £3 billion per year.

When considering all the alternatives to the EU, all will allow for the UK to be fully engaged with the international UN sponsored bodies that are increasingly setting regulations. However, the option of the customs union does not give the UK independent input into the WTO. And only the EEA/EFTA alternative keeps the UK at the heart of discussions in the European Union. Whilst the bespoke arrangement of a series of free trade agreements like the Swiss option may be preferable in the long term it will take time to deliver. Membership of the EEA is, however, an off-the-shelf almost instantly accessible alternative to the EU which offers much of what the UK has been publically saying it wants from 'Europe.' That is economic cooperation and trade without surrendering the micro-management of the nation to an interfering EU which is continuing to amass power in areas that have little to no relationship to jobs, growth, and prosperity. The fact that the rest of the world is growing, especially the countries in the Commonwealth and EFTA, shows that EU policies may actually be deeply prejudicial to the economy.

The European Economic Area may not be the perfect scenario; but membership of it can be categorised as 70% better than EU membership. It has the benefits of access to the Single Market and continuing influence over its development. Whilst at the same time reducing regulation by as much as $^2/_3$ and allowing for trade opportunities such as with the Commonwealth to be explored and enhanced. In the worst case scenario EFTA/EEA membership can simply serve as a transitional arrangement whilst the free trade agreements are negotiated and concluded. At which point Britain can exit the EEA; probably without fuss or fanfare as few have actually heard of it. Perhaps, however, with Britain as a member EFTA may grow in stature and have more authority in its negotiations with the EU. Other countries such as EFTA's original members may follow the UK's example by leaving the EU and re-joining the European Free Trade Association. The Republic of Ireland, a nation whose economy is more aligned to the rest of the world than to continental Europe, may also choose to join EFTA.

The modern, and perhaps brief, phenomenon of the UK – a global nation – seeking just a Eurocentric future has led to Britain failing to take advantage of other opportunities that lay outside of the continent of Europe. Can an alternative to the EU be found in the rest of the world?

The Commonwealth of Nations: Out of the European Union into the world

The economist Roger Bootle has said that 'In global terms, the EU is most assuredly in the slow lane. If we weren't in it already, surely this is a club we shouldn't want to join.' Furthermore, John Cridland, the Direcor General of the Confederation of British Industry, said in November 2011; "We've concentrated too much on Europe – we need to get out and build export markets in the rest of the world".

Which club is best suited to help the UK take advantage of new opportunities around the globe?

When the UK joined the EEC, and its customs union, in 1973 Britain did not just turn its back on its trade links with the EFTA states. The UK also abandoned its traditional economic ties and formal trade preferences with the Commonwealth upon joining the European project.

The Commonwealth, like EFTA, is an intergovernmental organisation which does not compromise its member's sovereignty. Whilst Queen Elizabeth II is the Head of the Commonwealth, its member states do not have to adopt the monarch as their Head of State.

What is more, the position of Head of the Commonwealth is not a hereditary one and is not automatically the preserve of the Sovereign of Britain and the other realms.

The main decision making body are Prime Ministers and Presidents of its member states. They formally meet on a biennial basis as the Commonwealth Heads of Government Meeting (CHOGM). This is supported by the Commonwealth Secretariat. This is based in London. Its role is to facilitate cooperation between the member states, organise meetings, and assists the development of policy amongst the Commonwealth members. The Secretariat also helps countries implementing the decisions and policies of the Commonwealth that have been established at the Commonwealth Heads of Government Meetings. The Commonwealth Secretary-General is the head of the Secretariat. This position is elected by the Heads of Government. Interestingly the Commonwealth Secretariat has Observer status at the United Nations. This gives the Commonwealth the right to speak at the UN's General Assembly meetings. It can also take part in votes on procedural matters and to sign and even sponsor United Nation's resolutions.

The Commonwealth is much more than one organisation. It is also an already existing and active network that is underpinned by a host of Commonwealth Family non-governmental organisations that seek to strengthen ties between the members and enhance cooperation and development in the fields of broadcasting, business, education, sport and importantly the law.

The Commonwealth in economic terms does already achieve a lot. What is more, this is on a limited budget. The Secretariat's budget is just around £15 million with contributions shared between the member states according to their ability to contribute. The Commonwealth Youth Programme (CYP) which helps young people in many member countries, and thus assists with the delivery of future development goals, has a budget of less than £3 million. This too is divided up fairly between the affiliates.

The Commonwealth also has the Commonwealth Fund for Technical Co-operation (CFTC). This establishes a network of Commonwealth experts that helps members that need the assistance with matters ranging from; international trade issues, including negotiations at the World Trade Organisation. It also helps with encouraging economic competitiveness and development in a whole host of areas. These range from; fostering investment, to advancing technology and to enabling the development of energy resources in both terms of renewables and natural resources. To create an environment where economic growth can take place this Commonwealth fund also helps member states draft legislation and enhance legislation to deliver more dynamism for growth.

This is on an annual budget of just £29 million. The CFTC does not operate on a top-down basis like the European Union, where member states have to adopt EU standards and international policies. Instead it offers advice and assistance. Another difference with the European Union is that contributions to the Commonwealth Fund for Technical Co-operation are voluntary.

The finances of the Commonwealth contrast sharply with those of the European Union. And one wonders what the Commonwealth of Nations could achieve if it benefitted from just a proportion of the largesse that the Brussels bureaucracy extracts from its member states.

Many of the fastest growing emerging markets in the world are members of the Commonwealth. These include notable fast developing states such as; Kenya, India, Pakistan and South Africa. Even the established economies of Australia and Canada are also continuing to grow. Both those Anglophone states weathered the 2008 international financial storm, and its aftermath, well.

Its membership includes 54 countries stretching across every inhabited continent on the planet; even Europe where the UK is not the only member. Both Malta and Cyprus are members of the Commonwealth.

The population of the Commonwealth is nearly two and a quarter billion people, approaching a third of the world's population, living on more than eleven and a half million square miles; nearly a quarter of the earth's land mass. What is more, this territory is rich in natural resources, which not only provide the global economy with the commodities that enable growth but can also give its member states real potential. Presently, the Chinese are forging links with these resource rich states; the UK's Eurocentric orientation is making Britain miss out on abundant opportunities abroad.

Currently the UK is not only prevented from creating its own specific bilateral investment treaties on its own terms with

Commonwealth countries, but the EU also prevents the UK from reaching trade agreements with these tigers. Interestingly, none of the other alternatives to the EU prevent the UK from exploring the option of a revitalised Commonwealth. This option is only excluded if the UK chooses to remain in the EU's customs union.

Perhaps there is scope to explore options for a revitalised Commonwealth in which Britain should take the lead in the formation of a Commonwealth Free Trade Area. Movements are already underway amongst some Commonwealth citizens to create a commonwealth free trade association and cement links between member states.

In 2005 a Canadian author called Brent Cameron wrote a book titled The Case for Commonwealth Free Trade. Here he stated that,

'If the Commonwealth today were an economic bloc, it would be equal in size to the United States; it would have 13 of the world's fastest growing economies; it would possess most of the world's leading knowledge economies outside of the US; it would have one third of the world's population; and would represent 40 per cent of the membership of the World Trade Organisation.'

If the UK will focus on helping to develop the Commonwealth as a trade association it will be working in a legal and commercial culture which the UK can easily fit into. The Commonwealth, as a trade association, will be more suited to many aspects that are shared between Britain and the Commonwealth; yet are not generic between the Uk and the EU. The English language is widely used, this makes trade even easier. Yet at present the UK is disbarred from entering into trade agreements with Britain's co-linguists. The homogeneity extends beyond language. The legal system used in many of these states is based upon English Common Law which is seen as placing individual rights at the heart of the legal system. Anything that is not specifically banned is allowed. This custom contrasts with the Corpus Juris Civilis tradition developed by the Byzantine Emperor Justinian I. This formed the basis for the Code Napoleon which in turn has inspired the legal systems of many countries in continental Europe.

Decisions derived in Common Law jurisdictions have an effect on developing the law in states that use the same system. Whilst these decisions will not form legally binding precedent in another state they can and do have an obiter dicta (things said by the way) effect. This gives rulings in other countries the opportunity to inform or guide future decision making in the Common Law family of countries. It is therefore almost an international open source system that can adapt and learn from other occurrences in other countries; important in a quickly developing world where new commercial opportunities are continually evolving.

Enhancing the body of knowledge surrounding the law is not just a matter of convenience. Common Law is seen as the basis for the commercial success of the states that use it. Rather than providing a broad and at times ambiguous set of principles, as in continental law, common law offers clear guidelines. The Anglo-Saxon system sets specific stipulations of what cannot be done; this provides businesses with surety as to the legal environment that they are operating. This means that a business can make commercial decisions safe in the knowledge that they will not breach the law or suffer at the whims of a politicised judgement. Many Commonwealth members have also accepted this Anglo-Saxon tradition of property rights, a concept that is a pre-requisite for growth and one that many European states have not always respected. The EU bail-in of bank deposits in the Commonwealth and EU state of Cyprus in March 2013 – where funds were seized – is underwritten by EU Directive 2012/0150 COD and will be a template for future confiscations of capital.

Exiting the European Union and enhancing links with the Commonwealth will not only disentangle the UK from the growing influence of Corpus Juris but also enhance links with nations that Britain has more in common with such as Australia, Canada and New Zealand. The Commonwealth network also extends beyond its own membership. It has members that belong to other international organisations such as the North American Free Trade Association, through Canada, and the Association of Southeast Asian Nations, through Malaysia and Singapore. And via Guyana into the South American free trade area known as Mercosur. Guyana, along with other Commonwealth states, is also a member of the Caribbean Community (CARICOM).

Not all Commonwealth members had been part of the British Empire. States such as Namibia joined though its links to South Africa, Papua New Guinea through its traditional ties to Australia and Samoa via New Zealand. Mozambique joined in 1995. Rwanda, recognising the economic benefits of the Commonwealth, became a member in 2009 even though it had been previously a German and then Belgium colony. The President of Rwanda, Paul Kagame, explained his country's reason for joining;

"We hope to tap into the trade and investment opportunities that the Commonwealth offers so that Rwanda can expand its economy and effectively participate in the global marketplace."

President Kagame is not alone. The Indian Urban Development Minister, Kamal Nath, stated in 2010 that,

"The Commonwealth is the ideal platform for business and trade ... I hope that India's ties with the Commonwealth will move from strength to strength, and that the new paradigm will only mean greater warmth, greater cooperation."

India is a fast growing and increasingly sizeable economy. Unlike China its population of 1.241 billion people will continue to grow as will its significant middle-class. According to the respected global management consultants, McKinsey & Company, the Indian middle-class will by 2025 number 583 million. Incidentally, this important sector of the Indian economy alone will be much greater than the current declining population of the European Union.

Research shows that a Commonwealth effect that expands investment and increases trade between its members above and beyond what would normally be expected already exists. This expands economic activity between Commonwealth member states even when 'regional trade agreements or geographical proximity are taken into account.'

What is more, research by the Royal Commonwealth Society shows that 'there is a clear relationship between Commonwealth membership and increased trade and investment.' This benefit is significant. The Commonwealth effect already gives a real advantage to its members.

'The value of trade is likely to be a third to a half more between Commonwealth member states compared to pairs of countries where one or both are not Commonwealth members. This effect can be seen even after controlling for a range of other factors that might also explain trade patterns.'

Clearly the Commonwealth can and does have a future with trade at its heart. And over the past two decades trade between commonwealth countries has risen by over a quarter. And this is achieved before the trade association is in place.

As the Royal Commonwealth Society argues if the research does indeed confirm that the Commonwealth is, 'an under-utilised resource which is able to be leveraged, then the possibilities of realising growth potential throughout the Commonwealth could be improved.' A Commonwealth Free Trade Association will build on the existing links that already enhance economic growth for its members.

Not all Commonwealth states will want to engage at first in such a free trade association. However, many may well appreciate the UK returning to the fold and the commercial opportunities this will offer them. Resentment caused through the EU's one sided trade deals with the African, Caribbean and Pacific Group of States will help Britain's case. EU trade policy has for many years acted in a prejudicial manner against their agricultural exports to the European Union.

Developments in international trade and growth may well in time change the power dynamic that the EU has been able to exert over developing nations. The Commonwealth share of GDP is set to overtake the European Union, what is more according to the IMF and World Economics population growth in the Commonwealth alone will increase by around twice as much as the population of the entire EU. By 2050 the world may be very different and it will make strategic sense for the UK to align with this group rather than to be subsumed within the Eurasian bloc.

Incidentally there are four states in the United States of America that do not describe themselves as states. Instead they call themselves Commonwealths. These are; Kentucky, Massachusetts, Pennsylvania and Virginia. It is not as yet proposed to readmit these back into the current Commonwealth of Nations organisation.

Whilst it is true that Britain had lost an empire but failed to find a role in the world, a factor in the decision to join the EU, the empire, however, did leave a potentially valuable legacy. This is the Commonwealth. Reinvigorating this will for the first time in four decades give Britain the potential for a leading role in what can become an important trade organisation. It was hoped that membership of the EEC and later the EU would deliver a suitable leading role for the UK. However, Britain's diminishing influence in the European Union shows that EU membership has not given the UK the position of importance which was once hoped. The EU remains dominated by the Franco-German axis.

Advocating and achieving a Commonwealth Free Trade Area will give the UK the bigger say in the world which it has sought since decolonisation. Such a position in international affairs and a positive role for a nation lost at sea since Macmillan abandoned the UK's global vision and sought a Eurocentric future, which even supporters of the EU can recognise has been far from happy, can be realised by looking to Britain's moat. The seas around the UK once guarded Britain from Europe's authoritarian tendencies and for several centuries it has served as a pathway to growing markets overseas many of which Britain originally established and nurtured. It is time to look again at the possibilities that exist overseas.

As the former British Prime Minister, the late Baroness Thatcher, wrote;

"That such an unnecessary and irrational project as building a European superstate was ever embarked upon will seem in future years to be perhaps the greatest folly of the modern era. And that Britain, with her traditional strengths and global destiny, should ever have been part of it will appear a political error of historic magnitude. There is, though, still time to choose a different and a better course."

This can be the Commonwealth. What is more, it can form part of a bigger picture that does not prevent the UK remaining in the European Economic Area and EFTA. What is more, like EFTA and the EEA, the Commonwealth is an organisation that is already in existence. Using its structures and links will be preferable to re-inventing the wheel. The trade benefits are already in existence for those countries that are free to develop their own trade policies. It is time that the UK took a fresh look at the Commonwealth of Nations and recognise that this will be the future for British trade. And as the Commonwealth develops a liberalised trade policy Ireland may join this institution as well. This will not only have an economic benefit for all concerned; it will also have the potential to help with reconciliation between the troubled parts of the British Isles.

Conclusion

"If Britain must choose between Europe and the open sea, she must always choose the open sea."
Prime Minister Sir Winston Churchill MP, 11th May 1953

National sovereignty has become national suzerainty. The distinction is rarely understood, and even more rarely discussed. In effect once independent nation-states now have limited autonomy and have become vassals of the European Union to which they must pay tribute.

For many continental countries democracy was just an interregnum. Many European nations as we know them emerged only relatively recently; Germany was founded in 1871, Italy was unified by 1866. Many states in Eastern Europe emerged after the chaos of World War One. Few enjoyed liberty for long. Most of the history of Europe has consisted of multi-national empires, not all of which were created by force. Some were created through established rights of succession passing a province to a foreign prince or potentate. This led to many occasions where power rested with elites who had little or no connection to the nationality that they governed - sometimes from afar.

Democracy was established for much of Europe when first the Nazi and then the much later Soviet occupation over their multi-national empire ceased in the late 1980s and early 1990s. Power however has now been ceded from national democracies to the distant institutions of the European Union essentially ending any semblance of national democracy. The status quo ante has been restored. What is more, the growth of supranational governance now grips the few European nation-states that were once bastions of freedom and limited government answerable to its citizens not to a distant elite. To the same extent as in Central and Eastern Europe; democracy has also been diminished in the northern European states of the Netherlands, Denmark, Sweden and Finland just as it has in the UK.

However, liberal nationalism that created and preserved many of the national democracies what we know today in Europe was the most important ideological force during the twentieth century. This reasoned belief in the nation was specifically the desire of a people to be self-governing and ruled according to their own laws and by their own institutions and not by those that are perceived to be from a different and unwelcome transnational polity. This desire for national freedom was a positive force for good as exemplified by the still relatively recent struggles against both Nazism and Communist tyranny on the Continent of Europe.

The nature of the modern adversary of national sovereignty, the bureaucratic class, is in no way comparable to the authoritarianism of some ideologies spawned on the continent. However, for the sake of those without jobs active liberal nationalism is once again needed to restrain the excesses of European political elites. Governance by far away institutions that are unresponsive to the diverse needs of the governed has created an economic catastrophe that has betrayed a generation to unemployment. Once some European nations traded democracy for dictatorship on the false prospectus that they would deliver prosperity; the EU made a similar promise. Yet, just like the undemocratic regimes that preceded it the EU has failed to be of economic benefit; moving power from accountable institutions to a sclerotic unreformable centralised system that operates beyond effective democratic oversight.

There is now a widening gulf between the institutions of the EU and the lives of the people which it has a growing influence over. This chasm will challenge Brussels' hegemony. The compact between the EU and the people, protecting and enhancing their economic well-being, is being undermined by the failure of the euro and the inability to meet the challenge of emerging economies of Brazil, India and China. The many failures of one-size-fits-all will inevitability lead to more opposition to the EU and a backlash against ever closer union.

History did not stop with the fall of the Berlin Wall and the collapse of communism. The issue of European, indeed global, centralisation versus preserving or enhancing national democracy is the great debate of our time. Whilst the European Union is far from being a totalitarian state, it is equally far from being either representative of its peoples or a direct democracy.

Apart from keeping some countries out of the EU, those who oppose the EU have achieved little in terms of practical public policy results. The debate however has dramatically shifted. Once to even state that Britain should never join the Single Currency was to invite accusations of extremism. Now, the UK's very membership of the EU is being called into question.

Some still call for reform, but changing the EU from within has so far proved to be impossible. The founding fathers of what became the European Union always intended it to be much more, a political union of overly powerful politicians and international bureaucrats. Internal reforms is simply impossible.

The faux reform strategy is still being played out. The British Prime Minister David Cameron recently claimed a victory at the 25th October 2013 meeting of the European Council. The PM argued that Barroso, the President of the Commission, had been persuaded into adopting Cameron's cutting red-tape agenda. The reality is that proposals to reduce bureaucracy had been brought forward by the European Commission which had actually won the support of David Cameron. Not vice versa. What is more, the proposals to reduce red tape will actually involve the combining of regulations and will give the Commission a further opportunity to 'gold-plate' their own legislation and build on the existing body of EU law.   Such is EU 'reform'.

Instead of calling for reform of the European Union it is better to look outside of the box and call for an expansion of the European Free Trade Association, which Britain can re-join, and for reform of the European Economic Area. Instead of pretending that the European Union can dramatically change in order to suit Britain's needs it is time to give serious consideration to alternatives to the EU. And the fact is that there are real alternative opportunities for Britain to explore in Europe and beyond.

Britain will be much better off in a reformed EFTA/EEA arrangement where the members of this EU-out group have perhaps more autonomy from Single Market legislation rule making and/or more influence over its formulation.

This can be achieved if Britain leaves the EU and re-joins the European Free Trade Association. Under the original conception of the European Economic Area, those states that were to be in the internal market but outside of the EU were to have co-decision over regulation. The UK realigning its international position can lead to this change.

Joining with Norway and forming and building on the existing group of EU-out states can lead to a new group of nations ranging from Ireland to the other Scandinavian states. Taking the long view, this is recreating the pre-1066 political arrangement. This was a time when North-Western European states were closely aligned politically, economically and socially and were quite independent of continental doctrines. Before Britain joined the EEC as the EU was then known trade with the Commonwealth and EFTA were compatible. They can be again. Yet membership of the EU is incompatible with a global Britain.

Perhaps EU will collapse before the UK exits leaving Britain as the only EU member, then the fun can begin. Until such time the UK has a choice; either to stay in the EU and try and balance France, Germany and the other interest groups that favour more centralisation or alternatively to try and arrest the development of the EU from outside and be an example to other European states, showing them that there is an alternative to EU Federalism. We have been here before.

As Pitt said all those years ago. "England has saved herself by her exertions, and will, as I trust, save Europe by her example." If Britain takes the right route she could again save herself by her actions, and Europe by her example.

The choice will ultimately be yours in a national referendum.

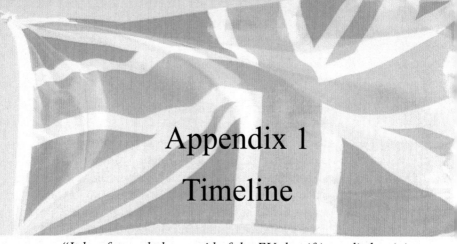

Appendix 1
Timeline

"It has famously been said of the EU that if it applied to join itself, it wouldn't get in. The EU doesn't meet the democratic criteria it demands of its members."
Larry Siedentop, political philosopher, from his book *Democracy in Europe*

1950
The Vision of a European Federation On 9th May the French Foreign Minister, Robert Schuman, made what became known as the Schuman Declaration. This called for a supranational higher authority above the governments of the European states. The 9th May has since been adopted as 'Europe Day.'

1951
The European Coal and Steel Community (ECSC) is formed The Treaty of Paris is signed by Luxembourg, Belgium, France, Italy, the Netherlands and West Germany. It ends tariffs and restrictions on imports on the trade of coal, iron ore and steel. It also handed decision making in these industries to a supranational authority.

1955
The Messina Conference Jean Monnet, a French economist and diplomat, convenes the Messina Conference which ran from 1st to 3rd June in the Sicilian city. Monnet was campaigning for the creation of the European Economic Community (EEC).

1957
The Treaty of Rome This creates the European Economic Community (EEC). The first goal according to the treaty's preamble was to 'lay the foundations of an ever closer union among the peoples of Europe.'

1958
The three European Communities On 1st January 1958 the EEC and Euratom come into force and exist alongside the European Coal and Steel Community.
The Common Agricultural Policy founded A policy to fund the French agricultural industry at the expense of first the German and later the British and German taxpayer.

1960
Britain leads in the creation of an alternative to EU Membership The European Free Trade Association (EFTA) was formed. This created free trade between its participants, Austria, Britain, Denmark, Norway, Portugal, Sweden and Switzerland. However, it did not have the supra-national aspirations of the EEC.

1961
Britain, Denmark and Ireland apply to join the EEC Searching for a post-Imperial role for Britain, British Prime Minister Harold Macmillan applies for Britain to join the EEC.

1963
France Rejects British membership On 14th January 1963 President De Gaulle of France vetoed the British application to join the EEC. De Gaulle said: "England's nature, England's structure, England's very situation differs profoundly from those of the continentals."

1965
The three communities merge The Brussels Treaty, is signed, merging the control of the EEC, Euratom and the ECSC creating the European Community (EC) under the control of common institutions.

1966
Full free trade in EFTA The European Free Trade Association achieves complete free trade between its members.

1970
The Werner Report Written by the Prime Minister of Luxembourg, Pierre Werner, its proposals were intended to create; "a European federal state, with a single currency." This was known and approved of by Edward Heath and the British government.

1972
Edward Heath pushes through the European Communities Act 1972.
Norway rejects EU membership On 25th September 1972 the Norwegians reject EU membership in a referendum.

1973
The UK, Ireland and Denmark to the EEC British Prime Minister Edward Heath stated: 'There are some in this country who fear that in going into Europe we shall in some way sacrifice independence and sovereignty. These fears, I need hardly say, are completely unjustified." He later admits this was untrue.

1975
The Wilson renegotiation Harold Wilson's Labour Government renegotiates Britain's terms of membership. He claims major concessions, but in reality there were only minimal adjustments on ancillary issues such as the terms of trade relating to New Zealand butter.
British Referendum on EEC membership British Harold Wilson holds a referendum on whether Britain should remain a member of the EEC. The public vote to stay in.

1977
EFTA/EEC free trade The EEC and the European Free Trade Association abolish tariffs on industrial products traded between the two organisations.

1979
The beginnings of monetary union In March the European Monetary System (EMS) and its European Exchange Rate Mechanism (ERM) is formed. This pegged together the currencies of the EEC. Britain had announced that it is staying out on 5th December 1978.

1981
Greece joins the EEC

1984
The budget rebate On 26th June 1984 British Prime Minister, Margaret Thatcher, wins the famous rebate on taxpayers' money paying for the EU's overblown agricultural payments at a meeting in Fontainebleau.

1985
Greenland withdraws from the EEC
Enter Jacques Delors On 7th January the French federalist Jacques Delors takes up the position of President of the European Commission. He becomes a driving force for further integration.

1986
Spain and Portugal join the EC.
Single European Act This gave the institutions of the EEC the power to create a regulation red-tape area over industry (the Single Market) in all member states.

1988
EC passports established On 5th April 1988 passports become standardised across the EC.
The Bruges Speech On 20th September 1888 Margaret Thatcher outlines an alternative vision for Europe, one of cooperating nation-states without 'ever-closer union'.

1990
Britain becomes a member of the European Exchange Rate Mechanism As a result of pressure from the then Chancellor of the Exchequer, John Major, and the Foreign Secretary, Douglas Hurd, the Thatcher government joined the ERM in October 1990. This pegged the pound with the Deutschmark.

1992
The Maastricht Treaty With its 30 areas of decision making moved to, or introduced subject to, Qualified Majority Voting it was a major step in centralising power in the EU. It

also established what we now call the European Union. The British Prime Minister John Major's attempt to force the treaty through the House of Commons was to scar his Premiership and highlight issues relating to the centralisation of the EU.

The formation of the European Economic Area association The EEA agreement is signed by all EFTA states, giving them free trade with the EU without political union.

The Danes vote 'Nej' to Maastricht Treaty Black or Golden Wednesday On 16th September, 1992 known by some as "Black Wednesday" and as "Golden Wednesday" to others, the UK leaves the ERM.

French Maastricht referendum On 20th September 1992 the French only narrowly approve the Maastricht Treaty.

Swiss reject EEA membership The Swiss reject joining the European Economic Area in a referendum. As a result the government halts negotiations to join the EU.

1993
Danes are asked to vote again On 18th May 1993 a second referendum is held in Denmark on the Maastricht Treaty. After securing a number of opt-outs most notably on the euro the Danes approve the Maastricht Treaty.

1994
The European Economic Area (EEA) On 1st January 1994 the EEA comes into force. Iceland, Liechtenstein and Norway become part of the EU's Single Market without being in the EU.

Norway again votes No to the EU The Norwegians again reject EU membership. Norway remains a member of the EEA.

1995
Austria, Finland and Sweden join the EU.

1997
Referendum pledges Sir James Goldsmith's Referendum Party forces both the Conservative and the Labour Parties to pledge to hold a referendum before joining the euro.

Treaty of Amsterdam In this treaty 24 areas of decision making were moved to Qualified Majority Voting. It also created the Common Foreign and Security Policy (CFSP). and the European System of Central Banks (ESCB) which includes the Bank of England.

1999
The EU adopts the Euro. Britain, Denmark and Sweden stay out.

Commission resignation Jacques Santer, the then President of the European Commission, along, with the rest of the Commissioners resigned following a report into corruption.

2000
Danes reject the euro Despite securing an opt-out for the euro which was needed to pass the Maastricht Treaty in Denmark, the Danes were asked to join the EU's Single Currency. The Danish people vote no.

2001
Swiss EU referendum On 4th March 2001 the Swiss vote no even to opening negotiations with the EU on membership.

The Treaty of Nice In this treaty 46 areas of decision making were moved from one where a member-state had a veto to Qualified Majority Voting.

Irish reject the Nice Treaty The Irish vote 'no' to Nice on 7th June 2001.

The Laeken Declaration Following the Irish rejection of the Nice Treaty, the European Council meeting in Laeken in Belgium issued a declaration on committing the Union to becoming more democratic, transparent and effective.

2002
Euro notes and coins On 1st January 2002 euro notes and coins are introduced.

Ireland's second Nice Treaty Referendum On 19th October 2002 the Irish had to vote again on the Nice Treaty. This time the voters approved the Nice Treaty.

2003
Treaty of Athens. This paved the way for a further ten states to join the European Union.

Draft Treaty establishing a Constitution for Europe The Convention on the Future of Europe completes its work and announces a Draft Treaty establishing a Constitution for Europe on 18th July 2003.

Sweden rejects the Single Currency On 14th September 2003 the Swedish keep the Krona and decide not to adopt the euro.

2004
EU Constitution referendum promise 20th April 2004 the then British Prime Minister

Tony Blair pledges to hold a referendum on the EU Constitution regardless of whether it was rejected by another state or not.

Expansion of the EU On 1st May Cyprus, the Czech Republic, Estonia, Hungary, Latvia, Lithuania, Malta, Poland, Slovakia and Slovenia join the EU.

The Treaty Establishing a Constitution for Europe (TEC) In an attempt to ape the symbolism behind the original treaty founding the EEC the final text of the TEC is signed in Rome on 29th October 2004.

Voters reject regionalisation On 4th November 2004 voters in the North-east England EU region vote 'no' to a regional assembly.

2005

All MPs pledge to hold a referendum On 5th May 2005 the UK holds a general election. All MPs' manifestos upon which they stood for election stated that they supported a referendum on the EU Constitution.

France says 'Non' On 29th May 2005 the French vote no to the EU Constitution in a referendum.

The Dutch vote 'Nee' The Dutch also vote no in a referendum on the EU Constitution held on 1st June 2005.

Referendum cancelled Following the rejections of the EU Constitution in France and the Netherlands the Blair government drops its commitment to put it to the vote.

Blair's Budget negotiations At the meeting of the European Council British Prime Minister Tony Blair agreed to the 2007–2013 EU budget. Blair agreed to give up £7 billion from the rebate in return for a promise to review all EU spending including funds spent on the Common Agricultural Policy. However, the expected cuts in CAP spending never took place.

2006

French help scuttle world trade liberalisation Whilst the EU was pressurising third world nations into opening up their markets the French had blocked reforms that would open up the European Union to agricultural products produced in developing nations.

2007

Balkanisation On 1st January 2007 the EU expands into the Balkans with Bulgaria and Romania joining the EU.

Expansion of the euro Slovenia adopts the Single Currency on 1st January 2007.

The EU's Golden Anniversary On 25th March the EU celebrated the 50th anniversary of the signing of the Treaty of Rome.

David Cameron's first referendum pledge On 26th September 2007 the then Leader of the Opposition states that; "Today, I will give this cast-iron guarantee: If I become PM a Conservative government will hold a referendum on any EU treaty that emerges from these negotiations." The treaty in question was to become known as the Lisbon Treaty.

The Lisbon Treaty The Treaty of Lisbon was signed on 13th December 2007 in the Portuguese capital. It entered into force on 1st December 2009. This amended the existing EU treaties in such a way that they became almost identical to the rejected EU Constitution. Despite, it's effects being almost indistinguishable from the EU Constitution The Lisbon Treaty was only subject to a referendum in the Republic of Ireland where it is a constitutional requirement.

2008

Two Commonwealth countries adopt the euro On 1st January 2008 both Cyprus and Malta join the eurozone.

Ireland rejects the Lisbon Treaty On 12th June 2008 the Republic of Ireland holds a referendum on the Lisbon Treaty. The Irish vote 'no' by 53.4% to 46.6%.

2009

More euro expansion Slovakia joins the eurozone on 1st January 2008.

The Irish are made to vote again On 2nd October 2009 Ireland holds a second referendum on the Lisbon Treaty. This time the treaty is approved.

David Cameron cancels his cast-iron guarantee On 3rd November 2009 the then leader of the Opposition, David Cameron, announces that he will not hold a referendum on the Lisbon Treaty.

The Lisbon Treaty comes into force On 1st December 2009 the rules of the Lisbon Treaty now apply. This treaty made almost every area of EU decision making, bar taxation and some parts of foreign policy decision making, subject to Qualified Majority Voting (QMV).

A government for Europe The Lisbon Treaty

also established the post of High Representative of the Union for Foreign Affairs and Security Policy and the position of President of the European Council. Baroness Catherine Ashton became the High Representative and the Belgian Herman Van Rompuy President of the European Council.

2010

First Greek bailout On 2nd May 2010 the so-called troika of the EU, the European Central Bank (ECB) and the International Monetary Fund (IMF) agree to give Greece a €110 billion bailout. Austerity measures including tax increases and spending cuts are part of the agreement. It is expected that this will resolve Greece's economic problems.

Irish bailout On 28th November 2010 an €85 billion bailout of the Republic of Ireland is agreed.

2011

Estonia joins the euro On 1st January 2011 Estonia adopts the euro as its currency replacing the Kroon.

Portuguese bailout On 3rd May 2011 a €78 billion bailout of Portugal is agreed.

Political rebellion On 24th October 2011 the biggest Conservative Party parliamentary rebellion on the EU takes place. In all 111 MPs, 81 of whom were Conservative, defied the whips and voted for a referendum to be held on Britain's membership of the EU.

The Cameron veto British Prime Minister, David Cameron, on 9th December 2011 vetoed a new EU treaty that would have awarded the EU more control over the budgets of the eurozone states. The Eurozone member states went ahead anyway by other means.

2012

Second Greek bailout On 21st February 2012 the EU agrees to a further €130 billion bailout of Greece.

European Fiscal Compact Despite David Cameron's objections the Fiscal Compact was signed on 2nd March 2012. It entered into force on 1st January 2013.

Spanish bailout On 9th June 2012 the EU agrees to bailout the Spanish banking sector by providing up to €100 billion.

House of Commons demand cut in EU spending On 31st October 2012, an amendment was passed calling for a real terms cut in the European Union budget. The

government, favouring a small increase in EU spending, opposed this motion. The vote was to serve as a landmark in Britain's negotiations with the EU.

2013

40 years of membership 1st January 2013 Britain has been a member of the European Union, including its previous incarnations, totalling four decades.

In/Out referendum pledge On 22nd January David Cameron, if he is re-elected as Prime Minister, following a renegotiation promises to hold a referendum on the UK's membership of the EU in 2017. The British Prime Minister pledged to renegotiate the terms of Britain's EU membership and put this to the vote.

EU leaders agree budget cut but Britain will pay more The EU agreed to a reduction in its spending over 2014–2020 from €993 billion euros to €960. However, the UK will still pay more than in the previous EU budget.

Cyprus bail-in Controversy was caused by the EU's appropriation of some bank deposits in Cyprus, these were seized in exchange for a €10 billion financial package.

The European Parliament rejects the EU budget deal On 13th May MEPs refused to agree to the budget deal reached between the EU leaders.

EU amends budget taking more UK cash. The UK opposed this but was out-voted and had to pay a further £770 million in 2013.

Iceland suspends EU accession talks. Following the 2008 financial crash and failure of Icelandic banks the Nordic island state applied to join the EU. However, the economy of Iceland recovered outside of the European Union the Icelandic currency, the Króna, was allowed to float freely.

Financial Framework finally confirmed The 2014 – 2020 budget was finally agreed by the European Parliament after concessions on spending.

Mounting speculation of a third Greek bailout Rumours grow that Greece may need yet another bailout.

2020

An independent Britain On 1st January 2020 the UK regains its sovereignty and political independence. It is now outside of the European Union. The process as to how this can be done is set out in this book but is yet to be agreed to by Eurosceptics, but will be.

Appendix 2
About the Author

The author, Robert Oulds M.A., is the longstanding Director of the Bruges Group, the respected think tank which for the last 20 years has been at the forefront of the debate about the UK's relationship with the EU and the wider world. Their findings, which informs both members of the press and politics, has accurately predicted the outcome of developments in the EU years in advance. In particular the grave crisis in the Eurozone and the illness at the heart of the European project.

Bruges Group research is often reported in the media. Robert Oulds regularly appears on the television and the radio debating topical issues. As such he is very familiar with the public policy process.

He has a keen interest in military affairs, politics and history. As matters relating to military operations are often closely intertwined with politics the author's involvement with both national and transnational affairs gives him a good grounding in international relations. And it gives him a useful understanding of the wider strategic significance of major questions regarding Britain's involvement in the world.

Robert Oulds' meticulous research skills have also been honed by his authorship of a great deal of material on many political and international issues, and this gives him the skill of making complex issues accessible to the general public. This allows him to uncover what you need to know about Britain and the European Union.

Robert Oulds is the author of Montgomery and the First War on Terror, published by Bretwalda Books. The book details a little known period of Monty's career. Bernard Law Montgomery, later Field Marshal Viscount Montgomery of Alamein, faced guerrilla forces in Ireland in the early 1920s and Palestine on the eve of the Second World War. That book explores the lessons of Monty's victories in those conflicts and how they should be applied today in the modern war on terror in Afghanistan.

Since 2002 the author has also served his community as a local government Councillor in a London Borough. This led him to become a Chairman of Planning and he was the Cabinet Member with responsibility for Education and Children's Services. His involvement in politics also led to his becoming a Chairman of two Parliamentary Constituency Associations.

Robert Oulds is the Standard Bearer and Treasurer for his local branch of the Royal British Legion (RBL). This is an organisation established to help the welfare of ex-Servicemen and it campaign on issues relating to the armed forces. The RBL is also the custodian of the nation's Remembrance services; and it organises and runs the annual Poppy Appeal which raises funds for the aid of our soldiers, sailors and airmen and women as well as their dependents.